The One Year Book
OF
Bible Prayers

THE ONE YEAR®

book of

Bible Prayers

General Editor
Bruce B. Barton

TYNDALE HOUSE PUBLISHERS, INC.
WHEATON, ILLINOIS

I love the LORD because he hears
and answers my prayers.
Because he bends down and listens,
I will pray as long as I have breath!

PSALM 116:1-2

Prayer is one of the greatest mysteries of life. Why does the infinite God choose to bend down and listen to our requests? Why does the Creator of the universe, the King of kings, answer us when we speak to him? To pray is to have access to God—to the one who spoke this world into existence and who can change us and our world as well.

God invites us to pray (2 Chronicles 7:14), for he delights in answering the prayers of his people (Proverbs 15:8). Yet, often we neglect prayer for a variety of reasons: We're busy; we're not certain how to pray; or we're reluctant to bring to God the concerns that really bother us.

The One Year Book of Bible Prayers is designed to help you pray. In it you will find prayers that are recorded in the Bible. These prayers express a wide range of needs, worship themes, and emotions. Some are cries for help. Others openly express doubts and discouragement. Still others celebrate God as the magnificent King of kings. You'll find in this book Job's cry of desperation, as well as Paul's intercession for the believers in Ephesus. You'll find Hannah's petition for a son, as well as Mary's enthusiastic thanksgiving to God. Through these prayers, you'll find the words to express many of your deepest longings to God as well.

The One Year Book of Bible Prayers is organized into short daily readings. Each day features an excerpt from a prayer in the Bible, a short meditation on that prayer that will help you focus your thoughts, and then a sentence you can use to start your own prayer. Although these daily readings begin with January 1, you can begin exploring the Bible's prayers on today's date.

My hope and prayer is that the scriptural prayers collected in this book will rejuvenate your prayer life.

Bruce B. Barton

**SOLOMON'S
PRAYER
FOR
WISDOM**

That night the Lord appeared to Solomon in a dream, and God said, "What do you want? Ask, and I will give it to you!"

Solomon replied, ". . . O Lord my God, now you have made me king instead of my father, David, but I am like a little child who doesn't know his way around. And here I am among your own chosen people, a nation so great they are too numerous to count! Give me an understanding mind so that I can govern your people well and know the difference between right and wrong. For who by himself is able to govern this great nation of yours?" 1 KINGS 3:5-9

Imagine Solomon, the heir to one of the wealthiest and most powerful nations at that time, beginning his inaugural address with a prayer for God to help him—a mere "little child." With all that was at his command, Solomon deliberately wielded the power of prayer. He knew that prayer was the key to his success. Solomon honestly evaluated his own abilities in light of the magnitude of his responsibilities as the king of Israel. He concluded: "Who by himself is able to govern this great nation of yours?"

As you begin this new year, let Solomon's prayer for wisdom guide your own prayer. Seek God's wisdom first; let him counsel you.

Dear Lord, I ask for your wisdom in my life this year . . .

**PRAISE TO
THE ONE
WHO
SUPPORTS
ME**

*God arms me with strength;
  he has made my way safe.
He makes me as surefooted as a deer,
  leading me safely along the mountain heights.
He prepares me for battle;
  he strengthens me to draw a bow of bronze.
You have given me the shield of your salvation.
  Your right hand supports me;
  your gentleness has made me great.
You have made a wide path for my feet
  to keep them from slipping.*

PSALM 18:32-36

Having narrowly escaped King Saul's murderous schemes, David could have boasted of his military skill—his talent with the bow and his extensive knowledge of the mountainous terrain. He certainly had bragging rights; he had just escaped King Saul's grasp. But David was a man of God. David praised the Lord God openly because his strength and skill came from the Lord. No earthly shield could have protected him from the arrows of his enemies. Only God could protect him and strengthen him for battle.

Has God strengthened and supported you in the last year? Thank the Lord for his support, and commit all your impossible situations to him.

Dear Lord, your right hand has supported me in these ways . . .

MORE THAN WE EVER DARE TO ASK

Now glory be to God! By his mighty power at work within us, he is able to accomplish infinitely more than we would ever dare to ask or hope. May he be given glory in the church and in Christ Jesus forever and ever through endless ages. Amen.

EPHESIANS 3:20-21

Paul's prayer of adoration is perhaps best summarized with one word, *more*. His praise rises to its feet in a standing ovation for the God he adores. To Paul, God not only is more mighty, he does more. We pray for a morsel, and he gives us a feast. We beg for the strength to get to first base; he answers with a grand slam. God answers our prayers with far more than we can ever dare, ask, or hope for.

Are your prayers characterized by the word, *more*? More praise than just the usual? More trust in the infinite and almighty God? Let the glory of God expand your prayer today.

Dear Lord, I praise you because you are able to do more than I would ever dare to ask . . .

January 4

**CONFESSING
INSTEAD OF
HIDING**

When I refused to confess my sin,
I was weak and miserable,
and I groaned all day long.
Day and night your hand of discipline was heavy on me.
My strength evaporated like water in the summer heat.
Finally, I confessed all my sins to you
and stopped trying to hide them.
I said to myself, "I will confess my rebellion to the Lord."
And you forgave me! All my guilt is gone.
Therefore, let all the godly confess their rebellion to you while
there is time.

PSALM 32:3-6

We find many ways to get around admitting our sin. We rationalize our sins away. We try to drown out the guilt with all types of distractions. But over time, our sins deplete our will to pray. David was intimately familiar with all the ways one can try to hide sin. He had exhausted himself covering up his own sins. But everything changed when he finally gave up running away from his sin: "Finally, I confessed all my sins to you."

Like David, we can find our prayer life renewed when we freely confess our sins to God. Confess your sin and let God restore your prayer life to what it can and should be.

Dear Lord, I don't want to hide my sins anymore; I want to confess them to you today . . .

CARRIED IN HIS ARMS

Praise the Lord; praise God our savior!
For each day he carries us in his arms.
Our God is a God who saves!
The Sovereign Lord rescues us from death.

PSALM 68:19-20

What do you picture in your mind when you pray to God? Do you picture a loving father listening to his child? Do you picture a mighty conqueror with the power of a vast army of angels at his disposal? Your answer likely depends on what you're praying for at the moment. David's prayer gives an intimate picture of God carrying his loved one in his arms.

Meditate on this picture for a moment. Imagine yourself in David's description. As you begin to speak with God about your needs and concerns, imagine his arms surrounding you in a protective embrace, and let his embrace comfort you.

Dear Lord, I thank you for carrying me in your arms today as I tell you what concerns me right now . . .

**THE
LORD'S
PRAYER**

*"Our Father in heaven,
    may your name be honored.
May your Kingdom come soon.
May your will be done here on earth,
    just as it is in heaven.
Give us our food for today,
and forgive us our sins,
    just as we have forgiven those who have sinned against us.
And don't let us yield to temptation,
    but deliver us from the evil one."*

MATTHEW 6:9-13

When you go to a restaurant, you don't just order "some food"; you make specific requests. In the same way, Jesus' prayer reminds us to be specific when we ask God for something.

Use the Lord's Prayer as a guide for specific prayer. Start by acknowledging the One you are approaching—the almighty God, whose name should be honored by everyone everywhere. Recommit yourself to his Kingdom and his purposes. Confess your sins, and pray that the Lord will protect you from succumbing to any further temptations. And finally, ask the Lord for what you need that day. God is waiting to pour out his blessing and resources on you—if you only will ask.

Dear Lord, may your will be done . . .

**PROCLAIMING
GOD'S
SAVING
POWER**

But I will keep on hoping for you to help me;
I will praise you more and more.
I will tell everyone about your righteousness.
All day long I will proclaim your saving power,
for I am overwhelmed by how much you have done for me.
I will praise your mighty deeds, O Sovereign Lord.
I will tell everyone that you alone are just and good.

PSALM 71:14-16

The psalmist had trusted God from his childhood and had continually proclaimed the Lord's goodness to others. At his peak, his life was a shining example to others. But as he grew older, people began to plot against him. In his old age, he started to feel abandoned by God. So in this passionate prayer, he appeals to the Lord and places his hope in him. He prays that God would give him the chance to proclaim the Lord's saving power among his people once again.

Do you have that same desire to tell others of God's goodness to you? Recall God's protection and guidance in your life and let someone know how much God has helped you.

Dear Lord, I am overwhelmed by how much you have
done for me, and I want to tell everyone . . .

EZRA'S PRAYER OF CONFESSION

I prayed, "O my God, I am utterly ashamed; I blush to lift up my face to you. For our sins are piled higher than our heads, and our guilt has reached to the heavens. Our whole history has been one of great sin. That is why we and our kings and our priests have been at the mercy of the pagan kings of the land. We have been killed, captured, robbed, and disgraced, just as we are today.

"But now we have been given a brief moment of grace, for the Lord our God has allowed a few of us to survive as a remnant. He has given us security in this holy place. Our God has brightened our eyes and granted us some relief from our slavery."

EZRA 9:6-8

Although the Israelites had accumulated "sins piled higher than" their heads, God had been merciful to them, allowing some of them to survive their exile to Babylon and return to Jerusalem. But the remnant of Israelites God saved had not learned their lesson. They immediately began disobeying God again. Because of this, Ezra is embarrassed to approach God on behalf of his people.

Sometimes confessing sin is embarrassing and awkward. At those times, remind yourself that the Lord loves to restore and forgive those who approach him with a humble and contrite heart.

Dear Lord, though I am ashamed of my sin, I know that you will not abandon me as I confess my sins to you . . .

A PRAYER
FOR
RESTORED
SUCCESS

Satisfy us in the morning with your unfailing love,
so we may sing for joy to the end of our lives.
Give us gladness in proportion to our former misery!
Replace the evil years with good.
Let us see your miracles again;
let our children see your glory at work.
And may the Lord our God show us his approval
and make our efforts successful.
Yes, make our efforts successful!

PSALM 90:14-17

In this prayer, Moses asked that God's unfailing love would greet his people every morning. He prayed for his people to see the miracles of God's work in their lives, and he asked for God's approval of their efforts.

Ask God to bless your endeavors: "Yes, make our efforts successful!" But remember your requests reveal how you measure success. When you spend time in prayer today, ask God for his blessings on your efforts. But first ask yourself what true success is.

Dear Lord, make my efforts successful in the following ways . . .

**EXPRESSING
OUR FEARS
TO GOD**

*"But who am I to appear before Pharaoh?" Moses asked
God. "How can you expect me to lead the Israelites out of
Egypt?"*

*Then God told him, "I will be with you. And this will
serve as proof that I have sent you: When you have brought
the Israelites out of Egypt, you will return here to worship
God at this very mountain."*

EXODUS 3:11-12

After fleeing from Egypt to escape Pharaoh's wrath, Moses settled
down to a quiet life in Midian. But God had different plans for Moses.
He wanted Moses to return to Egypt, confront Pharaoh, and lead the
Israelites out of slavery. When Moses heard this, he hesitated. "Who
am I?" he asked. "The people won't believe me. I'm not a good speaker."
But for every one of Moses' excuses, God had an answer. God
promised to be with him and to empower Moses each step of the way.

What challenging situation has God given you? Freely express
your misgivings and fears about the tasks God has given to you.
Commit those fears to God, and remind yourself of God's
willingness to empower you every step of the way.

*Dear God, be with me as I do your will, even though I
ask, "Who am I to do it?" . . .*

January 11

A Priceless Inheritance

All honor to the God and Father of our Lord Jesus Christ, for it is by his boundless mercy that God has given us the privilege of being born again. Now we live with a wonderful expectation because Jesus Christ rose again from the dead. For God has reserved a priceless inheritance for his children. It is kept in heaven for you, pure and undefiled, beyond the reach of change and decay.

1 PETER 1:3-4

Prayer keeps our hearts turned heavenward, while our feet remain firmly on this earth. Peter prayed for Christians facing persecution and rejection by their neighbors. He prayed to remind them of the prize awaiting them in heaven—even as they struggled here on earth.

Let your own troubled heart soar with wonderful expectation of all the treasures awaiting you in heaven. Let this prayer take your mind off the cares and struggles of this world. Refresh your soul with thoughts of the pure, undefiled inheritance reserved for you in heaven—an inheritance that cannot be destroyed.

Dear Lord, I praise you for reserving a priceless inheritance for me in heaven . . .

PRAISE TO THE LORD!

May the glory of the Lord last forever!
The Lord rejoices in all he has made!
The earth trembles at his glance;
the mountains burst into flame at his touch.
I will sing to the Lord as long as I live.
I will praise my God to my last breath!
May he be pleased by all these thoughts about him,
for I rejoice in the Lord.
Let all sinners vanish from the face of the earth;
let the wicked disappear forever.
As for me–I will praise the Lord!

PSALM 104:31-35

You'll never lack for ways to express yourself to God in prayer when you use Scripture in your prayers. This prayer provides a portrait of the Almighty that will jump-start anyone's prayer life. Immerse yourself in this beautiful prayer of praise to the Lord. Imagine the piercing power of his mere glance, which makes the entire earth tremble. The very mountains he created ignite at his touch.

What adversary are you facing? What mountain stands in your way? Nothing is too big for the Lord. Commit your adversaries, your worries, and your cares to him.

Dear Lord, may you be pleased by all these thoughts about you, for I rejoice in you . . .

January 13

PRAISE FOR GOD'S WORKMANSHIP

You made all the delicate, inner parts of my body
and knit me together in my mother's womb.
Thank you for making me so wonderfully complex!
Your workmanship is marvelous—and how well I know it.
You watched me as I was being formed in utter seclusion,
as I was woven together in the dark of the womb.
You saw me before I was born.
Every day of my life was recorded in your book.
Every moment was laid out
before a single day had passed.

PSALM 139:13-16

Any biology text can illustrate how wonderfully complex the human body is. From brain cells to blood cells—each intricate component of our bodies is carefully designed. You don't have to take a biology course to marvel at how our eyes can take in the bright blue color of the sky, how our ears can detect a pin drop, how our nose can enjoy the aroma of ground coffee or the scent of a beautiful flower. How exciting it is to enjoy the body God has made for us!

David expressed this same wonder as he prayed this prayer. Set aside a few minutes today to praise God for his sovereign care.

Dear Lord, thank you for making me with such
marvelous workmanship . . .

BOWING BEFORE OUR MAKER

Come, let us worship and bow down.
Let us kneel before the Lord our maker,
for he is our God.
We are the people he watches over,
the sheep under his care.
Oh, that you would listen to his voice today!

PSALM 95:6-7

This prayer is a grand call to worship—a summons to bow low before God, our maker. Like a shepherd, our almighty Creator looks after us. He guides us. He wants to protect us from danger. That's why we need to listen carefully to his voice and follow him.

The more we make psalms like these our own, the more prayer will become natural to us. We will learn what it means to bow before our Lord and trust him to care for us. Meditate on this psalm, and slowly pray it back to your loving Shepherd. Recommit yourself to listen to him and follow his direction.

Dear Lord, you are my God, and I am under your care . . .

PRAISE TO HIM WHO RULES FOREVER

All praise to him who loves us and has freed us from our sins by shedding his blood for us. He has made us his Kingdom and his priests who serve before God his Father. Give to him everlasting glory! He rules forever and ever! Amen!

REVELATION 1:5-6

"Who's in charge around here anyway?" we sometimes mutter under our breath. Burdens and trials can become so overwhelming that we become discouraged. Our prayers become stilted and awkward. In those times, we can draw strength from what the apostle John observed while in exile on the island of Patmos. The book of his visions—Revelation—is like a grand coronation ceremony of God's Son, Jesus Christ. It pictures Jesus as the King of kings, as the ultimate authority in heaven and on earth. This prayer exalts Jesus and proclaims his royal status.

Reflect on what it will be like to meet this glorious King of kings. Then with the apostle John, proclaim: "He rules forever and ever!"

Dear Lord, I want to give you everlasting glory! You rule forever and ever . . .

THE OWNER OF ALL THINGS

Then David praised the Lord in the presence of the whole assembly: "O Lord, the God of our ancestor Israel, may you be praised forever and ever! Yours, O Lord, is the greatness, the power, the glory, the victory, and the majesty. Everything in the heavens and on earth is yours, O Lord, and this is your kingdom. We adore you as the one who is over all things."

1 CHRONICLES 29:10-11

Most of us work long and hard to buy the things we have. It's all too easy to conclude: "I've earned all of this by my own efforts. It's all mine." Although King David was one of the richest men of his day—owning gold and silver, and governing the united kingdom of Israel—he didn't fall into the trap of thinking his possessions were his own. Instead, he reminded himself that everything in the heavens and on the earth belonged to the Lord. That's why David gave up many of his treasures to build the Lord's Temple.

Remember how great the Lord is; then pray with an attitude like David's.

Dear Lord, everything in the heavens and on earth is yours . . .

THE DESIRE TO OBEY

"May he give us the desire to do his will in everything and to obey all the commands, laws, and regulations that he gave our ancestors. And may these words that I have prayed in the presence of the Lord be before him constantly, day and night, so that the Lord our God may uphold my cause and the cause of his people Israel, fulfilling our daily needs."

1 KINGS 8:58-59

After spending seven years constructing the Temple, King Solomon led the Israelites in dedicating this magnificent structure to the Lord. First, Solomon praised the Lord for keeping his promises, for establishing the Israelites in the land, and for giving them the opportunity to build God's Temple. God had kept all the promises he had made to Solomon's father, King David. How should the Israelites respond to their God? King Solomon prayed that the Israelites would *want* to obey the Lord's commands so that the name of God would be exalted.

Is your prayer that your life will bring glory to God? Reflect on your motives for obeying God, then pray with a heart like Solomon's.

Dear Lord, give me the desire to do your will in everything . . .

CONFESSION

BEFORE

PETITION

Then I said, "O Lord, God of heaven, . . . listen to my prayer! Look down and see me praying night and day for your people Israel. I confess that we have sinned against you. Yes, even my own family and I have sinned! We have sinned terribly by not obeying the commands, laws, and regulations that you gave us through your servant Moses.

"Please remember what you told your servant Moses: 'If you sin, I will scatter you among the nations. But if you return to me and obey my commands, even if you are exiled to the ends of the earth, I will bring you back to the place I have chosen for my name to be honored.'" NEHEMIAH 1:5-9

When Nehemiah heard how his people were suffering back in the devastated province of Judah, he mourned, wept, fasted, and prayed. Nehemiah knew that unconfessed sin was a barrier to prayer. Only after he confessed his own sins, his family's sins, and those of his people did he ask God to grant him success before the king. God answered Nehemiah's prayer. The Lord moved the heart of King Artaxerxes to send Nehemiah back to Jerusalem to rebuild its walls.

Are you concerned about the condition of your own nation? Confess your own sins and the sins of your people, and then ask the Lord to intervene.

Dear Lord, I confess that we have sinned against you . . .

A PRAYER FOR HOLINESS

Now may the God of peace make you holy in every way, and may your whole spirit and soul and body be kept blameless until that day when our Lord Jesus Christ comes again. God, who calls you, is faithful; he will do this.

1 THESSALONIANS 5:23-24

As we grow up, our parents teach us how to become independent, beginning with small things and going from there. By the time we've become adults, we start believing we can do everything on our own. That type of attitude often spills over into our spiritual lives. The Scriptures teach us to live a holy life, and we determine to become holy by our own efforts. But in today's prayer, Paul doesn't tell them to *be* holy. Instead he prays: "May the God of peace *make you* holy."

In our own strength, we're not capable of becoming holy. But Paul reassures the Thessalonians that God "is faithful; he will do this." Take to heart Paul's message and pray that God will continue to make you holy.

Dear Lord, keep me blameless until that day when you come again . . .

PRAISING GOD FOR WISDOM

"Praise the name of God forever and ever,
for he alone has all wisdom and power.
He determines the course of world events;
he removes kings and sets others on the throne.
He gives wisdom to the wise
and knowledge to the scholars.
He reveals deep and mysterious things
and knows what lies hidden in darkness,
though he himself is surrounded by light.
I thank and praise you, God of my ancestors,
for you have given me wisdom and strength."

DANIEL 2:20-23

While Daniel and his friends were in exile, they were chosen to be advisers to King Nebuchadnezzar. One night, the king had a disturbing dream, so he demanded that his advisers tell him what he dreamed as well as their interpretation of the dream. If they couldn't do both, he would condemn them all to death—including Daniel and his friends.

Daniel and his friends responded by consulting God in prayer. Daniel couldn't know the thoughts of the king, but the all-knowing God could. The Lord answered their prayers, revealing the dream and its meaning to Daniel. So Daniel broke forth into praise and thanks to God.

The God who answered Daniel's prayer is also listening to you.

Dear Lord, you alone possess all wisdom and power . . .

REQUESTING CLARIFICATION

Moses said to the Lord, "You have been telling me, 'Take these people up to the Promised Land.' But you haven't told me whom you will send with me. You call me by name and tell me I have found favor with you. Please, if this is really so, show me your intentions so I will understand you more fully and do exactly what you want me to do. Besides, don't forget that this nation is your very own people."

And the Lord replied, "I will personally go with you, Moses. I will give you rest—everything will be fine for you."

EXODUS 33:12-14

God had already commanded Moses to lead the Israelites into the Promised Land. But since they had disobeyed him by worshiping the gold calf, God had refused to travel with such "stubborn, unruly people." That's why Moses prayed: "Show me your intentions so I will understand you more fully." God didn't reprimand Moses for stalling. Moses knew that moving ahead without the Lord's guidance, presence, and power would be disastrous, so he sought out the Lord.

God will answer those who seek him. Moses asked for understanding, and God gave himself. He promised to be with Moses to guide him every step of the way, and he will guide you as well.

Dear Lord, show me your intentions so I will do exactly what you want me to do . . .

COMPLAINING ABOUT RIDICULE

O Lord, you persuaded me, and I allowed myself to be persuaded. You are stronger than I am, and you overpowered me. Now I am mocked by everyone in the city. Whenever I speak, the words come out in a violent outburst. "Violence and destruction!" I shout. So these messages from the Lord have made me a household joke. And I can't stop! If I say I'll never mention the Lord or speak in his name, his word burns in my heart like a fire. It's like a fire in my bones! I am weary of holding it in!

JEREMIAH 20:7-9

When the Lord chose Jeremiah as his spokesman, the young man resisted. But God touched Jeremiah's mouth and said, "See, I have put my words in your mouth! Today I appoint you to stand up against nations and kingdoms" (Jer. 1:4-10). But in prayer, Jeremiah openly admitted to God that he was tired of being ridiculed. Even so, he couldn't stop speaking the word of God: "I can't stop! If I say I'll never mention the Lord or speak in his name, his word burns in my heart like a fire."

Speaking the truth for God is difficult and takes its toll. If you're frustrated with witnessing for God, tell the Lord. Admit that you're weak, and ask the Lord for strength. He will renew your zeal for the truth.

Dear heavenly Father, rekindle the fire in my heart to speak the words you've put in my mouth . . .

FROM HUMILITY TO PRAISE

Then the leaders of the Levites–Jeshua, Kadmiel, Bani, Hashabneiah, Sherebiah, Hodiah, Shebaniah, and Pethahiah–called out to the people: "Stand up and praise the Lord your God, for he lives from everlasting to everlasting!"

Then they continued, "Praise his glorious name! It is far greater than we can think or say. You alone are the Lord. You made the skies and the heavens and all the stars. You made the earth and the seas and everything in them. You preserve and give life to everything, and all the angels of heaven worship you."

NEHEMIAH 9:5-6

After rebuilding the walls of Jerusalem, the Israelites gathered for a time of dedication and worship. They expressed sorrow for their sins by fasting, dressing in sackcloth, and sprinkling dust on their heads. They confessed their sins and the sins of their ancestors. Then, they listened for three hours while the Book of the Law was read, followed by another three more hours of confession. Only after all this did the leaders command the people to stand up and praise their Creator.

Approach the Lord the way the Israelites did. Confess your sins. Humble yourself before the Lord. Then, let your confession lead into exuberant praise for the one who has forgiven your sins.

Everlasting Lord, I humble myself before you and give you praise . . .

JESUS' PRAYER FOR BELIEVERS

"O righteous Father, the world doesn't know you, but I do; and these disciples know you sent me. And I have revealed you to them and will keep on revealing you. I will do this so that your love for me may be in them and I in them."

JOHN 17:25-26

At the Last Supper, Jesus prepared his disciples for his approaching death. He washed their feet, talked about his coming betrayal, predicted Peter's denial, and told them about the Holy Spirit. Then Jesus prayed for them, asking the Father to "keep them safe from the evil one" and to "make them pure and holy by teaching them your words of truth" (17:15, 17). Even as he faced betrayal, denial, crucifixion, and death, Jesus was concerned about his followers. He didn't ask that they be kept from every trial, but he did pray that they remain in God's love.

We can take great comfort that Jesus included us in his prayer: "I am praying not only for these disciples but also for all who will ever believe in me because of their testimony" (17:20).

Dear Jesus, thank you for your concern for me that even in your last few hours on earth you prayed for me . . .

THANKS TO GOD, OUR SHELTER

But the Lord reigns forever,
executing judgment from his throne.
He will judge the world with justice
and rule the nations with fairness.
The Lord is a shelter for the oppressed,
a refuge in times of trouble.

PSALM 9:7-9

David certainly had times of trouble in his life. He had been a fugitive, fleeing from Saul, the most powerful man in the land (1 Samuel 23:25). Another time, even David's son turned against him (2 Samuel 15:14). So when David praised the Lord for being a *shelter* for the oppressed and a *refuge* in times of trouble, he wasn't talking about hypothetical, abstract concepts. Putting his trust in God was a life-and-death matter, and God had never abandoned him.

In times of trouble, remember that God is watching over us. He will never abandon those who call on him.

Dear Lord, thank you that we can find shelter in you,
who never abandons any who come to you . . .

PRAISE TO GOD, OUR MAJESTIC KING

*Your throne is founded on two strong pillars—righteousness
    and justice.*
Unfailing love and truth walk before you as attendants.
*Happy are those who hear the joyful call to worship,
    for they will walk in the light of your presence, Lord.*
*They rejoice all day long in your wonderful reputation.
    They exult in your righteousness.*
*You are their glorious strength.
    Our power is based on your favor.*
*Yes, our protection comes from the Lord,
    and he, the Holy One of Israel, has given us our king.*

PSALM 89:14-18

This psalm uses many lofty and majestic words to praise God for who he is. It pictures the Lord as an impressive king sitting on a throne supported by two strong pillars—his righteousness and his justice. Two attendants—unfailing love and truth—go before the Lord clearing the way for him. It is a joy for the Lord's subjects to worship him, for he alone does what is completely right. He alone judges with justice. He alone upholds truth.

What is most amazing is that this powerful King and righteous Judge loves his people and allows them to walk in his presence. Oh what a joy to walk in the light of God's presence and celebrate the King of kings!

O King of kings, with great joy I answer the call to worship you . . .

January 27

RESTING IN THE ETERNAL GOD

Lord, through all the generations
*   you have been our home!*
Before the mountains were created,
*   before you made the earth and the world,*
*   you are God, without beginning or end.*
You turn people back to dust, saying,
*   "Return to dust!"*
For you, a thousand years are as yesterday!
*   They are like a few hours!*
You sweep people away like dreams that disappear
or like grass that springs up in the morning.

PSALM 90:1-5

Where has all the time gone? we often wonder as the minutes, hours, days, and years slip by. We never have enough time to accomplish all that we desire to do. Moses pondered the brevity of life in the oldest prayer in the book of Psalms. Yet, he praised God: "For you, a thousand years are as yesterday!" God is not constrained by time, unlike ourselves. He is never rushed or exasperated by it, nor does he have a beginning or an end, for he is the Creator of time itself.

When you become painfully aware of your own limitations, seek peace in the Lord. Give all your moments over to God's care, and let him give eternal significance to all your daily efforts.

Eternal God, I know that a thousand years are like a
day to you . . .

**JOY IN
GOD'S
PRESENCE**

How lovely is your dwelling place,
  O Lord Almighty.
I long, yes, I faint with longing
  to enter the courts of the Lord.
With my whole being, body and soul,
  I will shout joyfully to the living God.
Even the sparrow finds a home there,
  and the swallow builds her nest
  and raises her young–
  at a place near your altar,
  O Lord Almighty, my King and my God!
How happy are those who can live in your house,
  always singing your praises.

PSALM 84:1-4

Unlike the temple musicians of Solomon's day, we don't have to go to a specific place to be in the Lord's presence (1 John 4:13). Like the sparrows at Solomon's temple, we have the privilege of being at home in the presence of the Lord, for the Spirit is with those who confess Jesus' name (John 16:7).

We can make our homes and our workplaces sacred places by consciously reminding ourselves of the Lord's presence and worshiping him. "How happy are those who can live in your house!"

O Lord Almighty, thank you for fulfilling my longing to be in your presence . . .

PRAISE TO OUR GENEROUS LORD

A single day in your courts
*   is better than a thousand anywhere else!*
I would rather be a gatekeeper in the house of my God
*   than live the good life in the homes of the wicked.*
For the Lord God is our light and protector.
*   He gives us grace and glory.*
No good thing will the Lord withhold
*   from those who do what is right.*
O Lord Almighty,
*   happy are those who trust in you.*

PSALM 84:10–12

Too often, we envy someone else's dream relationship, stunning appearance, or extravagant income. We too easily forget that such things alone will never satisfy us. Only a relationship with God can bring eternal joy. In this prayer of praise, the temple musicians sing, "No good thing will the Lord withhold from those who do what is right. . . . Happy are those who trust in you." They praised God for the blessings he gives to the obedient—mercy, protection, favor, honor, and joy.

God won't withhold his riches from those who obey him. God generously satisfies our needs.

Generous King, I praise you for blessing me with so many good things . . .

**AN URGENT
CRY FOR
HELP**

Bend down, O Lord, and hear my prayer;
answer me, for I need your help.
Protect me, for I am devoted to you.
Save me, for I serve you and trust you.
You are my God.
Be merciful, O Lord,
for I am calling on you constantly.
Give me happiness, O Lord,
for my life depends on you.
O Lord, you are so good, so ready to forgive,
so full of unfailing love for all who ask your aid.
Listen closely to my prayer, O Lord;
hear my urgent cry.

PSALM 86:1-6

In deep distress, David relied on the Lord. "My life depends on you," he cried. David didn't base his appeals for mercy on what he had done for God. No, he appealed to God's character instead: "O Lord, you are so good, so ready to forgive, so full of unfailing love for all who ask your aid." The Lord is truly a merciful God; and he wants to rescue those who are in trouble.

Like David, we should call on the Lord—not only when we're distressed, but at all times. We should approach the Lord in humility, relying on his steady character. Yet we can pray with confidence, for God will answer his faithful servants.

O merciful Master, my life depends on you . . .

PRAISING GOD'S FAITHFULNESS

I will sing of the tender mercies of the Lord forever!
Young and old will hear of your faithfulness.
Your unfailing love will last forever.
Your faithfulness is as enduring as the heavens.

PSALM 89:1-2

Early in David's reign, God promised David that his dynasty and his kingdom would "continue for all time" (2 Samuel 7:16). This prayer of Ethan reminds us how God had begun to fulfill his promises to David. This was evidence to Ethan of God's "unfailing love"—a love that would last forever and forever.

Jesus Christ has fulfilled God's promise to David. Jesus Christ—a descendant of David through his earthly father Joseph—was raised from the dead so he could rule at the right hand of God the Father (Mark 14:61-62; Acts 5:29-32). And the Lord has mercifully included us in his kingdom. Reflect on God's faithfulness to you through Christ.

Dear Lord, thank you for your unfailing love . . .

February 1

LONGING
FOR THE
LORD

As the deer pants for streams of water,
*   so I long for you, O God.*
I thirst for God, the living God.
*   When can I come and stand before him? . . .*
Why am I discouraged?
*   Why so sad?*
I will put my hope in God!
*   I will praise him again—*
*   my Savior and my God! . . .*
Through each day the Lord pours his unfailing love upon me,
*   and through each night I sing his songs,*
*   praying to God who gives me life.*

PSALM 42:1-2, 5-6, 8

When have you felt like God was far away? For the psalmist, being surrounded by his taunting enemies made him feel distant from God. The psalmist's enemies expressed his true thoughts in verse 3: "Where is this God of yours?" But their taunts only made him yearn for God even more, like a thirsty person awaiting a refreshing drink of water. So he freely admitted to God that he was discouraged. But he didn't let his discouragement be the final word. Instead, he began counting the ways God had poured out his unfailing love on him. In the end, he praised the Lord, who was graciously sustaining his life.

Does God seem far away? Express your longing to him. Then, start recounting the ways God has provided for you.

Dear Lord, I am discouraged, yet I put my hope in you . . .

**A PRAYER
DURING A
CRISIS**

*[Jehoshaphat] prayed, "O Lord, God of our ancestors, you
alone are the God who is in heaven. You are ruler of all the
kingdoms of the earth. You are powerful and mighty; no one
can stand against you! O our God, did you not drive out
those who lived in this land when your people arrived? And
did you not give this land forever to the descendants of your
friend Abraham? Your people settled here and built this
Temple for you. They said '. . . We can cry out to you to save
us, and you will hear us and rescue us.' . . .*

*"We are powerless against this mighty army that is about
to attack us. We do not know what to do, but we are looking
to you for help."* 2 CHRONICLES 20:6-9, 12

King Jehoshaphat was surrounded by enemy armies as he prayed
this prayer. But he knew God was a fortress that could withstand all
his enemies' assaults. Even though his situation seemed hopeless,
Jehoshaphat started recounting the ways God had faithfully
delivered his people in the past, and then he asked for his help in
the present. Jehoshaphat's trust was well-placed, for the next day the
Lord caused his enemies to turn on each other.

When you face impossible situations, take time to remind
yourself of the way God has taken care of you and your family in the
past. You may be powerless, but through prayer you have access to
an all-powerful God.

*Dear Lord, I am powerless, so I am looking to you for
help . . .*

A COMPLAINT CONCERNING INJUSTICE

Help, O Lord, for the godly are fast disappearing!
The faithful have vanished from the earth!
Neighbors lie to each other,
speaking with flattering lips and insincere hearts.
May the Lord bring their flattery to an end
and silence their proud tongues. . . .
Lord, we know you will protect the oppressed,
preserving them forever from this lying generation,
even though the wicked strut about,
and evil is praised throughout the land.

PSALM 12:1-3, 7-8

Why is it that those who get ahead always seem to be the ones who lie, cheat, and steal? They not only get away with their evil deeds, but their actions are admired and paraded around the world. Daydreaming about wicked people getting their just desserts may bring a smile to our face, but thinking about revenge isn't healthy for our soul. Instead, we should commit the wicked and the evil they do to God in prayer. We can't stop others from speaking lies or taking advantage of us, but we can and should cry out to the Lord who watches over his people. God knows the truth about all people, and he hears and responds to the cry of his people. This truth can give us peace amidst all the evil of those around us.

Dear Lord, thank you for watching over me as those around me plot evil . . .

February 4

PRAISE FOR SAFETY

David sang this song to the Lord after the Lord had rescued him from all his enemies and from Saul. These are the words he sang:

"The Lord is my rock, my fortress, and my savior;
my God is my rock, in whom I find protection.
He is my shield, the strength of my salvation, and my stronghold,
my high tower, my savior, the one who saves me from violence.
I will call on the Lord, who is worthy of praise,
for he saves me from my enemies."

2 SAMUEL 22:1-4

There's no greater feeling than getting home safe and sound, especially when the journey was difficult. Such experiences produce stories that we love to tell to others. But all too often we forget to give thanks to the Lord for protecting us.

When David was relaxing in complete safety, he remembered to praise the Lord for delivering him from King Saul. He acknowledged that it was God, not his own military prowess or physical strength, that saved him.

When the Lord rescues us from desperate situations, the threats of others, or simply our own mistakes, we must remember to stop and praise him.

O Lord, you are worthy of praise because you saved me from . . .

February 5

A REQUEST FOR PROTECTION

O God, listen to my cry!
Hear my prayer!
From the ends of the earth,
I will cry to you for help,
for my heart is overwhelmed.
Lead me to the towering rock of safety,
for you are my safe refuge,
a fortress where my enemies cannot reach me.
Let me live forever in your sanctuary,
safe beneath the shelter of your wings!

PSALM 61:1-4

As the commander of Israel's armies, David was an expert at analyzing an enemy's defenses and planning fortifications. Under David's leadership, the strong fortress of Zion (later called Jerusalem) was captured from the Jebusites. And after he captured it, David oversaw the building of additional fortifications around Zion (2 Samuel 5:6-10). But David didn't place his trust in the fortress he had built. He knew God was his true "towering rock of safety." There was no safer refuge than the Lord's sanctuary—the presence of the Almighty.

Although we might not realize it, we are just as vulnerable as King David was. We need to be led to God's rock of safety. Run to the Almighty in prayer and trust in him to keep you safe.

O God, lead me to the towering rock of safety, for you are my safe refuge . . .

February 6

A Prayer against Mockers

Then [Nehemiah] prayed, "Hear us, O our God, for we are being mocked. May their scoffing fall back on their own heads, and may they themselves become captives in a foreign land! Do not ignore their guilt. Do not blot out their sins, for they have provoked you to anger here in the presence of the builders."

NEHEMIAH 4:4-5

Nehemiah had come all the way from Persia to lead his people in the rebuilding of the walls of Jerusalem. When the people of Jerusalem finally got to work rebuilding the walls, they were greeted by a band of hecklers. "That stone wall would collapse if even a fox walked along the top of it!" Tobiah jeered. Nehemiah's response wasn't the natural one. He didn't try to silence the hecklers with a barrage of insults. He didn't get angry or violent. Instead he turned to God in prayer. He asked the Lord to hear their taunts.

Mocking and provocation shouldn't stop us from doing God's work. Instead, we, like Nehemiah, should look to God to deal with those who taunt us and faithfully continue about our task.

Dear Lord, hear those who are mocking me and rescue me . . .

PRAISE FOR GOD'S RESCUE

On the very day I call to you for help,
my enemies will retreat.
This I know: God is on my side.
O God, I praise your word.
Yes, Lord, I praise your word.
I trust in God, so why should I be afraid?
What can mere mortals do to me?
I will fulfill my vows to you, O God,
and offer a sacrifice of thanks for your help.
For you have rescued me from death;
you have kept my feet from slipping.
So now I can walk in your presence, O God,
in your life-giving light.

PSALM 56:9-13

Desperate people do desperate things, yet it is God who ultimately rescues them. When David fled to the Philistine city of Gath to escape King Saul, he quickly realized that his life was in danger, for he was an Israelite warrior who had no doubt killed many Philistines. So David acted as if he were insane, and the king of Gath allowed him to leave unhindered. David quickly found a safer hideout in the cave at Adullam (1 Samuel 21:10–22:1). It was probably there that David had the time to write this prayer, praising God for rescuing him from "mere mortals."

If you're facing a difficult situation, rely on God to rescue you. When you place you trust in the Almighty, you'll have no reason to fear.

Dear Lord, why should I be afraid when I am trusting you today for . . .

February 8

CALLING ON GOD'S NAME

But I called on your name, Lord, from deep within the well, and you heard me! You listened to my pleading; you heard my weeping! Yes, you came at my despairing cry and told me, "Do not fear."

Lord, you are my lawyer! Plead my case! For you have redeemed my life.

LAMENTATIONS 3:55-58

Parents take great care in choosing the right name for their baby. A child's name is certainly important, but how much more important is God's name? God's name reveals his character. Calling on God's name means remembering what kind of God we're calling upon. Jeremiah faced the anger of those who had rejected God's warnings of judgment. He called on the name of the Lord, asking him to represent him as both his lawyer and his redeemer. He asked the Lord to take up his cause and rescue him. The Lord answered him, coming to his defense and comforting him with these simple words: "Do not fear."

What a privilege we have to be able to call upon the same God Jeremiah did! Our God answers those who call on his name, calming our fears and defending our causes.

Dear Lord, plead my case and redeem me from . . .

Praying When Hope Seems Dim

Save me, O God,
for the floodwaters are up to my neck.
Deeper and deeper I sink into the mire;
I can't find a foothold to stand on.
I am in deep water,
and the floods overwhelm me.
I am exhausted from crying for help;
my throat is parched and dry.
My eyes are swollen with weeping,
waiting for my God to help me....
But I keep right on praying to you, Lord,
hoping this is the time you will show me favor.

PSALM 69:1-3, 13

David's prayer recorded in this psalm essentially amounts to a simple, "Save me, I'm sinking." It's the cry of a desperate man who can't even think of helping himself. But at least David knew whom he needed to ask for help. Although he was exhausted from crying to the Lord in prayer, he kept on shouting to his God, the only one who could save him.

When waves of adversity threaten to drown you in despair, pray to God. Remember David's persistence, and keep on asking God for help.

Dear Lord, I am exhausted from crying for help, but I will keep on praying to you.

February 10

REJOICING IN GOD'S PROTECTION

But let all who take refuge in you rejoice;
let them sing joyful praises forever.
Protect them,
so all who love your name may be filled with joy.
For you bless the godly, O Lord,
surrounding them with your shield of love.

PSALM 5:11-12

All of us want security. That's why we put up fences, install electronic detection systems, and lock our doors. We want assurance that no one can harm us.

In this prayer, David rejoiced in God's protection. David commanded fortresses and armies, but he knew he couldn't count on these alone to keep him safe. Only God could surround him with a shield of love when wicked people attacked, whether they wielded armies of men or vicious rumors and lies. Even when he was under attack, David had nothing to fear, for the Lord was his safe refuge.

Are you concerned about your future security? Commit yourself to God's care. Ask him to surround you with a shield of love. Then rejoice in the Lord's protection.

Dear Lord, surround me with your shield of love . . .

February 11

PRAYING WHEN GOD FEELS DISTANT

My God, my God! Why have you forsaken me?
Why do you remain so distant?
Why do you ignore my cries for help?
Every day I call to you, my God, but you do not answer.
Every night you hear my voice, but I find no relief.
Yet you are holy.
The praises of Israel surround your throne.
Our ancestors trusted in you,
and you rescued them.
You heard their cries for help and saved them.
They put their trust in you and were never disappointed.

PSALM 22:1-5

Trust is a precious commodity in any relationship—slow to build and all-too-easy to undermine. Faced by dark and hopeless circumstances, we can start feeling abandoned by God and lose our trust in him. Yet it may be comforting to know that we're not the only ones who have felt that way. "Why have you forsaken me?" David cried. Jesus repeated these same words as he suffered on the cross (Mark 15:34). But such a straightforward question implies an intimate and trusting relationship between the petitioner and God in the first place. And David didn't give up waiting for God to answer him, for he knew that God has always responded to the cries of his people.

Do you feel alone and abandoned by God? Remind yourself of some ways God has worked in your life. God never abandons his people.

O God, though I feel alone, I put my trust in you . . .

February 12

**A PRAYER
FOR LOVE**

*May God himself, our Father, and our Lord Jesus make it
possible for us to come to you very soon. And may the Lord
make your love grow and overflow to each other and to
everyone else, just as our love overflows toward you. As a
result, Christ will make your hearts strong, blameless, and
holy when you stand before God our Father on that day
when our Lord Jesus comes with all those who belong to him.*

1 THESSALONIANS 3:11-13

When Paul wrote to the Thessalonians, his love and concern for
them were apparent in every word. When he prayed for them, he asked
the Lord to make their love for one another overflow. Paul prayed that
the Thessalonian church might become a loving, supporting community
of faith. The strong, silent, loner Christian didn't fit into Paul's understanding of how God works among his people.

Each of us needs each other. God uses other believers to
strengthen us and make us holy. As you pray for strength to be
faithful to God, you should expect his answer to come through those
believers who worship every Sunday with you. Likewise, you should
earnestly pray that God might use you to strengthen other believers.

*O God, help my love to grow and overflow to other
believers . . .*

February 13

THE REQUEST OF ABRAHAM'S SERVANT

"O Lord, God of my master," he prayed. "Give me success and show kindness to my master, Abraham. Help me to accomplish the purpose of my journey. See, here I am, standing beside this spring, and the young women of the village are coming out to draw water. This is my request. I will ask one of them for a drink. If she says, 'Yes, certainly, and I will water your camels, too!'—let her be the one you have appointed as Isaac's wife. By this I will know that you have shown kindness to my master."

As he was still praying, a young woman named Rebekah arrived with a water jug on her shoulder. Her father was Bethuel, who was the son of Abraham's brother Nahor. GENESIS 24:12-15

When believers face momentous decisions, they long to be aligned with God's will and purposes. Abraham had asked his servant to find the right bride for his son, Isaac. Abraham's servant realized the great weight of the responsibility he carried, so he submitted the matter directly to God rather than depend solely on his own wisdom. He asked God for a sign, and God granted his request instantaneously. Before he finished praying, Rebekah arrived and offered to give him water for both himself and his camels. What a remarkable answer to prayer!

God wants to direct our lives as well. Do we have the courage to seek out God's direction and ask for his guidance as Abraham's servant did?

Dear Lord, help me to depend on you as I seek to do your will . . .

February 14

A Prayer to Know God's Love

And I pray that Christ will be more and more at home in your hearts as you trust in him. May your roots go down deep into the soil of God's marvelous love. And may you have the power to understand, as all God's people should, how wide, how long, how high, and how deep his love really is. May you experience the love of Christ, though it is so great you will never fully understand it. Then you will be filled with the fullness of life and power that comes from God.

EPHESIANS 3:17-19

To love and to be loved are among the most fulfilling of human experiences. But precisely because so many people want love, many counterfeits are offered. The word *love* has become increasingly cheap, sentimental, and commercialized. But the apostle Paul proved by the way he lived his life that he truly and unselfishly loved his converts. He desired that they would understand and experience the love of God—the real thing. He understood that the lives of his converts had to be rooted in something that would last—God's eternal love.

As we intercede in prayer for those we love most, we can ask nothing better than that they would establish their lives on God's everlasting love.

Lord God, I pray that the ones I love might experience the love of Christ . . .

PRAISE TO THE GOD WHO SATISFIES

> *I have seen you in your sanctuary*
> *   and gazed upon your power and glory.*
> *Your unfailing love is better to me than life itself;*
> *   how I praise you!*
> *I will honor you as long as I live,*
> *   lifting up my hands to you in prayer.*
> *You satisfy me more than the richest of foods.*
> *I will praise you with songs of joy.*
>
> PSALM 63:2-5

Many of us put a great deal of time and effort into the pursuit of a rather elusive goal: fulfillment. We seek it in our work, in our relationships, and in our possessions. But our search for fulfillment in these areas often turns up empty. We are constantly disappointed. In this prayer, however, David described to God a different type of search that leads to ultimate fulfillment. Having "gazed upon" God's power and glory, he had found a purpose and meaning for his life. God's love was better than life itself! That's why David stayed up at night meditating on God and honoring and praising him.

May our prayers reflect our excitement to come into the Lord's presence and the satisfaction we experience from his love.

O God, your unfailing love is better to me than life itself . . .

February 16

**A Prayer
to
Overflow
with Love**

*I pray that your love for each other will overflow more and
more, and that you will keep on growing in your knowledge
and understanding. For I want you to understand what
really matters, so that you may live pure and blameless lives
until Christ returns. May you always be filled with the fruit
of your salvation–those good things that are produced in your
life by Jesus Christ–for this will bring much glory and praise
to God.*   Philippians 1:9-11

The trademark of the Christian is love. Like fruit on a tree, it is
produced by the life that God gives, which courses within us. Jesus
said as much when he said, "Your love for one another will prove to
the world that you are my disciples" (John 13:35). The apostle Paul
prayed fervently for the new believers in Philippi and told them
what he prayed for: that they would *overflow* with love for each
other—not with a gooey, sentimental sort of love, but with real,
God-inspired love. Paul knew that their loving actions toward each
other would be the best testimony of Christ's work within them.

Reflect for a few moments on what it means to overflow with
God's love.

*Dear Lord, place within me a love that continuously
overflows to others . . .*

February 17

CALLING ON GOD

But I will call on God,
and the Lord will rescue me.
Morning, noon, and night
I plead aloud in my distress,
and the Lord hears my voice.
He rescues me and keeps me safe
from the battle waged against me,
even though many still oppose me.
God, who is king forever,
will hear me and will humble them.

PSALM 55:16-19

"Help!" Should you hear such a cry, wherever you are, you know that immediate and decisive action is required. The person in distress must be at the end of his or her resources, completely lost unless someone intervenes. For believers, whatever difficulty we encounter, the one to whom we can cry "Help!" is God himself. He always hears, and he is powerful enough to save. David knew this. In trying circumstances, David reminded himself that "the Lord hears my voice" and "rescues me."

The more desperate your situation, the more it makes sense to express your anguish to God, even aloud. Like David, you will find him responsive to your plea.

I will call on you, God, in my distress . . .

February 18

DELIGHT IN GOD'S PRESENCE

Oh, that you would burst from the heavens and come down! How the mountains would quake in your presence! As fire causes wood to burn and water to boil, your coming would make the nations tremble. Then your enemies would learn the reason for your fame! When you came down long ago, you did awesome things beyond our highest expectations. And oh, how the mountains quaked! For since the world began, no ear has heard, and no eye has seen a God like you, who works for those who wait for him! You welcome those who cheerfully do good, who follow godly ways. ISAIAH 64:1-5

Have you ever wished that God would reveal himself in frightening majesty? Apparently Isaiah, in his lonely and often unpopular role as prophet, sometimes longed for such a revelation to reinforce his message to the Israelites that they should renew their love toward God. As Isaiah reflected on what it would be like for God to burst forth from the heavens, he renewed his commitment to serve the Almighty no matter what the cost. He recalled how God had intervened on behalf of faithful believers in the past; he affirmed that God certainly "works for those who wait for him."

Take time today to calm your soul before the Lord. Commit your worries and problems to him, and wait on him to answer.

Holy God, you work on behalf of those who wait for you . . .

A PLEA FOR SAFETY

O Lord, you are my refuge;
never let me be disgraced.
Rescue me! Save me from my enemies, for you are just.
Turn your ear to listen and set me free.
Be to me a protecting rock of safety,
where I am always welcome.
Give the order to save me,
for you are my rock and my fortress.

PSALM 71:1-3

Life is full of uncertainty, turmoil, and danger. Sometimes these trials are more psychological or spiritual in nature than physical, but the threat is real nonetheless. Where can we turn to find a safe haven? The psalmist knew that God was his refuge. In fact, the Lord had been his only source of hope ever since he was a child. He knew that God is a just and compassionate God. The Lord wants to protect his people. If God would only give the order, the psalmist knew he would be saved, so it was only natural for him to shout, "Rescue me!"

Consider what sorts of "enemies" confront you today. With the psalmist, turn to your rock and fortress, who is always ready to save you.

O Lord, my refuge, rescue me from . . .

**A Prayer
to Walk
with God**

*Yet I still belong to you;
   you are holding my right hand.
You will keep on guiding me with your counsel,
   leading me to a glorious destiny.
Whom have I in heaven but you?
   I desire you more than anything on earth.
My health may fail, and my spirit may grow weak,
   but God remains the strength of my heart;
   he is mine forever. . . .
But as for me, how good it is to be near God!
   I have made the Sovereign Lord my shelter,
   and I will tell everyone about the wonderful things you do.*

PSALM 73:23-26, 28

Sometimes people are so "in love" that they would readily
proclaim they need nothing else as long as they have one another.
How much more do those in an intimate relationship with God
have everything they need? In this prayer, Asaph considered the
blessings that were his because he walked with God. God was guiding
him and leading him to a glorious destiny. Asaph even described
the Lord as "holding my right hand." To Asaph, the Lord was like a
prized possession—more to be desired than anything on earth,
outlasting even the breath of life itself.

Take a few moments in God's presence to reflect on the priceless
gift of your relationship with him. Tell him how and why you love
him. Ask him to keep you always close by his side.

O God, I desire you more than anything on earth . . .

BOASTING IN THE LORD

I will praise the Lord at all times.
I will constantly speak his praises.
I will boast only in the Lord;
let all who are discouraged take heart.
Come, let us tell of the Lord's greatness;
let us exalt his name together.
I prayed to the Lord, and he answered me,
freeing me from all my fears.
Those who look to him for help will be radiant with joy;
no shadow of shame will darken their faces.

PSALM 34:1-5

Sometimes people who come across with the most bravado are actually the most fearful. Their boasts mask a dark reality of fear. But there's another type of boasting grounded in reality: boasting in the Lord. In God, there's plenty to boast about. The Almighty has the power and the desire to save all who put their trust in him. In this prayer, David was boasting in God because he had narrowly escaped from his enemy. King Saul had wanted to murder him, but David, through some shrewd cunning, had escaped. But in this prayer, David gave all the credit to God. He viewed his deliverance as an answer to prayer.

From what near-disaster has God delivered you recently? With David, "boast" in the Lord and direct your thanks and praise to him.

O Lord, thank you for answering me when I prayed to you about . . .

February 22

A PETITION FOR MERCY

Oh, do not hold us guilty for our former sins!
  Let your tenderhearted mercies quickly meet our needs,
  for we are brought low to the dust.
Help us, O God of our salvation!
  Help us for the honor of your name.
Oh, save us and forgive our sins
  for the sake of your name. . . .
Then we your people, the sheep of your pasture,
  will thank you forever and ever,
  praising your greatness from generation to generation.

PSALM 79:8-9, 13

A plea to God for mercy presumes that the petitioner is guilty. It is the cry of someone brought low, dishonored, and in need of forgiveness. When God shows mercy, he isn't forgiving that person because of what he or she has done, but because God is compassionate to those who repent of their sins and ask for forgiveness. It is only because of God's goodness that sinners are forgiven. Asaph understood that it wasn't his worthiness but the Lord's greatness that prompted the Lord to rescue him. In light of this truth, Asaph dedicated this prayer to praising God for being so merciful.

Are you in need of God's mercy? His love and goodness are the source of your hope. Cast yourself on his mercy and let your lips overflow with grateful praise.

O Lord, do not hold me guilty for my sins . . .

HEALING THROUGH CONFESSION

Lord, have you completely rejected Judah? Do you really hate Jerusalem? Why have you wounded us past all hope of healing? We hoped for peace, but no peace came. We hoped for a time of healing but found only terror.

Lord, we confess our wickedness and that of our ancestors, too. We all have sinned against you. For the sake of your own name, Lord, do not abandon us. Do not disgrace yourself and the throne of your glory. Do not break your covenant with us. Please don't forget us! JEREMIAH 14:19-22

When Jeremiah prayed for the spiritual healing of the nation of Judah, he confessed the sins of his people first. Sin—either ours or the sins of others—inevitably brings pain and suffering. Often when Jesus healed a physical illness or infirmity, he addressed the sick person's sin first. When friends lowered a paralyzed man into a crowd before Jesus, he said: "Son, your sins are forgiven" (Luke 5:20). Jeremiah confessed his people's sins with an attitude of utter helplessness and dependence on God, his Savior. No other god but the Lord was his hope, so Jeremiah was determined to wait on the Lord to act.

When you know that you are suffering pain from sin, follow Jeremiah's lead and cast yourself on the Lord's mercy.

Lord, I confess my sin and trust that you will not abandon me . . .

PRAISE FOR GOD'S KNOWLEDGE OF US

You both precede and follow me.
*   You place your hand of blessing on my head.*
Such knowledge is too wonderful for me,
*   too great for me to know!...*
I could ask the darkness to hide me
*   and the light around me to become night—*
*   but even in darkness I cannot hide from you.*
To you the night shines as bright as day.
Darkness and light are both alike to you.

PSALM 139:5-6, 11-12

Because we know that God sees and knows all things, his presence can be either a source of comfort or a source of dread. Just as Adam and Eve hid after they had eaten the forbidden fruit (Genesis 3:10), we often hide our sins from God. Yet at the same time, it can be comforting to know that the darkness—symbolic of danger and hopelessness—is "as bright as day" to God. No sin, neither our own nor others', is too big for God to forgive, provided we repent and fall on his mercy. Through Christ's resurrection, darkness was forever shattered.

As you approach God in prayer today, take courage. Remind yourself of God's intimate knowledge of you and his commitment to guide you through the darkness into his eternal light.

Dear Lord, even in darkness I cannot hide from you . . .

**PRAISE TO
MY SAVIOR**

Teach me your ways, O Lord,
that I may live according to your truth!
Grant me purity of heart,
that I may honor you.
With all my heart I will praise you, O Lord my God.
I will give glory to your name forever,
for your love for me is very great.
You have rescued me from the depths of death!

PSALM 86:11-13

As we grasp the enormity of what God has done for us, we look for ways to declare our love for God. Because the Lord had saved David from death, David expressed his deep love for God in exuberant gratitude: "With all my heart I will praise you." Yet as he approached God in prayer, David realized his life didn't measure up to God's standards. But he still wanted to honor God with his life, so he prayed that God would grant him a pure heart. He wanted to remain in unbroken fellowship with God, so he asked God to teach him his ways.

When we pray, we need to remind ourselves what a privilege it is to approach the Lord. We were in the depths of sin, but the Lord has elevated us so that we can stand in his presence. Ask the Lord today to teach you how you should live according to *his* ways.

O Lord, I thank you for saving me and ask you to teach me your ways . . .

February 26

**FILLED
WITH AWE**

This prayer was sung by the prophet Habakkuk:
> *I have heard all about you, Lord, and I am filled with
> awe by the amazing things you have done. In this time of
> our deep need, begin again to help us, as you did in years
> gone by. Show us your power to save us. And in your anger,
> remember your mercy.*
>
> HABAKKUK 3:1-2

Habakkuk was a prophet of God in a time of "deep need"—a time when God's people were suffering disgrace and evil seemed to be winning the day. But Habakkuk didn't let the prominent events of his day discourage him. He reminded himself who God was and encouraged himself with memories of the "amazing things" God had accomplished in the past. He acknowledged that God's anger toward his people was justified. He knew, however, that God could save his generation as well as any other, for the Lord was merciful. So he laced his pleas for mercy and salvation with expressions of awe and praise.

In your time of need, let your prayers begin and end with praise for the God who is worthy of all glory and honor.

*O God, I am filled with awe by the amazing things you
have done . . .*

A PLEA FOR COMPASSION

O Lord, do not rebuke me in your anger
or discipline me in your rage.
Have compassion on me, Lord, for I am weak.
Heal me, Lord, for my body is in agony.
I am sick at heart.
How long, O Lord, until you restore me?
Return, O Lord, and rescue me.
Save me because of your unfailing love.

PSALM 6:1-4

Like children, we sometimes get ourselves into situations from which we cannot extricate ourselves. We know that our plight is the result of sin or foolishness. Anger certainly is a justifiable reaction on the part of our heavenly Father. In this psalm, David found himself in such a situation. He knew that God was the only one to whom he could appeal for compassion, so he prayed to God with unabashed candor. After all, God is both just and loving. He certainly disciplines, but he also forgives.

When you find yourself in a predicament, perhaps of your own making, don't hesitate to follow David's example and pour your heart out before God.

Dear Lord, have compassion on me, for I am weak . . .

PRAISE FOR GOD'S DISCIPLINE

Happy are those whom you discipline, Lord,
and those whom you teach from your law.
You give them relief from troubled times
until a pit is dug for the wicked.
The Lord will not reject his people;
he will not abandon his own special possession.
Judgment will come again for the righteous,
and those who are upright will have a reward.

PSALM 94:12-15

Does it ever seem as if those who try to live by God's laws are getting nowhere, while people with no thought of God seem to prosper? If so, you're not alone. The psalmist is one of many people in the Bible who pondered this problem in his prayers to the Lord. Yet the psalmist walked with God long enough to know that God's ways are just. The Lord had taught him, corrected him, and disciplined him so that the Lord's ways had become second nature to the psalmist. If we have that type of dynamic relationship with the Holy One, we are the ones who will ultimately prosper. The time will come when those who have ignored God's justice will face the tragic consequences of their evil actions.

Next time you become discouraged, join the psalmist in taking the long view. Remind yourself of the eternal destiny of those who follow God.

O Lord, thank you for disciplining me . . .

**MICAH'S
PRAISE FOR
GOD'S
COMPASSION**

O Lord, come and rule your people; lead your flock in green pastures. Help them to live in peace and prosperity. Let them enjoy the fertile pastures of Bashan and Gilead as they did long ago. . . .

Where is another God like you, who pardons the sins of the survivors among his people? You cannot stay angry with your people forever, because you delight in showing mercy. Once again you will have compassion on us. You will trample our sins under your feet and throw them into the depths of the ocean! MICAH 7:14, 18-19

In the course of his calling as a prophet to Judah, Micah often spoke *with* God as well as *for* God. He had a clear understanding of God's hatred of sin. This understanding enabled him to warn the people in no uncertain terms of God's coming judgment. But he also was intimately acquainted with God's compassionate nature. Though God might be justified in wiping out an entire nation, he consistently pardoned sinners who repented of their ways. In a beautiful word picture, Micah described God throwing the sins of his people into the depths of the ocean.

Today, we can approach the same merciful God. He wants to forgive those who turn away from their sins.

O God, who delights in showing mercy, restore me . . .

**AN OPEN
HEART
BEFORE
GOD**

*Search me, O God, and know my heart;
    test me and know my thoughts.
Point out anything in me that offends you,
    and lead me along the path of everlasting life.*

PSALM 139:23-24

In Psalm 139, David celebrated God's intimate knowledge of him—for "you saw me before I was born. Every day of my life was recorded in your book" (v. 16). David prayerfully realized that God knew everything he did and thought. David's response was to ask God to purify him. He knew that his own perception of sin was limited. There might be something in his life that offended the Almighty, something David wasn't aware of. So David prayed, "Point out anything in me that offends you."

We, too, should confess our sins and ask God to show us where we have wronged him. Quiet your heart before the Lord today, and ask God to search your heart and point out anything that offends him.

Holy Lord, point out anything in me that offends you . . .

A DESPERATE CONFESSION

"Lord, our wickedness has caught up with us. We have sinned against you. So please, help us for the sake of your own reputation."

JEREMIAH 14:7

When God brought a drought upon the people of Judah, they realized the extent of their sin and appealed to God. In essence, they had been "caught" in their sin. It was only when they could no longer deny the reality of their sin that they approached God in prayer. They prayed that the Lord might save them because of his own reputation. *Surely*, they thought, *God would not want the world to see his people wiped out.*

Sometimes we, too, suffer the disastrous consequences of our sins and are forced to admit, belatedly, that "our wickedness has caught up with us." Let us not offer God halfhearted repentance. Pray that genuine sorrow may take root in your heart, so that God can work lasting change in your life.

Dear Lord, my wickedness has caught up with me . . .

March 4

Who may worship in your sanctuary, Lord?
   Who may enter your presence on your holy hill?
Those who lead blameless lives
   and do what is right,
   speaking the truth from sincere hearts.
Those who refuse to slander others
   or harm their neighbors
   or speak evil of their friends.
Those who despise persistent sinners,
   and honor the faithful followers of the Lord
   and keep their promises even when it hurts.
Those who do not charge interest on the money they lend,
   and who refuse to accept bribes to testify against the innocent.
Such people will stand firm forever.

PSALM 15:1-5

Periodically, the people of Israel "went up" to the Temple in Jerusalem for feasts and celebrated God's saving acts on their behalf. In this prayer, David meditated on what characteristics should mark those who worship before the Lord at the Temple. Such people should be "blameless"—truthful, kind, generous, and loving.

Many church services include a time of confession in their worship services so that worshipers can prepare their hearts properly. As you enter God's presence for your own time of worship and prayer, ask the Lord to cleanse your life.

Dear Lord, as I enter your presence, cleanse me . . .

March 5

A PRAYER
FOR
STRENGTH

Come back, we beg you, O God Almighty.
Look down from heaven and see our plight.
Watch over and care for this vine
that you yourself have planted,
this son you have raised for yourself. . . .
Strengthen the man you love,
the son of your choice.
Then we will never forsake you again.
Revive us so we can call on your name once more.
Turn us again to yourself, O Lord God Almighty.
Make your face shine down upon us.
Only then will we be saved.

PSALM 80:14-15, 17-19

When we are exhausted—at the very end of our own strength—there is only one place to turn. God is our only hope for strength. Asaph, the psalmist, stated this truth in his prayer to God. Why should God revive us again and again? God created us to be in relationship with him. He wants us to call on his name. We are his vine, and as such we're completely dependent on the one who has planted us—God himself. We can't grow unless he provides moist soil, pure water, and sunshine. Leaving or forsaking our Provider is ultimately suicidal.

Dedicate some time today for praising and thanking God for his love for you. And when you feel like you can't go on, ask him to revive and strengthen you.

O Lord God Almighty, make your face shine down upon us . . .

**HEZEKIAH'S
PRAYER FOR
PURIFICATION**

*Most of those who came from Ephraim, Manasseh, Issachar,
and Zebulun had not purified themselves. But King
Hezekiah prayed for them, and they were allowed to eat the
Passover meal anyway, even though this was contrary to
God's laws. For Hezekiah said, "May the Lord, who is good,
pardon those who decide to follow the Lord, the God of their
ancestors, even though they are not properly cleansed for the
ceremony." And the Lord listened to Hezekiah's prayer and
healed the people.* 2 CHRONICLES 30:18-20

King Hezekiah's prayer illustrates the timeless truth that ultimately
we are made pure by God himself, not by our own works. The nations
of Israel and Judah had been separate for many years, but Hezekiah
boldly invited everyone from Israel and Judah to renew their faithful
observance of the Passover at the temple in Jerusalem. Most of the
Israelites spurned the invitation, but some from Israel "humbled
themselves and went to Jerusalem" (v. 11). Hezekiah's prayer for these
impure Israelites was in keeping with God's nature, and God forgave
them.

Although we must never take God's good will for granted, we can
be assured that if we approach him humbly, knowing that we are
incapable of justifying ourselves, he will purify us.

*May the Lord, who is good, pardon us who decide to
follow the Lord . . .*

March 7

PRAISE FOR GOD'S MERCY

Praise the Lord!
For he has heard my cry for mercy.
The Lord is my strength, my shield from every danger.
I trust in him with all my heart.
He helps me, and my heart is filled with joy.
I burst out in songs of thanksgiving.

PSALM 28:6-7

God is merciful! How many times, like David, have we felt that our backs were up against the wall, our situation hopeless unless God intervened? David experienced the Lord's strength many times, so he often expressed his gratitude with this type of praise: "He has heard my cry for mercy. The Lord is . . . my shield from every danger. I trust in him with all my heart," David joyfully concluded.

When we ask for God's mercy, we must never neglect to sing his praise, for he is our only hope, our strength, and our shield. Even as we wait for a solution to our current dilemma, we can praise him for his faithfulness to us in the past. This will encourage our faith and nurture our trust in the God of mercy.

I praise you, Lord, for you have heard my cry for mercy . . .

March 8

THE TAX COLLECTOR'S HUMBLE PRAYER

"The proud Pharisee stood by himself and prayed this prayer: 'I thank you, God, that I am not a sinner like everyone else, especially like that tax collector over there! For I never cheat, I don't sin, I don't commit adultery, I fast twice a week, and I give you a tenth of my income.'

"But the tax collector stood at a distance and dared not even lift his eyes to heaven as he prayed. Instead, he beat his chest in sorrow, saying, 'O God, be merciful to me, for I am a sinner.'"

LUKE 18:11-13

These two prayers stand in sharp contrast to one another. The Pharisee barely acknowledged God at all. He used his time in the Temple as an opportunity to justify himself. In the guise of thanking God, he cut down others and congratulated himself. There was no humility in him. The tax collector, on the other hand, was rightfully aware of his sin before the most holy God. He made no claims for himself. He didn't try to justify his action. He only admitted he was a sinner. Jesus declared that it was the humble tax collector, not the proud Pharisee, whom God was willing to justify.

May God give us the courage to admit our true condition before him. Take time to meditate on God's holiness, and give up justifying yourself. In humility, cast yourself on the Lord's mercy.

O God, be merciful to me, for I am a sinner . . .

A PRAYER FROM THE DISCOURAGED

I lie in the dust, completely discouraged;
*   revive me by your word.*
I told you my plans, and you answered.
*   Now teach me your principles.*
Help me understand the meaning of your commandments,
*   and I will meditate on your wonderful miracles.*
I weep with grief;
*   encourage me by your word.*
Keep me from lying to myself;
*   give me the privilege of knowing your law.*

PSALM 119:25-29

When you're completely discouraged, where do you turn? The psalmist turned to God's laws and commandments. They revived him, even though circumstances had left him lying in the dust. He wanted to know more about God and truly *understand* God's ways, and he meditated on God's amazing miracles. He reminded himself that it was a privilege to know God and his laws. After all, God's law kept him from lying to himself. It liberated him from the quicksand of self-deceit and placed him firmly on the solid ground of God's law.

In the secular and self-absorbed climate of our times, despair is common. Even in your deepest discouragement, ask God to help you to understand his truth.

Lord, I weep with grief. Encourage me by your word . . .

STEPHEN'S PRAYER FOR FORGIVENESS

As they stoned him, Stephen prayed, "Lord Jesus, receive my spirit." And he fell to his knees, shouting, "Lord, don't charge them with this sin!" And with that, he died. ACTS 7:59-60

Stephen, a deacon of the early church, courageously proclaimed to the Jews the true identity of Jesus and the purpose of his death and resurrection. For his forceful and persuasive proclamation of the Good News, he was stoned to death. As he was being pelted with stones, Stephen started praying. First, he committed himself to the Lord. He was completely at peace that God would receive him into his kingdom. Even more surprisingly, Stephen's last words before he died were a prayer for his killers—asking God to forgive them.

Many times in life we will experience mistreatment at the hands of others, perhaps even for taking a stand for the Lord. May God so infuse us with his love and mercy that we, like Stephen, may pray for those who persecute us.

Dear Lord, have mercy on . . .

RECOGNIZING OUR SIN

We are not godly. We are constant sinners, so your anger is heavy on us. How can people like us be saved? We are all infected and impure with sin. When we proudly display our righteous deeds, we find they are but filthy rags. Like autumn leaves, we wither and fall. And our sins, like the wind, sweep us away. Yet no one calls on your name or pleads with you for mercy. Therefore, you have turned away from us and turned us over to our sins.

And yet, Lord, you are our Father. We are the clay, and you are the potter. We are all formed by your hand. Oh, don't be so angry with us, Lord. Please don't remember our sins forever. Look at us, we pray, and see that we are all your people.

ISAIAH 64:5-9

There are times when we are overwhelmed with the harsh reality of our sin, and we, like Isaiah, must admit, "we are not godly." In the bright light of God's purity, all of the Israelites' "righteous deeds" were no better than filthy rags, and they were like windblown autumn leaves. But the Israelites still refused to call upon God, so the Lord had turned them over to their sins. Yet Isaiah was bold enough to remind God that they were his chosen people. He pleaded with God not to destroy them.

Like Isaiah, we need to realize how thoroughly saturated we are by sin. But lest we start despairing, we need to remind ourselves that God can forgive us and restore us once again.

Dear Lord, we are not godly, but you are merciful . . .

March 12

**A CRY FOR
GOD TO
HURRY**

Please, God, rescue me!
Come quickly, Lord, and help me. . . .
But may all who search for you
be filled with joy and gladness.
May those who love your salvation
repeatedly shout, "God is great!"
But I am poor and needy;
please hurry to my aid, O God.
You are my helper and my savior;
O Lord, do not delay!

PSALM 70:1, 4-5

Have you ever, like David, asked God to hurry? In this prayer, David asked God to defend him against his enemies. He asked that he might be given the opportunity once again to praise the Lord for his deliverance. Then he seemed to remember his desperation once again, and he prayed, "But I am poor and needy; please hurry to my aid, O God."

There will be times when you feel desperate and cry out to God for help. You may even remind yourself of God's faithfulness to you—and then panic! At those times, however, remember that you aren't alone. Faithful people of God have felt that kind of desperation in the past. But God will not turn a deaf ear to you. He will give you all that you need.

Dear Lord, my helper and my Savior, please hurry . . .

March 13

SOLOMON'S PRAYER THAT GOD MAY FORGIVE

"If they sin against you—and who has never sinned?—you may become angry with them and let their enemies conquer them and take them captive to a foreign land far or near. But in that land of exile, they may turn to you again in repentance and pray, 'We have sinned, done evil, and acted wickedly.' Then if they turn to you with their whole heart and soul and pray toward the land you gave to their ancestors, toward this city you have chosen, and toward this Temple I have built to honor your name, then hear their prayers from heaven where you live. Uphold their cause and forgive your people who have sinned against you."

2 CHRONICLES 6:36-39

King Solomon had been given the great honor of constructing the temple for the worship of the Almighty. His prayer to God at the dedication of the temple showed his wisdom and farsightedness. He foresaw the day when God would have to discipline his people because of their persistent sin. But Solomon also realized that the suffering of being captives in a foreign land might bring them to their senses. In that case, he asked God to hear their prayers and forgive them.

If we are honest with ourselves, we will realize that, despite our best intentions, we will disobey our Lord. We shouldn't pray that God would withhold his correction. Instead we should pray, as Solomon did, that we may repent and turn back to God and that God may forgive.

Dear Lord, when I sin against you, hear my cry of repentance . . .

March 14

**PRAISE FOR
THE GOD
WHO
HEARS**

*Come and listen, all you who fear God,
and I will tell you what he did for me.
For I cried out to him for help,
praising him as I spoke.
If I had not confessed the sin in my heart,
my Lord would not have listened.
But God did listen!
He paid attention to my prayer.
Praise God, who did not ignore my prayer
and did not withdraw his unfailing love from me.*

PSALM 66:16-20

Like the psalmist, we often ask God for help. The prayer in Psalm 66, however, is a good model for us. First, the psalmist remembered to praise God for who he is. Of course, God is always worthy; our praise doesn't change who God is. But we need to remind ourselves of the Lord's greatness. Next, and more importantly, the psalmist confessed his sin. He went so far as to say that if he had not confessed his sin, God would not have responded to his prayer!

Confession is a fitting prelude to petition. It aligns our heart with God's truth. It reminds us of our own unworthiness and the Lord's holiness. Before you make any requests of God today, take time to humbly confess your sins. Then praise God for hearing your prayer.

Praise God, who did not ignore my prayer . . .

**PRAISING
THE ONE
WHO
SATISFIES**

*Let them praise the Lord for his great love
and for all his wonderful deeds to them.
For he satisfies the thirsty
and fills the hungry with good things.*

PSALM 107:8-9

The words of this psalm were originally recited at one of Israel's religious festivals by those who knew what it was like to hunger and thirst, for it was spoken by those who had returned from exile in Babylon. These people spoke from experience of God's "great love," and they had seen him provide for his people in the midst of terrible trouble.

In a very small way, many of us can relate to the feelings of those exiles. Our lives are often filled with great need—whether physical, spiritual, emotional, or financial. Whatever needs you have now, express them to God. Ask him for the deep satisfaction that he alone can bring to each of your longings.

Dear Lord, I depend on you to meet my needs . . .

March 16

A PRAYER
IN SICKNESS

When Hezekiah heard this, he turned his face to the wall and prayed to the Lord, "Remember, O Lord, how I have always tried to be faithful to you and do what is pleasing in your sight." Then he broke down and wept bitterly.

But before Isaiah had left the middle courtyard, this message came to him from the Lord: "Go back to Hezekiah, the leader of my people. Tell him, 'This is what the Lord, the God of your ancestor David, says: I have heard your prayer and seen your tears. I will heal you, and three days from now you will get out of bed and go to the Temple of the Lord.'"

2 KINGS 20:2-5

Hezekiah was on his deathbed. But he knew of God's compassion and his power over disease, so he cried out to him. When God answered Hezekiah's prayer, he did so in a dramatic way. Within three days, the king was able to go to the temple.

God doesn't always respond to our prayers for healing in such a dramatic fashion. But we can be certain that God *can* and sometimes *will* act dramatically and suddenly to help us. In sickness and in health, God's wisdom is far beyond our own. Though we may never understand why things happen in our life, we can always know that God is loving, faithful, and powerful. No matter how hopeless your situation seems, trust in God's care for you and know that he is listening to your pleas.

O Lord, I cry out to you, for you are always faithful and loving . . .

March 17

SORROW FOR SIN

O Lord, don't rebuke me in your anger!
Don't discipline me in your rage!
Your arrows have struck deep,
and your blows are crushing me.
Because of your anger, my whole body is sick;
my health is broken because of my sins.
My guilt overwhelms me—
it is a burden too heavy to bear. . . .
But I confess my sins;
I am deeply sorry for what I have done.

PSALM 38:1-4, 18

Sometimes the gravity of our sin can overwhelm us. The physical and mental suffering can feel like God's heavy hand of judgment. This was David's situation as he prayed the words of Psalm 38. He spoke of God's anger and rage, of God's arrows striking deep and his blows crushing him. David realized that his own guilt was the cause of his suffering, and he knew where to turn for mercy and relief. He confessed his sin before God and knew he could receive forgiveness.

Sometimes when we are suffering because of sin, we are tempted to become bitter and turn away from God. Let us learn from David, who turned immediately to God. Confess your sin to God and stop the spiral of sin that sends us reeling away from God.

Lord, I confess my sins; I am deeply sorry for what I have done . . .

**PRAISE FOR
THE GOD
WHO IS
NEAR**

*The Lord is close to all who call on him,
    yes, to all who call on him sincerely.
He fulfills the desires of those who fear him;
    he hears their cries for help and rescues them.
The Lord protects all those who love him,
    but he destroys the wicked.
I will praise the Lord,
    and everyone on earth will bless his holy name
    forever and forever.*

PSALM 145:18-21

Does God ever seem far away? In this prayer, David reminded himself that God is *close* to all who call on him sincerely. He went on to praise the Lord for consistently answering the prayers of his people and fulfilling the desires of those who fear God.

Sometimes, like David, we may need to remind ourselves of God's great kindness, of his history of fulfilling the desires of those who fear him. If we reflect on how God has heard the cries of his people and rescued them, we will be more likely to call on God in faith. Although we may have our doubts sometimes, it is indeed true that God watches over all those who love him.

O Lord, you are close to all who call on you . . .

SEARCHING AFTER GOD

> *But for those who are righteous,*
> *the path is not steep and rough.*
> *You are a God of justice,*
> *and you smooth out the road ahead of them.*
> *Lord, we love to obey your laws;*
> *our heart's desire is to glorify your name.*
> *All night long I search for you;*
> *earnestly I seek for God.*
> *For only when you come to judge the earth*
> *will people turn from wickedness and do what is right.*
>
> ISAIAH 26:7-9

In every situation, the Lord God is the one we need. Isaiah knew this truth intimately. Isaiah wanted God to smooth out the road ahead for him. The path may have appeared steep and rough; but it wasn't impassable for those aligned with the Holy One. The world around Isaiah seemed to be going from bad to worse; but he cultivated an attitude of waiting for God. He knew the power to face every situation resided in God alone. Likewise, the writer of Revelation ended the record of his visions of coming apostasy and wrath with the same heartfelt cry: "Amen! Come, Lord Jesus!" (Revelation 22:20).

We, too, should nurture a longing for God to rescue us from the sin within and around us. He is our ultimate hope.

O Lord, all night long I search for you . . .

March 20

RESPONDING TO ANSWERED PRAYER

What mighty praise, O God,
belongs to you in Zion.
We will fulfill our vows to you,
for you answer our prayers,
and to you all people will come.
Though our hearts are filled with sins,
you forgive them all.
What joy for those you choose to bring near,
those who live in your holy courts.
What joys await us
inside your holy Temple.
You faithfully answer our prayers with awesome deeds,
O God our savior.

PSALM 65:1-5

God is worthy of our praise. He *does* answer our prayers. Moreover, he forgives our sins. David rejoiced in this truth and ecstatically exclaimed, "What joys await us inside your holy Temple." For David, entering God's presence was the greatest joy he could imagine. He made sure that the Lord knew of his joy and showered praises on him.

On countless occasions, God has forgiven our sins and answered our prayers. With the same fervency that we pray for his help, let us remember to sing his praises, and let us follow through on our promises to the Lord.

Dear Lord, I will fulfill my vows to you, for you answer my prayers . . .

**CELEBRATING
GOD'S
FAITHFUL
LOVE**

*Give thanks to the Lord, for he is good!
His faithful love endures forever.
Let the congregation of Israel repeat:
"His faithful love endures forever."
Let Aaron's descendants, the priests, repeat:
"His faithful love endures forever."
Let all who fear the Lord repeat:
"His faithful love endures forever."*

PSALM 118:1-4

Dependable. Reliable. Faithful. All of us want such qualities in our friends—dependable when the going gets tough, reliable when you have to count on them, and faithful to the end. As this psalm attests, such qualities are perfectly demonstrated in God himself. He came to our rescue when we were mired in our sin and could do nothing for ourselves. Such faithful love is something to celebrate, so praise him by saying: "His faithful love endures forever."

Each day, celebrate God's faithfulness. Meditate on the many ways God has blessed you and those you love. Rejoice over the many ways he has fulfilled his promises to you. Give him the thanks and praise he so deserves.

Dear Lord, your faithful love for me endures forever . . .

FORGIVENESS FOR GOD'S PEOPLE

"O our God, hear your servant's prayer! Listen as I plead. For your own sake, Lord, smile again on your desolate sanctuary.

"O my God, listen to me and hear my request. Open your eyes and see our wretchedness. See how your city lies in ruins—for everyone knows that it is yours. We do not ask because we deserve help, but because you are so merciful.

"O Lord, hear. O Lord, forgive. O Lord, listen and act! For your own sake, O my God, do not delay, for your people and your city bear your name." DANIEL 9:17-19

Most of us can think of one or two "inherited consequences" in our lives. Others may have made bad decisions, but we seem to be suffering the results. This is what Daniel was experiencing in Babylon. He knew he was there because his nation was being punished for generations of sinfulness. So he prayed for his people—God's people. From the land of punishment, he begged the Lord for forgiveness. His plea for mercy was based solely on God's compassionate character.

The Lord still disciplines his people when they refuse to walk in his ways, only now God's people are the church rather than an actual nation. Do you see the results of sin in your church? Spend some time today praying for the Lord's forgiveness and guidance.

Dear Lord, for your own sake, smile again on your desolate sanctuary . . .

Waiting Patiently for God

Teach me how to live, O Lord.
 Lead me along the path of honesty. . . .
Yet I am confident that I will see the Lord's goodness
 while I am here in the land of the living.
Wait patiently for the Lord.
 Be brave and courageous.
 Yes, wait patiently for the Lord.

PSALM 27:11, 13-14

David knew what it meant to be under pressure, surrounded by a vast army of enemies seeking his downfall. But even in those desperate times, David appealed to God for assistance with language that prepared his own soul for God's pace. Although David certainly had his own ideas on how God could fix his situation, he submitted himself to God's way. He asked the Lord to teach and lead him. Although David could have been tempted to frantic action, he quieted his heart and decided to wait on the Lord.

All too often we expect instant answers from the Lord. But God often uses the difficult situations in our life to forge character. Like David, we can be confident we will "see the Lord's goodness." But God will ultimately control the timing of his answers.

O Lord, teach me how to live and help me to wait patiently on you . . .

*Is it not the Most High who helps one and harms another?
Then why should we, mere humans, complain when we are
punished for our sins?*

*Instead, let us test and examine our ways. Let us turn
again in repentance to the Lord. Let us lift our hearts and
hands to God in heaven and say, "We have sinned and
rebelled, and you have not forgiven us."*

LAMENTATIONS 3:38-42

If we can read Lamentations without having our pride pierced, we may have hardened our heart toward God. In this prayer, Jeremiah attacks our tendency to call God to account for his actions. All too often, we presume to be the judge of God's ways, yet we avoid examining our own sinful ways. The weeping prophet points out the cost of such behavior: We miss God's forgiveness. The problem isn't God's punishment but our unwillingness to repent.

Today, consider the ways you have sat in judgment of God. In prayer, submit your own heart to the Lord's scrutiny, and confess to him all that he brings to mind.

Dear Lord, help me to examine and test my ways . . .

ABRAHAM'S PRAYER FOR MERCY

Abraham approached him and said, "Will you destroy both innocent and guilty alike? Suppose you find fifty innocent people there within the city—will you still destroy it, and not spare it for their sakes? Surely you wouldn't do such a thing, destroying the innocent with the guilty. Why, you would be treating the innocent and the guilty exactly the same! Surely you wouldn't do that! Should not the Judge of all the earth do what is right?"

GENESIS 18:23-25

In the days before their fiery judgment, the citizens of Sodom and Gomorrah probably had no idea that their neighbor Abraham was agonizing with God over their fate. Abraham saw the need for justice; but he also begged God to show them his mercy. He asked God to spare the city for just a handful of righteous people, and God agreed. In addition, God sent his angels to protect Lot's innocent family and get them out of harm's way. But as Sodom and Gomorrah's destruction illustrates, there's a limit to his mercy, for the God of justice will not let sin go unpunished forever.

Just as he listened to righteous Abraham long ago, God will listen to your cries for justice and your pleas for mercy. In the end, God will do what is right.

Righteous Judge, have mercy on me, a sinner . . .

March 26

A Prayer for Rescue

O God, insolent people rise up against me;
violent people are trying to kill me.
And you mean nothing to them.
But you, O Lord, are a merciful and gracious God,
slow to get angry,
full of unfailing love and truth.
Look down and have mercy on me.
Give strength to your servant;
yes, save me, for I am your servant.

Psalm 86:14-16

What situations have revealed your weakness and vulnerability the most? When have you most needed God's power? In this prayer, David described to God the predicament he found himself in. Arrogant people were opposing him, and some wanted to murder him. The odds against him were overwhelming, and he frankly admitted that to God. Yet David used a simple word to turn his prayer around—the word *but.* He used the word *but* to move his thoughts from his sizeable problems to his infinite and almighty God.

Once you have listed and lifted your troubles to God, follow David's example and acknowledge that no matter how daunting your situation may be, God is greater. He is the source of power—now and always.

Almighty God, give me strength and save me, for I am your servant . . .

SOLOMON'S DEDICATION OF THE TEMPLE

But will God really live on earth? Why, even the highest heavens cannot contain you. How much less this Temple I have built! Listen to my prayer and my request, O Lord my God. Hear the cry and the prayer that your servant is making to you today. May you watch over this Temple both day and night, this place where you have said you would put your name. May you always hear the prayers I make toward this place. May you hear the humble and earnest requests from me and your people Israel when we pray toward this place. Yes, hear us from heaven where you live, and when you hear, forgive.

1 KINGS 8:27-30

Standing before the magnificent temple in Jerusalem, Solomon considered the folly of limiting God to a building made of wood and stone. Solomon knew his temple was only a small tribute to the God who cannot be contained in the entire universe. But Solomon also realized that setting apart a place for prayer and worship doesn't necessarily mean that we believe God is confined there. Holy places serve as reminders and markers of our fellowship with God. Church buildings can't offer forgiveness or provide us with a relationship with God, but the God whom we meet there certainly does.

What places serve as reminders of God's presence in your life? How do they make you accountable before your holy Lord?

Infinite Lord, hear my prayer and forgive . . .

March 28

REJOICING OVER GOD'S FAVOR

O Lord my God, I cried out to you for help,
*   and you restored my health.*
You brought me up from the grave, O Lord.
*   You kept me from falling into the pit of death.*
Sing to the Lord, all you godly ones!
*   Praise his holy name.*
His anger lasts for a moment,
*   but his favor lasts a lifetime!*
Weeping may go on all night,
*   but joy comes with the morning.*

PSALM 30:2-5

Although God prevented David from building the great temple in Jerusalem, this prayer of David was sung when the temple was dedicated. The prayer's words echo the experience of someone who had survived God's anger and was rejoicing in God's mercy. Even a moment of God's anger created a night of weeping for David. But the darkness and sorrow of the night were always followed by a joy-filled morning—a restoration of David's relationship with his Lord. David knew God didn't get angry without reason, and the appropriate response to God's anger was repentance.

In your nights of painful waiting, remember that the Lord will surely bring about a morning of joy. Rejoice that one day he will wipe away every tear forever.

Dear Lord, I look to you to bring me favor and joy once again . . .

SILENT BEFORE GOD

Then the Lord said to Job, "Do you still want to argue with the Almighty? You are God's critic, but do you have the answers?"

Then Job replied to the Lord, "I am nothing—how could I ever find the answers? I will put my hand over my mouth in silence. I have said too much already. I have nothing more to say."

JOB 40:1-5

Job lost everything: his children, his possessions, his health, and the loyalty of his wife. He was left with friends who tried to explain it all by accusing him of doing wrong. Job and his friends tried to understand all that transpired, but in the end, they overlooked God's infinite wisdom and absolute sovereignty. The Almighty doesn't answer to anyone. His knowledge and power far surpass our own. We may never completely understand his ways. But God has revealed more than enough of his loving character so that we can fully trust him.

It's okay to ask God your difficult questions. But be careful not to use those questions as an excuse to accuse God or abandon him. Remind yourself that God is righteous, that his ways and thoughts are far above your own. Then sit in humble silence before the Almighty.

Righteous God, I don't understand, but I quietly trust that you have the answers . . .

MEDITATING ON GOD'S WORD

Teach me, O Lord,
*   to follow every one of your principles.*
Give me understanding and I will obey your law;
*   I will put it into practice with all my heart.*
Make me walk along the path of your commands,
*   for that is where my happiness is found.*
Give me an eagerness for your decrees;
*   do not inflict me with love for money!*
Turn my eyes from worthless things,
*   and give me life through your word.*

PSALM 119:33-37

Psalm 119 is one long, poetic prayer that praises and extols God's law. What a privilege to know what God says and to be able to walk on the path that leads to eternal life! The poet who penned this prayer knew he couldn't always follow God's law. He knew he needed someone to teach him God's law and help him understand the Lord's decrees. But more importantly, he needed a heart that eagerly sought out the Lord's will instead of his own will. He had experienced the lure of possessions, so he prayed to God, asking for the eagerness to follow God's ways.

One of the disciplines of the spiritual life is reading and studying God's Word. Ask the Lord today to increase your hunger for his Word and to enable you to to obey his commands, for in them you will find life.

Dear Lord, give me life through your Word . . .

A PRAYER TO THE UNCHANGING GOD

But Lord, you remain the same forever! Your throne continues from generation to generation. Why do you continue to forget us? Why have you forsaken us for so long? Restore us, O Lord, and bring us back to you again! Give us back the joys we once had! LAMENTATIONS 5:19-21

Jeremiah possessed one unshakable conviction: God doesn't change. Our faithfulness and our feelings are as fleeting as a breeze, but God remains the same. We wander away; God brings us back. We surrender our joy; God renews it. Though Jeremiah was praying for his people, his words can help us put our own lives into perspective. The eternal God is in control, and he is able to raise us up when we fall.

Acknowledging our complete dependence upon God in our prayers should be one of the first steps we take in prayer, for it's on that basis that we keep coming to him with our humble requests. God remains forever the same; we are the ones who have wandered from him. Today, take time to praise the Lord for his unchanging character.

Eternal God, bring me back to you again . . .

April 1

Praise at the Triumphal Entry

Most of the crowd spread their coats on the road ahead of Jesus, and others cut branches from the trees and spread them on the road. He was in the center of the procession, and the crowds all around him were shouting,

"Praise God for the Son of David!
Bless the one who comes in the name of the Lord!
Praise God in highest heaven!"

MATTHEW 21:8-9

The Jews, who gathered for the annual Passover celebration, knew what it meant to praise their Savior. Every year, they assembled at the Temple in Jerusalem to celebrate the God who had miraculously delivered their ancestors from slavery in Egypt. During the Passover feast, the people prayed and sang Psalms 113–118, which are hymns of praise to God, their Deliverer. So it was natural for the crowd of Passover pilgrims to greet Jesus with the words above, which are from Psalm 118:26. Why wouldn't they enthusiastically welcome Jesus—who had obviously come in God's name—to their grand celebration?

Let your prayer time be a celebration of God and his Son, Jesus. Today, use the words of the people of Israel to celebrate Jesus.

Dear Lord, I praise you for sending the Son of David . . .

April 2

AWE FOR THE CREATOR

The Lord merely spoke,
*   and the heavens were created.*
He breathed the word,
*   and all the stars were born.*
He gave the sea its boundaries
*   and locked the oceans in vast reservoirs.*
Let everyone in the world fear the Lord,
*   and let everyone stand in awe of him.*
For when he spoke, the world began!
*   It appeared at his command.*

PSALM 33:6-9

When was the last time you took time to admire God's handiwork in nature? The brilliant stars hanging in the sky and the oceans crashing against the coastline give us reasons to stand in awe of God, the Creator of it all. God merely spoke, and these wonders came into being. At times, God's creation—the vast universe populated by innumerable stars—makes us all feel so small and insignificant. How much more should we bow before the infinite God who can command the cosmos into existence or wipe it out in a moment!

Focus on some aspect of nature that inspires awe in you, whether it be a sparkling river, a peaceful lake, a spectacular skyline, or whatever. Then offer your praises to its great Creator.

Dear Lord, you merely spoke, and the heavens were created . . .

Heavenly Praise for the Lamb

After this I saw a vast crowd, too great to count, from every nation and tribe and people and language, standing in front of the throne and before the Lamb. They were clothed in white and held palm branches in their hands. And they were shouting with a mighty shout, "Salvation comes from our God on the throne and from the Lamb!" REVELATION 7:9-10

Many times our prayers tend to focus on this world and the struggles we encounter in our lives. God understands and accepts these prayers, but we must also direct our thoughts and prayers to the victory we will share with Christ. In Revelation, God gives us a splendid portrayal of that final victory. In a vision, the apostle John sees a magnificent scene: a vast multitude celebrating the triumph of the Lamb of God. Waving palm branches, the traditional symbol of victory, people from all over the world extol God for the salvation he has provided through his Son.

As followers of Christ, today, we are privileged to be part of this multitude—the communion of believers. Because Jesus has overcome death, a new life of wholeness and peace through him has opened up to us. This is worth shouting about—praising God with all that is in us!

Dear Lord, I join your praying people through the ages to shout about that salvation that comes from you . . .

April 4

RECALLING GOD'S WONDERFUL DEEDS

I recall all you have done, O Lord;
I remember your wonderful deeds of long ago.
They are constantly in my thoughts.
I cannot stop thinking about them.
O God, your ways are holy.
Is there any god as mighty as you?
You are the God of miracles and wonders!
You demonstrate your awesome power among the nations.
You have redeemed your people by your strength,
the descendants of Jacob and of Joseph by your might.

PSALM 77:11-15

How pleasurable it is to recall with our friends and loved ones those amusing and fun experiences we've shared together! Psalm 77 helps us remember God's wonderful works and praise him for them. But the writer of this psalm wasn't simply remembering God's deeds for fun. It was a necessity for him. Asaph was in trouble and desperately needed God's help. Recalling the ways God had miraculously and powerfully intervened in the lives of the Israelites in the past helped to reassure him that God would act in his distressing situation as well.

Remind yourself of what God did for his people long ago. Then look back on your own life and find the ways God has worked as well.

Almighty Lord, I recall all you have done for me . . .

GLORY TO GOD'S NAME

"Now my soul is deeply troubled. Should I pray, 'Father, save me from what lies ahead'? But that is the very reason why I came! Father, bring glory to your name."

Then a voice spoke from heaven, saying, "I have already brought it glory, and I will do it again." JOHN 12:27-28

When faced with a difficult situation, we often pray that our troubles will go away. Certainly, God is our deliverer from all evil, and it is appropriate to pray in this manner. Jesus, too, asked his Father to spare him from the agony of suffering a cruel death on a cross (Luke 22:42). But Jesus knew that enduring such suffering would bring greater glory to God the Father. By Jesus' death on the cross, God offered salvation to all who believed in him.

When we are apprehensive about events that loom in the future, we may certainly ask our Father to keep us from harm. But following our Savior's example, we may also pray that, whatever will come our way, God's name might be honored in our lives.

Dear Father, bring glory to your name, whatever I must pass through in the days to come . . .

April 6

GRATITUDE FOR GOD'S MERCY

The Lord is merciful and gracious;
*   he is slow to get angry and full of unfailing love.*
He will not constantly accuse us,
*   nor remain angry forever.*
He has not punished us for all our sins,
*   nor does he deal with us as we deserve.*
For his unfailing love toward those who fear him
*   is as great as the height of the heavens above the earth.*
He has removed our rebellious acts
*   as far away from us as the east is from the west.*

PSALM 103:8-12

We often pray for friends, family members, loved ones, missionaries, and those in need, but some of our prayers should be all about God. This was the case with David's prayer in Psalm 103. "Praise the Lord," David intoned, because the Lord doesn't remain angry forever, nor does he punish us to the extent we deserve. The greatness of God's love is as high as the heavens are above the earth. He has removed our sins from us as far as the east is from the west! With these beautiful and intriguing metaphors, David expressed his gratitude and awe for God's immeasurable greatness.

In the next few moments, try to express the extent of your gratitude to God. Then, offer this as a praise-gift to your Lord.

Dear Lord, you are merciful and gracious, slow to get angry and full of unfailing love . . .

April 7

A PRAYER FOR GOD'S WILL

He went on a little farther and fell face down on the ground, praying, "My Father! If it is possible, let this cup of suffering be taken away from me. Yet I want your will, not mine."

MATTHEW 26:39

Submitting to God's will for our lives can be a formidable challenge. At times, our dreams and aspirations conflict with God's will for us. Jesus wrestled with this issue in prayer in the Garden of Gethsemane. At stake, for Jesus, was the way God wanted to accomplish the salvation of his people. God's way included suffering and death on a cross. Jesus saw the difficult road ahead and spent a night agonizing in prayer over it. The strength and courage he found in prayer that night helped him withstand the suffering he faced the next day.

The choices we must make are less momentous than Jesus' choices, but they may still be agonizing enough to drive us to our knees before the Father. As his will becomes clearer, may God give us the ability to yield to his will, as Jesus did.

Dear Lord, I want your will, not mine, to be done . . .

April 8

**Revering
the Lord**

*All he does is just and good,
    and all his commandments are trustworthy.
They are forever true,
    to be obeyed faithfully and with integrity.
He has paid a full ransom for his people.
    He has guaranteed his covenant with them forever.
    What a holy, awe-inspiring name he has!
Reverence for the Lord is the foundation of true wisdom.
    The rewards of wisdom come to all who obey him.
Praise his name forever!*

PSALM 111:7-10

Much of society today no longer values reverence. Instead, our culture tends to uphold the irreverent—those who don't hold anything or anyone sacred. But this doesn't mean that God is any less worthy of reverence today than when the psalmist penned these words. God should be honored because all he does and says is just and good. We shouldn't approach God with a flippant or demanding attitude, but rather, with respect, honor, and reverence. True wisdom is knowing to whom we owe our very existence. And there are tangible rewards for those who align their life with this truth.

Revisit the foundation of your faith and the fount of all wisdom today. Bow before the Lord and give him the reverence he deserves.

Holy God, all you do is just and good. I honor, worship, and revere you . . .

JESUS' PRAYER FOR GLORY

When Jesus had finished saying all these things, he looked up to heaven and said, "Father, the time has come. Glorify your Son so he can give glory back to you. For you have given him authority over everyone in all the earth. He gives eternal life to each one you have given him. And this is the way to have eternal life—to know you, the only true God, and Jesus Christ, the one you sent to earth. I brought glory to you here on earth by doing everything you told me to do. And now, Father, bring me into the glory we shared before the world began."

JOHN 17:1-5

At the Last Supper, the night of his betrayal, Jesus prayed this prayer. In preparation for the suffering he would endure in the days ahead, Jesus prayed that God would be glorified in his life. We often think the road to glory is lined with success. Yet Jesus' road to glory was lined with suffering and seeming defeat in the form of a horrible death on the cross. How could this "defeat" bring God glory? Jesus explained in his prayer that God received glory through Jesus' obedience.

Rarely do we view our suffering and defeat as giving glory to God. But we also rarely have God's view of our circumstances. God's glory is reflected in our acts of obedience, love, and faithfulness in this life. Follow Christ's example today by praying that God might be glorified in your life.

Dear Father, let me bring glory to you here on earth by doing everything you have told me to do . . .

**PLACING
OUR HOPE
IN GOD**

Sing out your thanks to the Lord;
sing praises to our God, accompanied by harps.
He covers the heavens with clouds,
provides rain for the earth,
and makes the green grass grow in mountain pastures.
He feeds the wild animals,
and the young ravens cry to him for food.
The strength of a horse does not impress him;
how puny in his sight is the strength of a man.
Rather, the Lord's delight is in those who honor him,
those who put their hope in his unfailing love.

PSALM 147:7-11

God isn't impressed by the things that impress most people. People tend to value wealth, power, and prestige, while God is looking for those who depend on him and honor him. Psalm 147 was written after a group of Jews had returned from exile in Babylon. These people had learned the hard way that their true purpose was to honor God and submit to him. The psalmist in this prayer pointed out that all creation is dependent on God. God is the one who provides the rain. He allows the grass to grow. God himself gives food to the animals. Jesus later pointed out, "If God cares so wonderfully for flowers that are here today and gone tomorrow, won't he more surely care for you?" (Luke 12:28).

In your prayer today, acknowledge your dependence on God and thank him for providing for you.

O Lord, I put my hope in your unfailing love . . .

April 11

**JESUS'
MERCIFUL
PRAYER**

*Jesus said, "Father, forgive these people, because they don't
know what they are doing." And the soldiers gambled for his
clothes by throwing dice.*   LUKE 23:34

It is hard enough to forgive those who offend and injure us, but it
is even more difficult to forgive those who mock and taunt us when
we're suffering. Not realizing that Jesus was the Lord of glory, his
unwitting opponents fulfilled the prophecies in the Scriptures by
putting Jesus to death. Yet Jesus' grace—his willingness to forgive—
is evident even at the time when he was suffering the worst insults.
Here, on the cross, we can see most clearly who Jesus is. His prayer,
"Father, forgive them," shows us divine love like nothing else can.

As followers of Christ, let us pray the same prayer for our own
enemies.

*Lord Jesus, help me to forgive those who have wronged
me . . .*

SINGING PRAISES TO OUR GOD

Sing praises to God, our strength.
Sing to the God of Israel.
Sing! Beat the tambourine.
Play the sweet lyre and the harp.

PSALM 81:1-2

Almost any celebration—whether it's an orchestrated wedding or a small gathering of friends—involves music. Music and song can express the emotions of the human heart as nothing else can. That's why believers sing when they gather to worship God. Together in song, we remind ourselves of how majestic God is and express in harmonious melodies how happy we are to be his people. Psalm 81 calls God's people to worshipful prayer by directing them to sing their praises to God. What a wonderful way to begin one's own prayer time!

As you pray to God today, praise him for his strength. If you have access to hymnals, praise books, or recordings of worshipful songs, use these to help you wholeheartedly express your gratitude to God.

O God our strength, I sing praises to you . . .

JESUS' CRY TO HIS FATHER

At about three o'clock, Jesus called out with a loud voice, "Eli, Eli, lema sabachthani?" which means, "My God, my God, why have you forsaken me?" MATTHEW 27:46

From the earliest centuries of the church, Christians have pondered the significance of Jesus' cry from the cross. Was Jesus really abandoned by God the Father to bear in isolated torment the sin of all people for all time? Perhaps the best way to approach this unusual prayer is to place it in its biblical context. In Jesus' day, teachers would identify a Scripture passage by quoting its opening words. Jesus' prayer is a quote from the first verse of Psalm 22—a psalm which ends not in abandonment by God but in God's deliverance. Perhaps, Jesus was thinking of the entire psalm, including its concluding thoughts: "For he has not ignored the suffering of the needy. He has not turned and walked away. He has listened to their cries for help" (Psalm 22:24). Certainly, Jesus knew that his suffering on the cross wasn't God's *ultimate* abandonment of him. As the writer of Hebrews says, "He was willing to die a shameful death on the cross because of the joy he knew would be his afterward" (Hebrew 12:2).

Although we will never suffer as much as our remarkable Savior, we will encounter trials. When we do, we must look beyond our trials to our triumph with God.

My God, when I feel abandoned, help me to see that you are listening . . .

April 14

And they sang in a mighty chorus:

WORTHY IS THE LAMB

"The Lamb is worthy—the Lamb who was killed.
He is worthy to receive power and riches
and wisdom and strength
and honor and glory and blessing."

And then I heard every creature in heaven and on earth
and under the earth and in the sea. They also sang:

"Blessing and honor and glory and power
belong to the one sitting on the throne
and to the Lamb forever and ever."

REVELATION 5:12-13

Scripture encourages Christians to offer prayers of praise and thanksgiving to their God continually (1 Thessalonians 5:17-18). But as important as our personal worship of God may be, a vital dimension is missing until we join our prayers of praise with those of others. To be caught up in adoration of the Lord together with his people is the fulfillment of our calling to be his worshipers, for it is to a people (gathered from all places and all eras) that the Lord will come to receive the homage he richly deserves. His people will respond to his coming with a unified hymn of blessing, exalting the Lord God and the Lamb.

May we ever be found in the fellowship of that praising, prayerful people!

Blessing and honor, glory and power to you, Lord God . . .

**A PRAYER
FOR
COURAGE**

Then all the believers were united as they lifted their voices in prayer: "O Sovereign Lord, Creator of heaven and earth, the sea, and everything in them . . . Herod Antipas, Pontius Pilate the governor, the Gentiles, and the people of Israel were all united against Jesus, your holy servant, whom you anointed. In fact, everything they did occurred according to your eternal will and plan. And now, O Lord, hear their threats, and give your servants great boldness in their preaching. Send your healing power; may miraculous signs and wonders be done through the name of your holy servant Jesus."

ACTS 4:24, 27-30

Before his ascension into heaven, Jesus told his followers: "You will receive power and will tell people about me everywhere" (Acts 1:8). On the day of Pentecost, they did receive that power, but they still faced opposition—such as threats from the Jewish council against preaching the Good News. So the believers met together to pray. Their prayer is instructive. They didn't ask for the destruction of opposition but rather for boldness, and for God to demonstrate his power through them. They reported to God the threats they had received and reminded themselves of the way religious leaders had opposed Jesus, their Savior.

Today, ask Jesus to give you the courage and power to proclaim the Good News to those around you.

Dear Lord, grant me great boldness in my witness for you . . .

April 16

THE JOY OF GOD'S PRESENCE

No wonder my heart is filled with joy,
and my mouth shouts his praises!
My body rests in safety.
For you will not leave my soul among the dead
or allow your godly one to rot in the grave.
You will show me the way of life,
granting me the joy of your presence
and the pleasures of living with you forever.

PSALM 16:9-11

Often the fears and difficulties of this life fill our prayers with all kinds of concerns that center on ourselves. In this prayer, David described what it meant for him to enter God's presence. No longer did he have to be concerned about protecting and defending himself, for his loving God was his protector. Entering the Lord's presence released him from self-absorption to a joyful celebration of the King. For in prayer, David encountered one who was so awesome, yet comforting, that he focused not on himself but on his Creator.

The joy of God's presence should bring our lives into perspective and supply the power to continue serving the Lord in this life. Ask God to fill your life with his presence.

Lord, grant me the joy of your presence . . .

April 17

A Prayer for Resources

And now, may the God of peace, who brought again from the dead our Lord Jesus, equip you with all you need for doing his will. May he produce in you, through the power of Jesus Christ, all that is pleasing to him. Jesus is the great Shepherd of the sheep by an everlasting covenant, signed with his blood. To him be glory forever and ever. Amen.

HEBREWS 13:20-21

In the Bible God's people are continually compared to a flock of sheep, which are wholly dependent upon the Shepherd's leadership for food and protection. Although most of us now live and work in settings where individual achievement is prized, we should never imagine that we can be all the Lord wants us to be by "doing it alone." We belong to a people who have been brought into a covenant relationship with the Lord, and with one another, through the blood of Jesus. That is why the author of Hebrews wrote down his prayer for believers. He wanted all believers to join him in praying for the resources to do God's work together.

Pray that God might equip you and the believers in your local church to accomplish God's work together.

O Lord, our Shepherd, equip your people with all they need to do your will . . .

April 18

THANKS FOR GOD'S FORGIVENESS

Lord, you have poured out amazing blessings on your land!
You have restored the fortunes of Israel.
You have forgiven the guilt of your people—
yes, you have covered all their sins.
You have withdrawn your fury.
You have ended your blazing anger.
Now turn to us again, O God of our salvation.
Put aside your anger against us.

PSALM 85:1-4

However much our culture denies the reality and effect of guilt, there are many today who live under its burden. Many people still have the sense that their lives are not what they ought to be. This sense of guilt may actually be a gift from God to help redirect us to his way—the pathway that leads to a productive and joyful life. But God's greater gift to us is his mercy, which enables us to start anew on the path of right living. In this prayer to God, the psalmist thanks the Lord for forgiving his people and restoring his land. He had learned from his experience that when people ask God for forgiveness, he doesn't turn them away.

Remind yourself of the ways the Lord has forgiven you and renewed your life. Then offer your praises to your Savior.

Thank you, Lord, that you have forgiven my guilt and covered all my sin . . .

April 19

GRATITUDE FOR GOD'S REIGN

"We give thanks to you, Lord God Almighty,
the one who is and who always was,
for now you have assumed your great power
and have begun to reign.
The nations were angry with you,
but now the time of your wrath has come.
It is time to judge the dead and reward your servants.
You will reward your prophets and your holy people,
all who fear your name, from the least to the greatest.
And you will destroy all who have caused destruction on the
earth."

REVELATION 11:17-18

When evil goes unpunished, we might despair of ever obtaining justice and even question why we're serving the Lord. The Scriptures, however, encourage us to take the long-range view of history. The twenty-four elders, who sit in God's throne room, paint this long-range view for us in their prayer of praise to the Almighty. They thank the "one who is and who always was" for controlling all of history. They praise him for administering his perfect justice at the appropriate time. God's justice will ultimately prevail, and God's servants will ultimately be vindicated.

Take a moment to envision yourself before God's throne room at the end of time. What prayer of praise will you offer the Lord?

Sovereign Lord, I give thanks that you will one day
bring about justice . . .

PRAISE FOR GOD'S BLESSINGS

Praise the Lord, I tell myself;
   with my whole heart, I will praise his holy name.
Praise the Lord, I tell myself,
   and never forget the good things he does for me.
He forgives all my sins
   and heals all my diseases.
He ransoms me from death
   and surrounds me with love and tender mercies.
He fills my life with good things.
   My youth is renewed like the eagle's!

PSALM 103:1-5

Almost every firm with a sizable workforce gives a benefits package to its workers, and these benefits usually include health care, life, and disability insurance. In this prayer, David listed God's "benefits package," so to speak. First of all, David's very life and health came directly from God's hand. Yet God also filled David's life with many good things. But David recognized that the key benefit God gave to him was forgiveness—God's grace, which broke down the barrier of sin between God and him. David freely acknowledged that his life was thoroughly dependent on the merciful life-giver.

During your prayer time, list the many benefits God has given you. Then, refer to that list throughout the day and praise the Lord.

Dear Lord, I praise you for all your blessings toward me . . .

April 21

In that day you will sing:

"Praise the Lord!
He was angry with me,
but now he comforts me.
See, God has come to save me.
I will trust in him and not be afraid.
The Lord GOD is my strength and my song;
he has become my salvation."

ISAIAH 12:1-2

These verses, which echo Moses' praise in Exodus 15:2, contain the collective prayer that will issue from the lips of God's people when Christ reigns over the earth forever. God's people will greet Christ with a short prayer of praise that aptly describes their marvelous relationship with him. Though once angry at the sin of his people, God will comfort them. He won't come to judge the remnant but to save them. What a joy it is to know that, though we deserve judgment, we do not have to live in fear of God—our Savior.

Today, our prayers of praise are linked with all believers who have gone before us and all who will follow us. This praise is the cry of the redeemed—those who realize that God was willing to sacrifice his own Son in order to heal and save them. Join your voice in this prayer today.

Dear Lord, I praise you as my strength, my song, and my salvation . . .

April 22

GOD ANSWERS PRAYER

I cried out to you, O Lord.
I begged the Lord for mercy, saying,
"What will you gain if I die,
if I sink down into the grave?
Can my dust praise you from the grave?
Can it tell the world of your faithfulness?
Hear me, Lord, and have mercy on me.
Help me, O Lord."
You have turned my mourning into joyful dancing.
You have taken away my clothes of mourning and clothed
me with joy,
that I might sing praises to you and not be silent.
O Lord my God, I will give you thanks forever!

PSALM 30:8-12

God certainly knows what is best for us before we voice our requests. So why does the all-knowing, all-powerful God work out his plan through our simple requests? David possessed some insight into this question. He realized answered prayers demonstrate God's love and mercy to the world. Too often, we don't recognize God's work in our lives. In contrast, an answered prayer is a clear sign to us of God at work. God treasures the heartfelt gratitude and the joyful praise of those who recognize his loving hand in their lives.

When we receive answers to prayer, may we, like David, never take that miracle for granted.

Dear Lord, thank you for answering my prayers . . .

April 23

SINGING OF GOD'S GLORIOUS DEEDS

Let the whole earth sing to the Lord!
Each day proclaim the good news that he saves.
Publish his glorious deeds among the nations.
Tell everyone about the amazing things he does.
Great is the Lord! He is most worthy of praise!
He is to be revered above all gods.

1 CHRONICLES 16:23-25

Sometimes on beautiful spring days, with the glory of renewal evident all around us, we long to blend our expressions of praise with something much larger than ourselves. This prayer of David captured this same sentiment: "Let the whole earth sing to the Lord!" For David, every day was an occasion to proclaim the good news of salvation and God's amazing deeds. But this prayer was written for a special celebration: when David brought the ark of God into the special tent he had prepared for it. Especially on such occasions it was appropriate to declare God's greatness with much enthusiasm.

Imagine, for a moment, a whole gathering of believers, plus all of nature for miles around, united in a prayer of praise to God. What would it sound like? What words would you use to praise your Lord?

O Lord, let the whole earth sing praises to you . . .

**DELIGHT IN
GOD'S LOVE**

*Your unfailing love, O Lord, is as vast as the heavens;
    your faithfulness reaches beyond the clouds.
Your righteousness is like the mighty mountains,
    your justice like the ocean depths.
You care for people and animals alike, O Lord.
    How precious is your unfailing love, O God!
All humanity finds shelter
    in the shadow of your wings.
You feed them from the abundance of your own house,
    letting them drink from your rivers of delight.*

PSALM 36:5-8

In this prayer, David uses what he can see—the sky, the mountains, and the oceans—to illustrate what he can't see—the Lord's unfailing love, his faithfulness to his people, his righteousness, and his commitment to justice. And the fact that God daily feeds his creation—both people and animals alike—clearly demonstrates the depths of his love for all that he has made. In fact, God loves to allow his people to experience the "rivers of delight."

Take some time today to see the world around you and the simple elements of your daily life from David's vantage point. Our God is very great; and his signature is everywhere. Let us bow before him in worship and awe.

How precious is your unfailing love, O God . . .

REMEMBERING GOD'S MERCY

The unfailing love of the Lord never ends! By his mercies we have been kept from complete destruction. Great is his faithfulness; his mercies begin afresh each day. I say to myself, "The Lord is my inheritance; therefore, I will hope in him!"

The Lord is wonderfully good to those who wait for him and seek him. So it is good to wait quietly for salvation from the Lord.

LAMENTATIONS 3:22-26

In the book of Lamentations, the prophet Jeremiah expressed his anguish over the fall of Jerusalem—the culmination of God's judgment, which he himself had foretold over a period of years. Yet even through his tears over his destitute people, Jeremiah had an occasion to praise God. He dared to hope in God's undying love for his people. He recalled God's faithfulness and mercy. God himself was the reason the nation of Israel had been rescued from slavery and established in a prosperous land. God himself was the reason that Israel and Judah were not completely destroyed.

Hope is born from this kind of remembering of what God has done. And once our hope is revived, we find ourselves able—even eager—to wait quietly for his salvation, which surely will come.

Dear Lord, you are wonderfully good to those who wait for you and seek you . . .

April 26

GRATITUDE FOR GOD'S CARE

When I look at the night sky and see the work of your fingers—
the moon and the stars you have set in place—
what are mortals that you should think of us,
mere humans that you should care for us?
For you made us only a little lower than God,
and you crowned us with glory and honor....
O Lord, our Lord, the majesty of your name fills the earth!

PSALM 8:3-5, 9

After pondering the beauty and immensity of just one aspect of God's creation—the stars in the heavens, David was moved to say, "What are mortals that you should think of us?" We are mere specks in the vast universe in which we live. Yet the marvel is that God made us only a little lower than himself! He granted us great honor—by first creating us as the pinnacle of all other life on this earth and later, when we had sinned, by sending his own Son to save us.

When we are moved by the majesty or intricacy of something God has created in the physical world, we should remind ourselves that the God who created this amazing world has showered his infinite love on us. In prayer, express your wonder and gratitude to God today.

O Father, I praise you for crowning me with glory and honor . . .

THANKS FOR CHRIST'S VICTORY

But thanks be to God, who made us his captives and leads us along in Christ's triumphal procession. Now wherever we go he uses us to tell others about the Lord and to spread the Good News like a sweet perfume.   2 CORINTHIANS 2:14

Ancient Roman generals, returning from a victory in a distant land, would parade down the main streets with the spoils of battle—including a throng of captives. In this prayer of thanksgiving, Paul uses this image of a triumphal procession to thank Christ for defeating the evil forces of this world. Interestingly, Paul identifies believers as Christ's captives. We were once part of Satan's army; but Jesus has taken us captive. As such, our transformed lives clearly proclaim Christ's great victory. But unlike the captives of Roman conquerors, we aren't destined to be sold into demeaning servitude. Instead, Christ has freed us from our old evil master to become his adopted sons and daughters.

Thank God, today, that you are included in Christ's victory parade.

Thanks be to you, O God, who made me your captive in Christ's triumphal procession . . .

CALLING ON CREATION TO PRAISE GOD

Let the heavens be glad, and let the earth rejoice!
Let the sea and everything in it shout his praise!
Let the fields and their crops burst forth with joy!
Let the trees of the forest rustle with praise
before the Lord!
For the Lord is coming!
He is coming to judge the earth.
He will judge the world with righteousness
and all the nations with his truth.

PSALM 96:11-13

Sometimes our hearts are slow to comprehend what a privilege it is to approach the infinite God in prayer. Too often, we rush into God's presence with a hasty word of thanks or a list of requests. In contrast, the author of Psalm 96 took the time to contemplate to whom he was praying. The psalmist was so overwhelmed with God's greatness that he called upon the heavens and the earth to extol him. The entire earth was a magnificent instrument designed to sing the Lord's praises. The wheat and barley were bursting with joy before the Lord, while the wind was playing a beautiful melody of praise on the leaves and branches of the forest.

In prayer today, take a moment to appreciate the world God has created and rejoice in it.

Righteous Lord, I join all creation in praising you . . .

April 29

O Lord, you are my rock of safety.
  Please help me; don't refuse to answer me.
For if you are silent,
  I might as well give up and die.
Listen to my prayer for mercy
  as I cry out to you for help,
  as I lift my hands toward your holy sanctuary.

PSALM 28:1-2

There are times when God seems so far away. We pray . . . and pray . . . and pray . . . and there is no answer. Where is God? Does he really hear us? In Psalm 28, David expressed this same frustration about his prayer. He had called out to God for help, yet all he heard was silence. But instead of turning *away* from God, David turned *to* God and renewed his plea for God to listen. He refused to give up on God, for he knew he could count on God alone to save him.

The good news is that David wasn't disappointed. The second half of David's prayer describes how God heard David and answered his prayers (Psalm 28:6). Today, rejoice with David in God's commitment to hear and answer the prayers of his people.

O Lord, listen to my prayer for mercy as I cry out to you for help . . .

April 30

**HOPING IN
GOD ALONE**

*We depend on the Lord alone to save us.
Only he can help us, protecting us like a shield.
In him our hearts rejoice,
for we are trusting in his holy name.
Let your unfailing love surround us, Lord,
for our hope is in you alone.*

PSALM 33:20-22

We all crave security. When difficult circumstances threaten to overtake us, most of us lean heavily upon our friends and family to help us persevere. But this prayer reminds us that only almighty God can ultimately rescue and protect us. It is good to acknowledge our dependence on the Lord when we approach him in prayer. Remember that he is our shield. As we concentrate on this marvelous truth, our fear can turn to rejoicing.

Stop for a few moments to consider the ways you seek security—in small matters and in large matters. Then, before God, acknowledge that ultimately you depend on him *alone*.

O Lord our hope, surround us with your unfailing love . . .

May 1

Give thanks to the Lord and proclaim his greatness.
Let the whole world know what he has done.
Sing to him; yes, sing his praises.
Tell everyone about his miracles.
Exult in his holy name;
O worshipers of the Lord, rejoice!
Search for the Lord and for his strength,
and keep on searching.
Think of the wonderful works he has done,
the miracles and the judgments he handed down.

PSALM 105:1-5

Small crises can set us on a frantic search. Losing a ring or a key can set us on a search that leaves no sofa cushion unturned. The quest for a missing child can make the evening news and tie up an entire police department. But the psalmist speaks of a search that probably won't make the evening news: the search for the living God. In this prayer, the psalmist led God's people in thanking and praising the Lord for the wonderful things he had done for them. He encouraged God's people to search out the ways God was working in their lives and thank him for it.

What a marvelous search! Before you move ahead in the promise of this new spring month, search your life for the delightful blessings God has given you.

Dear Lord, I praise your for the wonderful works you have done . . .

May 2

SPIRITUAL BLESSINGS

How we praise God, the Father of our Lord Jesus Christ, who has blessed us with every spiritual blessing in the heavenly realms because we belong to Christ. Long ago, even before he made the world, God loved us and chose us in Christ to be holy and without fault in his eyes.

EPHESIANS 1:3-4

Although penned in prison, Paul's letter to the Ephesians is one of encouragement. Ephesus was one of the more prominent and strong churches that Paul established on an earlier missionary journey. Paul encouraged this church to praise God for the abundance of blessings they were enjoying. Paul lifted their eyes beyond this world toward heaven for the spiritual blessings God had provided for them.

In like manner, we, too, should praise God for all the spiritual blessings he has given us—our salvation, our inheritance in heaven, our promised new bodies. As you begin to pray today, thank God for the eternal blessings you can't see—joy, inner peace, and hope. Praise our gracious God, from whom our spiritual blessings flow.

Dear Lord, I praise you for the spiritual blessings in my life . . .

May 3

I will thank you, Lord, with all my heart;
I will tell of all the marvelous things you have done.
I will be filled with joy because of you.
I will sing praises to your name, O Most High. . . .
For you have judged in my favor;
from your throne, you have judged with fairness.

PSALM 9:1-2, 4

"It's not fair." How often that phrase comes to our minds when we feel we are mistreated! Yet in this prayer, David resisted the all too human temptation to complain about injustice. Instead, he reaffirmed his faith in God's justice, even though he had personally suffered and faced death at the hands of his enemies. Such mistreatment could have defeated David's hope in God. But he refused to dwell on his cruel enemies or on the injustices that he was suffering. Instead, he concentrated on his just and all-powerful God.

Instead of praying for God's ultimate revenge on your enemies, pray that God's justice will be carried out and leave the matter in his hands. Trust that he is sovereign and that we can trust our problems with others to him.

Dear Lord, I praise you for being a God of justice . . .

May 4

DAVID'S PRAYER FOR A CLEAN HEART

Create in me a clean heart, O God.
Renew a right spirit within me.
Do not banish me from your presence,
and don't take your Holy Spirit from me.
Restore to me again the joy of your salvation,
and make me willing to obey you.
Then I will teach your ways to sinners,
and they will return to you.

PSALM 51:10-13

Through the prophet Nathan, a web of selfishness, adultery, betrayal, lies, and murder in David's life had just been exposed. In that moment of crushing self-examination, David saw how sinful his heart was. Instead of withdrawing into a cocoon of self-pity, he prayed to the Lord. At this point in his prayer, David had turned the corner from ruthless self-examination to hopeful meditation. His sins were on his mind, but so was God's mercy. He knew that the remedy for his guilt wasn't self-sacrifice or a determination to make it right. No, David knew God was the only one who could save him from his sins and clean his filthy life.

Perhaps like David, you are due for a heart exam by God. Whatever the condition of your heart, God is the only physician with an unfailing cure.

O God, create in me a clean heart . . .

May 5

A PRAYER FOR SPIRITUAL WISDOM

I have never stopped thanking God for you. I pray for you constantly, asking God, the glorious Father of our Lord Jesus Christ, to give you spiritual wisdom and understanding, so that you might grow in your knowledge of God.

EPHESIANS 1:16-17

During his stay in Rome, Paul's chains reminded him of his limitations. Although his new converts in Ephesus needed more spiritual guidance, he couldn't be there to guide them. During that time when he could do the least, Paul utilized the power of prayer. He began his letter to the Ephesians by revealing to them the pages of his prayer journal. His prayers had one theme: that the Ephesians might gain spiritual wisdom from God. Like good news that is spread throughout a family, a copy of his prayers was circulated among the churches around Ephesus.

Are there loved ones for whom you need to pray, asking that they will gain further insight into who God is? Better yet, do they need to know that you pray for them on a regular basis? May Paul's heartfelt prayer lead you to pray for those you love.

Dear Lord, I pray for spiritual wisdom for . . .

May 6

LOVE FOR GOD'S SANCTUARY

I wash my hands to declare my innocence.
I come to your altar, O Lord,
singing a song of thanksgiving
and telling of all your miracles.
I love your sanctuary, Lord,
the place where your glory shines.

PSALM 26:6-8

We often approach worship on Sunday morning with little enthusiasm. In this prayer of David, however, we find an enthusiasm and joy for God's sanctuary. He describes what he did in the temple: After washing his hands and heart before God, he came to God's altar. There he sang a song of thanksgiving and told fellow worshipers of God's miracles. David yearned to join God's people to celebrate the Lord of the universe. David could think of no better place to be than standing in God's presence, among his people, praising the Lord who cared so much for him.

Let David's prayer inspire you to renew your commitment to God and his people.

Dear Lord, I love your sanctuary, where I tell others
about your miracles and sing songs of thanksgiving . . .

ASKING FORGIVENESS FOR PAST SINS

> *Forgive the rebellious sins of my youth;*
> *look instead through the eyes of your unfailing love,*
> *for you are merciful, O Lord.*
> *The Lord is good and does what is right;*
> *he shows the proper path to those who go astray.*
> *He leads the humble in what is right,*
> *teaching them his way.*
> *The Lord leads with unfailing love and faithfulness*
> *all those who keep his covenant and obey his decrees.*
>
> PSALM 25:7-10

We all have something we've done or said in the past that we deeply regret—whether it's a caustic, unloving remark or some selfish action. Often we allow such sins to impede our prayers today. We feel that we dare not ask God for too much, since we know we have deeply offended him. Even David had such thoughts. But instead of letting his past determine his future, David prayed for the Lord to forgive him and recognized that the Lord would show his people how to live in an upright way.

What sins still pester you? Today, ask the Lord to forgive and forget your past failures. But don't end your prayer there. Ask the Lord to teach you how to live differently.

Dear Lord, forgive me and show me the right way to deal with my problems today . . .

HONORING
OUR
FAITHFUL
GOD

"Praise the Lord who has given rest to his people Israel, just as he promised. Not one word has failed of all the wonderful promises he gave through his servant Moses. May the Lord our God be with us as he was with our ancestors; may he never forsake us."

1 KINGS 8:56-57

As King Solomon surveyed the magnificent Temple God had allowed him to build in Jerusalem, he reflected on how much the Lord had blessed his people. Their ancestors had wandered the deserts as nomads for decades, but now the Israelites owned their own land. They had endured several invasions, but now they enjoyed peace. Solomon wisely recognized that this was from the Lord's hand and praised him for these things. What a marvelous God! Not one of God's promises had failed through all those generations!

Take some time to review how God has blessed you. How has he provided you with food and shelter? In what ways has he given you rest? Remind yourself of God's promise to give believers an eternal rest from the sufferings of this world. Then, offer your praise to God.

Faithful Lord, I praise you that not one of your promises has failed . . .

**FINDING
SECURITY IN
GOD**

*But I cried to him, "My God, who lives forever,
don't take my life while I am still so young!
In ages past you laid the foundation of the earth,
and the heavens are the work of your hands.
Even they will perish, but you remain forever;
they will wear out like old clothing.
You will change them like a garment,
and they will fade away.
But you are always the same;
your years never end.
The children of your people
will live in security."*

PSALM 102:24-28

This anonymous prayer reflects the lament of someone in great distress. The words could be a journal entry of almost anyone whose problems are overwhelming. And yet, this troubled soul, after pouring out his problems before the Lord, sees a ray of hope in his desperate situation: He remembers he is a child of the eternal God. This God transcends not only our problems but also all of space and time. He is willing and able to preserve his people and bring them to live eternally in his secure presence.

If today you are troubled by the concerns of this life, take this prayer as your own. Voice your cares to God, and then thank him for providing stability in your ever-changing world.

Eternal God, I thank you for making me secure . . .

**PRAISING
GOD FOR
HOPE**

O Lord, you alone are my hope.
I've trusted you, O Lord, from childhood.
Yes, you have been with me from birth;
from my mother's womb you have cared for me.
No wonder I am always praising you!
My life is an example to many,
because you have been my strength and protection.
That is why I can never stop praising you;
I declare your glory all day long.

PSALM 71:5-8

This prayer may be from the aging King David, who looked back over his life and praised God for being ever present throughout his life. He thanked God for comforting and protecting him in his youth when almost everyone had abandoned him, as well as for upholding him in his old age. The essence of David's experience with God was hope. God gave him hope when everything else was going wrong.

How would you describe God's role in your life thus far? As the one who saves? strengthens? comforts? Through prayer, we can daily communicate our hope in God and reaffirm our love for him.

Dear Lord, you alone are my hope. I trust in you . . .

May 11

"The Lord brings both death and life;
he brings some down to the grave but raises others up.
The Lord makes one poor and another rich;
he brings one down and lifts another up.
He lifts the poor from the dust—
yes, from a pile of ashes!
He treats them like princes,
placing them in seats of honor.
"For all the earth is the Lord's,
and he has set the world in order."

1 SAMUEL 2:6-8

How easy it would have been for Hannah to use the birth of her son Samuel as an occasion for pride. She could have easily felt vengeful and triumphant over her rival, Peninnah. Hannah had not only a son, but also the love of the husband they shared. Plagued for years by Peninnah, Hannah could have spewed back sharp words. Instead of doing this, she offered her praise and thanks to God for answering her prayer for a son, for lifting her up out of her despair.

When faced with a troubling or difficult situation, do you find yourself embittered? Or are you inclined to prayer? Are you tempted to lash out in biting words? Remember Hannah's prayer and example before you do. Speak to God instead.

Dear Lord, I praise you for honoring and lifting me up . . .

May 12

**PRAISING
GOD FOR
STRENGTH**

*Let them all praise the name of the Lord.
For his name is very great;
his glory towers over the earth and heaven!
He has made his people strong,
honoring his godly ones—
the people of Israel who are close to him.
Praise the Lord!*

PSALM 148:13-14

This prayer summons all creation to praise God for his power and glory. Although we as mere human beings live with our weaknesses and limitations, this prayer reminds us of God's supernatural strength. All creation praises God, for his name alone is "great." Our wealth, our possessions, even our friends and family, can't save us from our troubles. God alone "towers" over our earthly problems and provides strength to endure hardships and overcome temptations. No prayer is powerless, for prayer connects us with the ultimate power of the universe.

So as you approach God in prayer today, repeat the words of this psalm as a testament to his strength.

Dear Lord, I praise you for making me strong . . .

May 13

AN APPEAL FOR HELP

But God is my helper.
The Lord is the one who keeps me alive!
May my enemies' plans for evil be turned against them.
Do as you promised and put an end to them.
I will sacrifice a voluntary offering to you;
I will praise your name, O Lord,
for it is good.
For you will rescue me from my troubles
and help me to triumph over my enemies.

PSALM 54:4-7

David prayed these words when he was on the run. He was fleeing from the murderous grasp of King Saul because the people living in the Desert of Ziph had revealed David's location. Because of their betrayal, Saul's men were hot on David's trail. It is a story fit for a movie—a desperate man fleeing for his life because of the betrayal of his so-called friends. Such a person doesn't hold back when asking for help. He throws himself into the arms of his rescuers.

When you face a serious problem, feel entirely alone, or are betrayed by someone you trusted, calm your soul by appealing to God for help. When you face a crisis, turn to your Helper in prayer, asking him to rescue you.

Dear Lord, I need you to come to my rescue today . . .

REJOICING IN GOD'S SURE STRENGTH

"O Lord, you are my light;
yes, Lord, you light up my darkness.
In your strength I can crush an army;
with my God I can scale any wall.
"As for God, his way is perfect.
All the Lord's promises prove true.
He is a shield for all who look to him for protection.
For who is God except the Lord?
Who but our God is a solid rock?
God is my strong fortress;
he has made my way safe.
He makes me as surefooted as a deer,
leading me safely along the mountain heights."

2 SAMUEL 22:29-34

Although we strive to follow through on our promises, we all fall short at one time or another. But not so with our God! Toward the end of his reign, King David praised God, proclaiming, "All the Lord's promises prove true." David described God as a rock, a protective shield, and a fortress. And God leads his people along the mountain heights like surefooted deer. All these images imply that danger and difficult circumstances still surround God's people, but God provides security in the midst of these things.

Today, whether your circumstances put you in bright sunshine or dark shadow, consider the trustworthiness of our God and offer him your worship in prayer.

Lord God, all of your promises prove true . . .

**GIVING
THANKS
MORNING
AND NIGHT**

*It is good to give thanks to the Lord,
    to sing praises to the Most High.
It is good to proclaim your unfailing love in the morning,
    your faithfulness in the evening,
accompanied by the harp and lute
    and the harmony of the lyre.
You thrill me, Lord, with all you have done for me!
I sing for joy because of what you have done.*

PSALM 92:1-4

What a way to start the day! This psalm was one of the first prayers on the priests' lips on the Sabbath day: "You thrill me, Lord, with all you have done for me!"

What if before you read your morning paper, before you head out the door, before you start the countless tasks you have to do for each day, you determine that you're going to start your day with praise for how God has "thrilled" you? Right now, you have the chance to start afresh. A new spring day is before you. Why not start things off right with a regimen of praise instead of the old routine? In prayer today, proclaim his unfailing love, and tonight, before going to bed, praise him again for his faithfulness.

Dear Lord, I praise you for your unfailing love in the morning . . .

$\mathcal{M}$ a y 16

DAVID'S PRAYER FOR CLEANSING

Have mercy on me, O God,
because of your unfailing love.
Because of your great compassion,
blot out the stain of my sins.
Wash me clean from my guilt.
Purify me from my sin.
For I recognize my shameful deeds—
they haunt me day and night.
Against you, and you alone, have I sinned;
I have done what is evil in your sight.
You will be proved right in what you say,
and your judgment against me is just.

PSALM 51:1-4

Sometimes a prayer for simple forgiveness seems inadequate. Our sins feel like an indelible stain. When the prophet Nathan confronted King David with his sin of adultery with Bathsheba and his murder of her husband, David was convicted. He didn't have to be persuaded of the justice of God's case against him. Despite the harm he had done to specific people and to the honor of the nation, his greatest concern was for the damage he had caused to his relationship with the Lord.

When you feel the Holy Spirit convicting you of sin, make sure your first concern is the disruption of your relationship with God. Like David, accept God's judgment and cast yourself upon his compassion. He alone is the one who can cleanse and purify you.

Holy God, purify me from my sin, for I recognize my shameful deeds . . .

JOYFUL PRAISES TO GOD

Shout joyful praises to God, all the earth!
  Sing about the glory of his name!
  Tell the world how glorious he is.
Say to God, "How awesome are your deeds!
  Your enemies cringe before your mighty power.
Everything on earth will worship you;
  they will sing your praises,
  shouting your name in glorious songs."

PSALM 66:1-4

God answers prayer! And when he does, we should shout out his praises and give him thanks. Psalm 66 was written after a great victory in battle. Perhaps, like many of Israel's victories, it had been won against all odds. Clearly, in these circumstances, God's people saw his miraculous intervention on their behalf. They wanted to tell one another, tell the world, and tell God himself how great he was. What joy to be aligned with God, who makes his enemies cringe!

Often, our prayers are heartfelt and fervent when we are petitioning God about some pressing need. But may our gratitude overflow with equal zeal when we see answers to those prayers.

O God, we praise you for all you have done . . .

May 18

JESUS' PRAISE FOR GOD'S WAYS

Then Jesus prayed this prayer: "O Father, Lord of heaven and earth, thank you for hiding the truth from those who think themselves so wise and clever, and for revealing it to the childlike. Yes, Father, it pleased you to do it this way!"

MATTHEW 11:25-26

When Jesus walked this earth, he prayed within the hearing of his disciples. We might well assume that he did this for their instruction. In this prayer, found in Matthew 11, Jesus thanked God for his marvelous ways. Indeed, God's ways are inscrutable to many people, especially those who think they are self-sufficient and already know enough. Often those who are "wise" in the ways of this world don't see a need for God. The Lord, therefore, chooses to reveal his truth instead to those who are humble and willing to listen to him.

Praise God that he reveals his truth to anyone who comes to him to learn. May God give us tender and receptive hearts to approach him in humility and trust. May we learn to seek wisdom and knowledge in God.

Dear God, thank you for hiding the truth from those who think themselves so wise and clever, and for revealing it to the childlike . . .

May 19

PRAISE FOR THE GOD WHO ANSWERS

*I love the Lord because he hears
and answers my prayers.
Because he bends down and listens,
I will pray as long as I have breath!*

PSALM 116:1-2

Children easily discern which adults are going to pay attention to them and who will likely "tune them out." And when they do find someone who pays attention to them, often they are eager to interact with them. This prayer pictures God as one who "bends down and listens." Like a caring father, he comes down to our level to let us know that we are heard, cared about, and valued. Like that discerning child, we should continue to come to God in prayer because he has proven to be trustworthy. He hears; but not only that, he answers, too, in his perfect timing and wisdom.

How the Lord deserves our adoration and trust! May God grant us eyes to see the trustworthiness of his character.

Dear Lord, thank you for hearing and answering my prayers . . .

**PRAISE FOR
ULTIMATE
JUSTICE**

*O Lord, what great miracles you do!
   And how deep are your thoughts.
Only an ignorant person would not know this!
   Only a fool would not understand it.
Although the wicked flourish like weeds,
   and evildoers blossom with success,
   there is only eternal destruction ahead of them.
But you are exalted in the heavens.
   You, O Lord, continue forever.*

PSALM 92:5-8

Eternity provides us with excellent perspective for the present. When we consider God's unlimited power and glory, the problems of this earthly life are cut down to size. "Although the wicked flourish like weeds, and evildoers blossom with success," we know that in the end God will bring about justice, though we may never see it ourselves. No power on earth, no matter how formidable it may seem, can last forever in its rebellion against the Lord of all creation.

What injustices cause you frustration in life? Reflect for a moment on the fact that God is eternal and just. Give praise to him for ensuring that his people will one day be rewarded and the wicked will be punished.

Almighty Lord, I praise you for your eternal justice . . .

PRAYING FOR EYES TO BE OPENED

Then Elisha prayed, "O Lord, open his eyes and let him see!" The Lord opened his servant's eyes, and when he looked up, he saw that the hillside around Elisha was filled with horses and chariots of fire.

As the Aramean army advanced toward them, Elisha prayed, "O Lord, please make them blind." And the Lord did as Elisha asked. 2 KINGS 6:17-18

Elisha the prophet had a price on his head. The king of Aram was tired of the prophet warning the king of Israel every time he tried to set an ambush for the Israelites. So this king decided to go after Elisha. Elisha's servant went out and saw all of the enemy troops amassed against his master and began to despair. But Elisha prayed simply that the servant's eyes would be opened. After God answered, Elisha asked God to blind the enemy. Again, God answered immediately and powerfully.

If you ever find yourself overwhelmed by the forces gathered against you, as Elisha's servant was, pray for your own eyes to be opened. Ask God to show you how he is protecting you.

O Lord, open my eyes and let me see your protection . . .

May 22

Your word is a lamp for my feet
and a light for my path.
I've promised it once, and I'll promise again:
I will obey your wonderful laws.
I have suffered much, O Lord;
restore my life again, just as you promised.
Lord, accept my grateful thanks
and teach me your laws.
My life constantly hangs in the balance,
but I will not stop obeying your law.

PSALM 119:105-109

In this psalm, a lamp symbolizes the guidance, wisdom, and knowledge that come from God's Word. Just as a lamp helps a traveler see in the dark, the Bible is a lamp for our feet and a light for our path. In this life, we walk through a dark forest of evil. But the Bible can be our light to show us the way, so we don't stumble as we walk. The psalmist prayed that God might give him more light—more understanding of God's Word—to keep him on the path of life.

Ask God to guide you through circumstances that may trip you up in your spiritual walk. Recommit yourself to God's Word as the psalmist did: "My life constantly hangs in the balance, but I will not stop obeying your law."

Dear Lord, your word is a lamp for my feet and a light
for my path . . .

May 23

But as for me, I will sing about your power.
I will shout with joy each morning because of your
unfailing love.
For you have been my refuge,
a place of safety in the day of distress.
O my Strength, to you I sing praises,
for you, O God, are my refuge,
the God who shows me unfailing love.

PSALM 59:16-17

Human love can be both a source of great joy and a source of great pain—especially when someone's love is fickle and fallible. God's love, in contrast, is *unfailing!* David wrote one of his great songs for worship on this theme. He sang the praises of God's power as well as his love. Because of who God is, he is a safe haven for us in the "day of distress." For this psalm, David's day of distress was the time King Saul sent men to wait outside his home to kill him. On that day, David called out to God and learned that he was his "strength." David praised the Lord for showing him unfailing love.

When you encounter your own "day of distress," find your strength and your hiding place in the God who loves you unfailingly.

You, O God, are my refuge. You show me unfailing love . . .

A PRAYER

FOR THE

WHOLE

EARTH

May God be merciful and bless us.
May his face shine with favor upon us.
May your ways be known throughout the earth,
*   your saving power among people everywhere.*
May the nations praise you, O God.
Yes, may all the nations praise you.

PSALM 67:1-3

God's salvation was meant not only for his chosen people, Israel, but also for all the peoples of the earth. This prayer first asks God to show his favor to Israel, but the psalmist goes on to ask that God's ways and his saving power be made known "among people everywhere," so that God would receive the praises due him from *all nations*—not just Israel. The birth, death, and resurrection of his Son answered this prayer. When Jesus ascended into heaven, he told his disciples, "With my authority, take this message of repentance to all the nations, beginning in Jerusalem: 'There is forgiveness of sins for all who turn to me'" (Luke 24:47).

May God grant us the understanding of his will so that we, too, will pray for the salvation of all nations.

May your ways be known throughout the earth, your saving power among people everywhere . . .

May 25

MOSES' PRAYER OF PRAISE

"The Lord is a warrior;
yes, the Lord is his name!
Pharaoh's chariots and armies,
he has thrown into the sea.
The very best of Pharaoh's officers
have been drowned in the Red Sea.
The deep waters have covered them;
they sank to the bottom like a stone.
"Your right hand, O Lord,
is glorious in power.
Your right hand, O Lord,
dashes the enemy to pieces."

EXODUS 15:3-6

Only after God struck the Egyptians with a series of plagues did Pharaoh agree to let the enslaved Israelites go. But after the Israelites set off into the desert, Pharaoh changed his mind again and pursued them with chariots and horsemen. Yet God miraculously pushed back the Red Sea. And when the Israelites had all made it to the other side, he flooded it back onto the Egyptians. God had shown himself to be the ruler of all nations and the deliverer of Israel. This miracle inspired awe in the hearts of the Israelites, and so they praised him for it.

Today, this miracle stands as a symbol of our own deliverance from sin. He is the God of the helpless. He is undaunted by the strength of the proud; and for this, he deserves our heartfelt praise.

Your right hand, O Lord, is glorious in power . . .

MAY EVERYONE PRAISE THE LORD

Praise the Lord!
Yes, give praise, O servants of the Lord.
*   Praise the name of the Lord!*
Blessed be the name of the Lord
*   forever and ever.*
Everywhere–from east to west–
*   praise the name of the Lord.*
For the Lord is high above the nations;
*   his glory is far greater than the heavens.*

PSALM 113:1-4

The God we worship reigns over all nations. He is the God of the poor and rich alike, the Lord of all races and nationalities. Our God is also the Lord of all time—from the time of Abraham's day to our own. This prayer calls on people everywhere and in every age to bless the name of the Lord. Why is he worthy of our continual praise? Because he is "high above the nations" and "his glory is far greater than the heavens."

When you approach God in prayer today, first praise him for being Lord of all times, all places, and all people. Reflect on God's character and his purposes for the whole earth, and bless his name.

Mighty God, you are high above the nations; your glory is far greater than the heavens . . .

May 27

**IN AWE
OF THE
ALL-
POWERFUL
KING**

*O nations of the world, recognize the Lord;
    recognize that the Lord is glorious and strong.
Give to the Lord the glory he deserves!
    Bring your offering and come to worship him.
Worship the Lord in all his holy splendor.
    Let all the earth tremble before him.
Tell all the nations that the Lord is king.
    The world is firmly established and cannot be shaken.
He will judge all peoples fairly.*

PSALM 96:7-10

In the presence of powerful people, our typical reaction is awe. How much more should we experience reverence and fear before the all-powerful Lord of the universe! Throughout Scripture, people who have caught a glimpse of God's glory have fallen face-down before him. But our response should not stop there. Psalm 96 encourages us to "give to the Lord the glory he deserves." We do so by bringing offerings to him, worshiping him in public gatherings, and telling others the good news. "Tell all the nations that the Lord is king," declares the writer.

As you come to God in prayer today, consider how he reigns over all the earth. Then worship him and express your awe at his greatness. Ask him to lead all people everywhere to recognize him as king.

Sovereign Lord, you reign over all the earth . . .

HEZEKIAH'S PRAYER FOR DELIVERANCE

And Hezekiah prayed this prayer before the Lord: "O Lord, God of Israel, you are enthroned between the mighty cherubim! You alone are God of all the kingdoms of the earth. You alone created the heavens and the earth. Listen to me, O Lord, and hear! Open your eyes, O Lord, and see! Listen to Sennacherib's words of defiance against the living God. . . .

"Now, O Lord our God, rescue us from his power; then all the kingdoms of the earth will know that you alone, O Lord, are God."

2 KINGS 19:15-16, 19

When King Hezekiah ruled in Jerusalem, the Assyrians were the scourge of the peoples around them. Their king, Sennacherib, scoffed at Judah's faith in God. He taunted them with arrogant claims that their God would be as powerless against the advancing Assyrian army as had been the gods of every other nation the Assyrians had conquered. When Hezekiah went to ask for God's help, he appealed, in a sense, to God's "pride." He asked God to clear his own name and to prove Sennacherib wrong in his predictions.

There may be instances when, with all humility and holy fear, we can ask God to intervene on our behalf in order to defend the holiness of *his* name. At those times, don't be afraid to ask God to defend his reputation by saving you.

O God, defend the honor of your name and rescue me . . .

May 29

**CELEBRATING
GOD'S
POWER**

*The Lord is good to everyone.
   He showers compassion on all his creation.
All of your works will thank you, Lord,
   and your faithful followers will bless you.
They will talk together about the glory of your kingdom;
   they will celebrate examples of your power.
They will tell about your mighty deeds
   and about the majesty and glory of your reign.
For your kingdom is an everlasting kingdom.
   You rule generation after generation.*

PSALM 145:9-13

David couldn't stop praising the extraordinary reign of the Lord over all of creation. God's power was so awesome to David that he couldn't imagine only people praising God's goodness. In this prayer, David described all of creation as praising the Lord: "All of your works will thank you, Lord." He portrayed God's people and all of God's creation excitedly "talking together" about God, celebrating his powerful deeds, and telling others of the wonderful things the Lord had done.

Look around you today. Imagine all of creation—including the wildflowers of the fields—expressing in their own nonverbal ways their thanks to God. Join in that chorus with your own expression of thanks to your Creator.

O Lord, our Creator, I join with creation and bless you . . .

PRAYING FOR GOD'S CORRECTION

I know, Lord, that a person's life is not his own. No one is able to plan his own course. So correct me, Lord, but please be gentle. Do not correct me in anger, for I would die.

JEREMIAH 10:23-24

When we get impatient for God to show us what he wants us to do, it's so easy to move ahead, plotting our own course. When that happens, we lose perspective, and we need someone to correct us. We need someone to tell us that we're off course and that we need to change directions. It's not always easy to accept that correction, but it's necessary. Jeremiah must have sensed that he was making his own plans and following his own way. "So correct me, Lord," he prayed, "but please be gentle. Do not correct me in anger, for I would die."

The Lord has a plan for us, a course he wants us to follow. When we get "off course," we would do well to pray as Jeremiah did and ask the Lord to make the necessary correction in our life.

Heavenly Father, correct me with mercy and lead me in the right path . . .

**DECLARING
GOD'S
AWESOME
POWER**

Sing to the one who rides across the ancient heavens,
*   his mighty voice thundering from the sky.*
Tell everyone about God's power.
*   His majesty shines down on Israel;*
*   his strength is mighty in the heavens.*
God is awesome in his sanctuary.
*   The God of Israel gives power and strength to his people.*
Praise be to God!

PSALM 68:33-35

In this prayer, David attempted to find images that adequately describe God's power and might. So he used the sun and thunder as illustrations of God's power. God holds the power that gives the sun its brilliance and the storm its terrifying thunderclaps. And remarkably, he gives power and strength to his people. Surely the Almighty is worthy of praise. David's desire was that the whole assembly of God's people would raise their voices as one to praise the God of Israel.

We, too, can receive God's power and strength just as David did. Take time today to meditate on God's power. Find an image that communicates power and strength in an awesome way to you personally. Then, praise the God who made those things.

O God of Israel, you give power and strength to your
people . . .

DEBORAH'S PRAISE FOR GOD'S VICTORY

"Listen, you kings!
  Pay attention, you mighty rulers!
For I will sing to the Lord.
  I will lift up my song to the Lord, the God of Israel.
"Lord, when you set out from Seir
  and marched across the fields of Edom,
the earth trembled
  and the cloudy skies poured down rain.
The mountains quaked at the coming of the Lord.
  Even Mount Sinai shook in the presence of the Lord, the
  God of Israel."

JUDGES 5:3-5

Deborah wasn't the type of woman to sit idly by and wait for others to act. When God told her that the Israelites should attack Sisera's army, she immediately gave Balak the news. And when Balak hesitated, she encouraged him by promising to march into battle with him. Her courage and trust in God inspired Israel to win the battle. Another woman, Jael, killed the enemy, Sisera, when she had the chance. At the victory celebration, Deborah took the lead again. She didn't take all the glory for herself. Neither did she praise Balak or Jael for their courage. She praised the Almighty for the victory.

Where has God given you a victory in your life? Where has he shown his power? Praise the Lord for working in your life and tell others how great he is.

Dear Lord, the mountains quake at your coming . . .

June 2

TRUSTING IN GOD'S JUSTICE

God is my shield,
*   saving those whose hearts are true and right.*
God is a judge who is perfectly fair.
*   He is angry with the wicked every day. . . .*
I will thank the Lord because he is just;
*   I will sing praise to the name of the Lord Most High.*

PSALM 7:10-11, 17

Often we turn to God in prayer when we are facing a difficult circumstance. David was facing such a situation. Apparently Cush, a lifelong enemy of David, had found an opportunity to accuse him. David didn't respond to Cush's accusations with counteraccusations. Instead, he brought his case before God, the perfect Judge. He trusted God's ability to judge the situation correctly and defend his cause.

When have you felt unjustly accused? Are there people in your life that seem out to get you? Commit these situations and people to the God who promises one day to bring justice.

God of justice, I entrust my life to your care . . .

**PRAISE FOR
ANSWERED
PRAYER**

*I give you thanks, O Lord, with all my heart;
   I will sing your praises before the gods.
I bow before your holy Temple as I worship.
   I will give thanks to your name
     for your unfailing love and faithfulness,
because your promises are backed
   by all the honor of your name.
When I pray, you answer me;
   you encourage me by giving me the strength I need.*

PSALM 138:1-3

God answers prayer. He is faithful. But all too often, we don't look for the ways God is working in our lives. We abandon our prayers, stop anticipating answers, and forget to thank him for how he does answer. But David kept track of what he prayed for and how God had answered him. The long list of answered prayers in David's life inspired him to thank the Lord with all his being. He sang his thanks to God, bowed before God in reverence, and offered an animal sacrifice as a thank offering. His thanksgiving included gestures and symbols, incense, and music.

What are some prayers God has answered for you in the past? Express your thanks to God and commit yourself to continue praying, anticipating that God will respond with the best answer in his perfect timing.

Dear Lord, I give you thanks with all my heart . . .

June 4

**GOD DOES
AS HE
WISHES**

*Not to us, O Lord, but to you goes all the glory
for your unfailing love and faithfulness.
Why let the nations say,
"Where is their God?"
For our God is in the heavens,
and he does as he wishes.*

PSALM 115:1-3

In the cycle of the growing seasons, June is often the waiting time. The crops have been planted, the spring rains have fallen, and fall's bounty is now in God's hands. Often the waiting time brings questions. Will the crops grow? Will God provide for us? On a global scale, as history trudges on and we await Christ's return, similar questions may arise. People don't see the results yet, so they begin to doubt. But God will not be held accountable to them, nor will he be rushed into accomplishing his plans. God has given people abundant reasons to trust him, and he does not need to prove himself again and again.

Instead of questioning, our response should be, "Your will be done. May your plans be accomplished on earth, and may all the glory go to you."

Heavenly Father, you do as you wish. Help me to trust you . . .

June 5

MANOAH'S PRAYER FOR INSTRUCTION

Then Manoah prayed to the Lord. He said, "Lord, please let the man of God come back to us again and give us more instructions about this son who is to be born."

God answered his prayer, and the angel of God appeared once again to his wife as she was sitting in the field. But her husband, Manoah, was not with her. JUDGES 13:8-9

Manoah and his wife were surprised by the news that they would be the parents of a special son. For this infertile couple, the possibility of pregnancy was unexpected enough. Yet God had even greater plans. Manoah wisely recognized that he needed more instruction on how to handle the responsibilities for raising this special boy. So Manoah simply prayed, "Give us more instructions," and God answered by sending an angel.

Unexpected developments often reveal our inadequacies. When they do, our spiritual maturity will be measured by our willingness to ask God for help. "If you need wisdom—if you want to know what God wants you to do—ask him, and he will gladly tell you. He will not resent your asking" (James 1:5).

Dear Lord, give me more instructions about . . .

Waiting on the Lord

> I wait quietly before God,
> for my salvation comes from him.
> He alone is my rock and my salvation,
> my fortress where I will never be shaken.
> So many enemies against one man—
> all of them trying to kill me.
> To them I'm just a broken-down wall
> or a tottering fence. . . .
> I wait quietly before God,
> for my hope is in him.

PSALM 62:1 3, 5

Surrounded by enemies, David felt like a broken-down wall, ready to collapse at any time. Just as a tottering fence can't withstand the battering of a persistent bull, David knew he couldn't withstand the attacks of his enemies. David didn't bemoan his circumstances. He didn't frantically try to counter every assault and every lie. Instead, he quietly waited on the Lord—the only one who could deliver him.

When you feel surrounded by your enemies and feel broken, express your feelings and concerns to God. But also resolve to trust in the Lord no matter what situation comes your way today, and refrain from taking matters into your own hands.

Dear Lord, I wait quietly before you, for my hope is in you . . .

June 7

PRAISE FOR THE GOD BEYOND COMPARISON

Who can be compared with the Lord our God,
who is enthroned on high?
Far below him are the heavens and the earth.
He stoops to look,
and he lifts the poor from the dirt
and the needy from the garbage dump.
He sets them among princes,
even the princes of his own people!
He gives the barren woman a home,
so that she becomes a happy mother.
Praise the Lord!

PSALM 113:5-9

Who can be compared to God? Comparisons only work between things in the same category. It's foolish to compare the speed of a runner with the speed of an ice-skater. The two are participating in entirely different types of races. We run into the same problem when it comes to God. There is no one in God's category! Who is strong enough for us to compare to the Almighty? The only way we can describe our infinite God is to recount what he has done for his people. He has lifted up the poor out of poverty. He has given children to the barren. Who else could do such things?

Remind yourself of how great God is. Recount the ways God has worked in your life and in the lives of others. Then praise the Lord for his love and concern for you.

Almighty God, you are beyond compare . . .

June 8

**WHERE DO
WE PUT
OUR HOPE?**

And so, Lord, where do I put my hope?
My only hope is in you. . . .
Hear my prayer, O Lord!
Listen to my cries for help!
Don't ignore my tears.
For I am your guest—
a traveler passing through,
as my ancestors were before me.
Spare me so I can smile again
before I am gone and exist no more.

PSALM 39:7, 12-13

"What do I have to hope in, anymore?" This is a common question for those experiencing depression or going through a tragic situation—as David was when he prayed this psalm. Hope is the fuel of life, giving people the ability to endure daily frustrations. But where there is no hope, life and vitality are slowly drained away. In this prayer, David reminded himself of the shortness of his own life. As the king of Israel, David would have possessed great power and resources, yet he quickly realized he couldn't place his hope in these things. His only hope was God.

Take a moment to reflect on where you place your hope. Is it in your possessions? your abilities? your relationships? Place your hope in God alone.

Dear Lord, my only hope is in you . . .

June 9

In Awe of God

All heaven will praise your miracles, Lord;
myriads of angels will praise you for your faithfulness.
For who in all of heaven can compare with the Lord?
What mightiest angel is anything like the Lord?
The highest angelic powers stand in awe of God.
He is far more awesome than those who surround his
throne.
O Lord God Almighty!
Where is there anyone as mighty as you, Lord?
Faithfulness is your very character.

PSALM 89:5-8

People have always been fascinated by angels. The thought of compassionate spirit beings watching over us comforts many. But when Scripture describes people meeting angels, it usually depicts the person in shock and awe. The glory and power of these beings are beyond our imagination. Yet, angelic glory is only a reflection of the glory of their Creator. Angels, as awesome as they may be, owe reverence and praise to the even mightier Lord of the heavens. In this prayer, the psalmist exalted and honored God by contemplating heaven's throne room, where the greatest angelic powers bow in awe before the Lord.

God alone is worthy of our worship. Reflect on what it will be like to join the myriads of angels in exalting and praising God. Offer your praise to God today.

Holy God, I join your angels in praising you . . .

**PONDERING
GOD'S
PRECIOUS
THOUGHTS**

*How precious are your thoughts about me, O God!
They are innumerable!
I can't even count them;
they outnumber the grains of sand!
And when I wake up in the morning,
you are still with me!*

PSALM 139:17-18

When a couple falls in love, they fondly think about each other many times throughout the day. They look forward to the time when they can be together again. During the times when they are apart, they try to imagine what each other is doing; and they make note of experiences they would like to share with each other later. If the thoughts of lovers are so consumed with each other, how much more are God's thoughts focused on us—the ones he loves with eternal love! God's thoughts about *you,* an individual he has created, are "precious" and "innumerable," outnumbering the grains of sand.

Take some time to ponder and marvel at the immensity of God's love for you. Thank him for caring about you.

How precious are your thoughts about me, O God . . .

June 11

**REJOICING
IN GOD'S
LAWS**

*I have hidden your word in my heart,
    that I might not sin against you.
Blessed are you, O Lord;
    teach me your principles.
I have recited aloud
    all the laws you have given us.
I have rejoiced in your decrees
    as much as in riches.
I will study your commandments
    and reflect on your ways.*

PSALM 119:11-15

Psalm 119 is a long prayer that celebrates God's law. Why would anyone rejoice over laws? Most of us find laws restricting. They tell us what we can't do. But the psalmist praised God's laws. He even committed himself to memorizing them and reciting them aloud. Why was he so eager to learn God's ways? Because he had discovered that in these laws there is *life!* Sin separates us from God and from the fullness of life God offers. Those who reject God's law are on a path that leads to self-destruction and death. Knowing what God's law says can keep us from sinning against him.

As you approach God in prayer today, ask him to teach you his law. Ask him to show you how you should apply it to your life.

Dear Lord, help me to hide your Word in my heart so that I might not sin against you . . .

June 12

MOSES' PRAYER TO ENTER THE LAND

"At that time I pleaded with the Lord and said, 'O Sovereign Lord, I am your servant. You have only begun to show me your greatness and power. Is there any god in heaven or on earth who can perform such great deeds as yours? Please let me cross the Jordan to see the wonderful land on the other side, the beautiful hill country and the Lebanon mountains.'"   DEUTERONOMY 3:23-25

One can detect wistfulness in Moses' desperate prayer. He wanted to enter the land God had promised his people so long ago. He wanted to see the land flowing with milk and honey. But unfortunately, Moses had allowed his anger with the Israelites to affect how he obeyed God's directions, so the Lord would not let him enter the land. Even though Moses faced a no to his prayer, however, he knew God had a good plan for his life and submitted himself to it. When God says no, there's a reason. His no is always loving; he always has our best interests at heart.

It's never wrong to ask God for our desires. As you approach God in prayer today, submit your longings to him. Then ask him to prepare you for his good plan for your life.

Sovereign Lord, I, too, am your servant. Help me accept your good plan for me . . .

June 13

I will praise you, my God and King,
and bless your name forever and ever.
I will bless you every day,
and I will praise you forever.
Great is the Lord! He is most worthy of praise!
His greatness is beyond discovery!

PSALM 145:1-3

There are many reasons to praise the Lord. Not only has he made us and given us life, but he has provided for our needs and placed us in a community of believers, among whom we can grow into the person he wants us to be. Above all, he has reconciled us to himself through Jesus Christ. But David here celebrated none of the above. Instead, he praised God simply for being his great King. God's position alone makes him worthy of praise! What is more, David not only praised God but *blessed him!* What an incredible thought! God receives some blessing, or satisfaction, as we turn to him in worship and prayer.

For a few moments, meditate on how God reigns over the entire universe. In prayer, praise and bless the great King of kings.

O God my King, I praise you and bless you, for you are most worthy . . .

June 14

The Lord is my light and my salvation—
so why should I be afraid?
The Lord protects me from danger—
so why should I tremble?
When evil people come to destroy me,
when my enemies and foes attack me,
they will stumble and fall.
Though a mighty army surrounds me,
my heart will know no fear.
Even if they attack me,
I remain confident.

PSALM 27:1-3

In his first inaugural address, President Franklin D. Roosevelt tried to assure a worried nation going through the Great Depression that "the only thing we have to fear is fear itself." Fear can be paralyzing. Fear of an uncertain future can rob us of our peace and joy; and fear of failure can keep us from stepping out in faith and doing something God wants us to do. In this prayer, David declared that even if a mighty army were to surround and attack him, he would remain confident, and his heart would know no fear. David could say that because the Lord was his "light" and his "salvation."

If fear threatens to paralyze you and rob you of your joy, take courage that the Lord is watching over you. In prayer, place your trust in God, your Savior.

Dear Lord, my light and my salvation, take away the
fear in my heart and help me to trust you . . .

June 15

PRAISING OUR RIGHTEOUS KING

The Lord is king!
Let the nations tremble!
He sits on his throne between the cherubim.
Let the whole earth quake!
The Lord sits in majesty in Jerusalem,
supreme above all the nations.
Let them praise your great and awesome name.
Your name is holy!
Mighty king, lover of justice,
you have established fairness.
You have acted with justice
and righteousness throughout Israel.
Exalt the Lord our God!
Bow low before his feet, for he is holy!

PSALM 99:1-5

"God is King!" The Psalms are filled with declarations of God's just and righteous reign. The Israelites certainly knew what it was like to live under less than perfect kings—weak kings, unjust kings, and evil kings. When the rule of law breaks down in a country, injustice, fear, and terror reign. But God's reign brings justice, peace, and life.

To be a glad servant of the great King of kings should be the joy and delight of every worshiper. But too often, we want to put ourselves on the throne and have our own way. Join the psalmist in bowing low before the King of kings in prayer.

I exalt you, O Lord, my God. I bow before you, for you alone are King . . .

June 16

**FIXING OUR
THOUGHTS
ON GOD**

*In that day, everyone in the land of Judah will sing this
song:*

*Our city is now strong!
   We are surrounded by the walls of God's salvation.
Open the gates to all who are righteous;
   allow the faithful to enter.
You will keep in perfect peace all who trust in you,
   whose thoughts are fixed on you!
Trust in the Lord always,
   for the Lord GOD is the eternal Rock.*

ISAIAH 26:1-4

We all want to be secure—to feel safe from the attacks of strangers
and enemies. In Israel, security meant living in a city with strong
walls to keep out invaders. In this prayer of praise, believers
proclaim that their security is in the Lord. While a stone wall may
one day fall to the ground, God will be the Protector and the Savior
of the righteous forever. Who or what should believers fear?
Nothing, for our future is secure, and this gives us peace of mind.

Fix your thoughts on your almighty God, as this prayer instructs
all of us to do. Reaffirm your trust in God today, and know the
peace that such trust brings.

*Sovereign Lord, help me to fix my thoughts on you and
trust in you always, for you are my eternal Rock . . .*

REJOICING IN OUR MAKER

Praise the Lord!
Sing to the Lord a new song.
Sing his praises in the assembly of the faithful.
O Israel, rejoice in your Maker.
O people of Jerusalem, exult in your King.
Praise his name with dancing,
accompanied by tambourine and harp.
For the Lord delights in his people;
he crowns the humble with salvation.
Let the faithful rejoice in this honor.
Let them sing for joy as they lie on their beds.

PSALM 149:1-5

Psalm 149 is the prayer of a joyful group of believers. Together in this prayer, they rejoice with one another because God is their King, and they praise God through the many expressive gifts God has given them—dancing, singing, and playing various instruments. The message of this psalm is that God takes delight in his people and saves those who humble themselves before him. Being included in this celebration has nothing to do with anyone deserving anything. It has everything to do with God's goodness.

Rejoice over the goodness of God and reaffirm your commitment to worship the Lord in your church with the talents God has given you.

O Lord our Maker, I rejoice in you and sing your praises in the assembly of the faithful . . .

June 18

A CRY FOR GOD'S PROTECTION

O Lord, I have so many enemies;
so many are against me.
So many are saying,
"God will never rescue him!"
But you, O Lord, are a shield around me,
my glory, and the one who lifts my head high.
I cried out to the Lord,
and he answered me from his holy mountain.
I lay down and slept.
I woke up in safety,
for the Lord was watching over me.

PSALM 3:1-5

When David's son Absalom rebelled, he tried to kill David and take over his throne. David fled for his life, hiding from his son and his powerful army. Some of David's enemies were saying, "God will never rescue him." In the midst of those problems, David was able to lie down and sleep. He was unafraid because he knew God was his shield. God was watching over him.

It may seem that your enemies are pursuing you to death. Some may even be saying to your face, "God will never rescue you!" Do what David did. Cry out to God, your shield, for protection. Then lie down and sleep in peace, for God will watch over you.

Dear Lord, I know you are watching over me. Be my shield . . .

June 19

MEDITATING ON GOD'S SPLENDOR

*Let each generation tell its children
of your mighty acts.
I will meditate on your majestic, glorious splendor
and your wonderful miracles.
Your awe-inspiring deeds will be on every tongue;
I will proclaim your greatness.
Everyone will share the story of your wonderful goodness;
they will sing with joy of your righteousness.*

PSALM 145:4-7

In just these few verses of prayerful meditation, David mentioned many things about God that make him worthy of our praise and worship: his majesty, his glorious splendor, his wonderful miracles, his greatness, his goodness, and his righteousness. He also praised God for his kindness, unfailing love, mercy, and compassion. No wonder David's prayer was full of praise. No wonder he encouraged each generation to tell others of God's mighty acts. No wonder he foresaw the day when God's awe-inspiring deeds would be on every tongue.

Take a few moments to meditate on God's splendor, and let David's prayer of praise lead you in praise to the Almighty. Then tell someone else this week about what God has done for you.

*Dear God, you are surrounded by majestic splendor.
Help me to tell others of your mighty acts . . .*

**PROCLAIMING
GOD'S
PERFECTION**

> *"I will proclaim the name of the Lord;*
> *how glorious is our God!*
> *He is the Rock; his work is perfect.*
> *Everything he does is just and fair.*
> *He is a faithful God who does no wrong;*
> *how just and upright he is!"*
>
> DEUTERONOMY 32:3-4

God is perfect! This was the theme of the song of praise that Moses taught the people toward the end of his life. No matter how much we admire other people, neither we nor they would ever claim perfection. But everything God does is "just and fair." If this is true, then we will sometimes need to adjust our perspective on life's trials and troubles. From our own limited vantage point, we cannot always understand why things happen and what they mean. But in those times of difficulty, we need to remind ourselves that God does no wrong; he is faithful, just, and upright.

Join your voice with that of Moses and many other believers through the centuries. Praise our holy and perfect God!

Dear God, your work is perfect. Everything you do is just and fair . . .

REJOICING OVER OUR INHERITANCE

I said to the Lord, "You are my Master!
All the good things I have are from you." . . .
Lord, you alone are my inheritance, my cup of blessing.
You guard all that is mine.
The land you have given me is a pleasant land.
What a wonderful inheritance!

PSALM 16:2, 5-6

We've all heard of families who are divided forever because they disagreed over an inheritance. Brothers and sisters who once loved each other spend the rest of their lives greedily fighting to protect what they have inherited from their parents, while others go to their grave hating and resenting their siblings who got a bigger share than they did. How refreshing to hear David say to the Lord, "The land you have given me is a pleasant land. What a wonderful inheritance!"

Are we satisfied with what the Lord has given us, no matter how great or small? Can you say—and really mean it—"I have you, Lord, and that's enough"? List in your mind all God has given to you. Then rejoice over your inheritance, over all the good things God has given you.

Dear Lord, you alone are my inheritance. All the good things I have are from you . . .

June 22

**AN APPEAL
FOR GOD TO
LISTEN**

Listen to my pleading, O Lord.
Be merciful and answer me!
My heart has heard you say, "Come and talk with me."
And my heart responds, "Lord, I am coming."
Do not hide yourself from me.
Do not reject your servant in anger.
You have always been my helper.
Don't leave me now; don't abandon me,
O God of my salvation!
Even if my father and mother abandon me,
the Lord will hold me close.

PSALM 27:7-10

David went through times when he felt abandoned by God. In this psalm, David pleads for God to hear his prayer and answer him. We, too, will go through "dark nights of the soul"—when it seems there's a wall between us and God—when it feels like he is far away. We, too, will cry out with a heart of anguish, "Are you listening, Lord? Please listen to my pleading and answer me!" Even before David received an answer, as he struggled in this storm of doubt, he prayed, "Even if my father and mother abandon me, the Lord will hold me close." He reassured his troubled soul that God was close—no matter how he felt.

During those times when God seems so distant, we must remind ourselves that God is near to those who call out to him.

Dear Lord, listen to my pleading. I know that even if my father and mother abandon me, you will hold me close . . .

LOOKING TO GOD FOR SAFETY

I look to you for help, O Sovereign Lord.
You are my refuge; don't let them kill me.
Keep me out of the traps they have set for me,
out of the snares of those who do evil.
Let the wicked fall into their own snares,
but let me escape.

PSALM 141:8-10

A newspaper story told of a lost hiker who wandered in a blinding snowstorm for hours without seeing any sign of life. Finally, exhausted, hungry, numb from the cold, and ready to give up, he saw a log cabin through the trees. While not luxurious, the abandoned cabin provided warmth and shelter until rescuers found the young man. What a welcome sight that rustic cabin must have been to that lost hiker! It was his shelter, his refuge—a place of safety. That warm cabin literally saved his life. Similarly, in this psalm, David described the Lord as a refuge from the dangers that surrounded him.

It's comforting to know that when enemies surround us, we can turn to the Lord. Today, commit your troubles to God in prayer.

Dear Lord, I look to you for help. You are my refuge . . .

June 24

LOOKING TO GOD FOR OUR NEEDS

For your kingdom is an everlasting kingdom.
You rule generation after generation.
The Lord is faithful in all he says;
he is gracious in all he does.
The Lord helps the fallen
and lifts up those bent beneath their loads.
All eyes look to you for help;
you give them their food as they need it.
When you open your hand,
you satisfy the hunger and thirst of every living thing.

PSALM 145:13-16

Life presents us with many competing demands—children asking for attention, bosses asking for greater productivity, and spouses asking for help with chores at home. While we are trying to attend to all these responsibilities, we may feel as if we need more and more as well. We may even begin to wonder if God himself is capable of providing for all our needs. But God, through his actions in the past, has demonstrated again and again that he can provide for our needs. He has promised to help us with our heavy burdens and even to help us when we stumble and fall. What a comfort to know that the Lord will provide for us!

Jesus told us not to worry, for God will provide for our needs (Matthew 6:31-33). In prayer today, commit your worries to him and trust him to provide for you.

Dear God, I look to you for help. Open your hand and satisfy my needs . . .

Praying for Strength from the Lord

Then Samson prayed to the Lord, "Sovereign Lord, remember me again. O God, please strengthen me one more time so that I may pay back the Philistines for the loss of my eyes." Then Samson put his hands on the center pillars of the temple and pushed against them with all his might. "Let me die with the Philistines," he prayed. And the temple crashed down on the Philistine leaders and all the people. So he killed more people when he died than he had during his entire lifetime.

JUDGES 16:28-30

Before Samson's birth, an angel of the Lord told his mother she would have a son. His hair was never to be cut. He was to be dedicated to God, and he was destined to rescue Israel from the Philistines. Samson was dedicated to God at birth, and he grew into a man of great strength. He served the Lord for years but later strayed away from God. Now, languishing in a Philistine prison, blind, weak, and far from God, he remembered the source of his strength. He prayed and asked God to strengthen him once again. The Lord answered his prayer, and Samson was able to win a great victory over the Philistines.

If you seem to be languishing in your walk with God, remember the source of your strength. Pray that God may strengthen you to win the battles he has prepared for you.

Dear God, strengthen me and help me to rely upon you rather than myself . . .

June 26

LOOKING TO GOD FOR MERCY

I lift my eyes to you,
O God, enthroned in heaven.
We look to the Lord our God for his mercy,
just as servants keep their eyes on their master,
as a slave girl watches her mistress for the slightest signal.
Have mercy on us, Lord, have mercy,
for we have had our fill of contempt.

PSALM 123:1-3

One of the most difficult things to do in life is wait. Our desire is to have the finished product or get to our intended goal immediately. But the psalmist in this prayer knew that waiting on the Lord was best, so he was going to wait as long as it took to see God's mercy revealed in his life. God grants us mercy, not because we deserve it but because he loves us, and he will grant it in his own timing. Like servants who keep their eyes on their master or a slave girl who watches her mistress for the slightest signal, we should be attentive to God's leading and patiently wait on God for his help.

Lift your eyes to God and look to him for mercy. Wait expectantly for him to help you. Then remember to thank God for his kindness and mercy toward you.

Dear Lord, I lift my eyes to you to find mercy . . .

FINDING STRENGTH IN TIMES OF TROUBLE

But Lord, be merciful to us, for we have waited for you. Be our strength each day and our salvation in times of trouble. The enemy runs at the sound of your voice. When you stand up, the nations flee!

ISAIAH 33:2-3

Right after this prayer for God to rescue Israel, the prophet Isaiah described the Israelites' desperate plight: The Assyrians had refused their petition for peace. All the land was in trouble. The roads were deserted, and no one dared to travel them anymore. Lebanon had been destroyed, the Plain of Sharon was a wilderness, and Bashan and Carmel had been plundered (Isaiah 33:7-9). Yet Isaiah's trust in the Lord never wavered during this difficult time. Because he believed God's promise to protect and deliver his people, Isaiah could pray with confidence, "Be our strength and our salvation in times of trouble."

God's promises haven't changed. He is still our strength each day and our salvation in times of trouble. In our time of trouble, we can call upon him as Isaiah did.

Dear Lord, even though I'm weak and in trouble, I believe your promise. Be my strength each day . . .

June 28

**RECOGNIZING
GOD'S
GREATNESS**

*I know the greatness of the Lord—
  that our Lord is greater than any other god.
The Lord does whatever pleases him
  throughout all heaven and earth,
  and on the seas and in their depths. . . .
Your name, O Lord, endures forever;
  your fame, O Lord, is known to every generation.
For the Lord will vindicate his people
  and have compassion on his servants.*

PSALM 135:5-6, 13-14

What is greatness? The writer of Psalm 135 contrasted the greatness of the living God with the pagan gods that were worshiped at his time. Simply put, there is no comparison: "Our Lord is greater than any other god." While other gods were thought to exercise control over different parts of creation (for instance, there was a rain god, a god of the seas, and so on), "the Lord does whatever pleases him throughout all heaven and earth." He can do anything he wants. Yet God uses his power to help his people and provide them with all they need. He willingly answers those who call on him. What a loving and compassionate God!

Take some time today to meditate on the greatness of the Lord.

Dear Lord, you indeed are great. Thank you for having compassion on me . . .

June 29

INTERCEDING FOR THOSE WHO HURT US

As the cloud moved from above the Tabernacle, Miriam suddenly became white as snow with leprosy. When Aaron saw what had happened, he cried out to Moses, "Oh, my lord! Please don't punish us for this sin we have so foolishly committed. Don't let her be like a stillborn baby, already decayed at birth."

So Moses cried out to the Lord, "Heal her, O God, I beg you!"

NUMBERS 12:10-13

As the Israelites camped in the wilderness near Hazeroth, Aaron and Miriam criticized Moses for marrying a Cushite woman. As punishment, God caused Miriam to be infected with a terrible skin disease. Aaron appealed to Moses to intercede on Miriam's behalf, and Moses did. He earnestly prayed and begged the Lord to heal her. God answered Moses' prayer; Miriam was healed, though she was placed outside the camp for seven days. Even though Miriam had criticized Moses, he was still willing to intercede in prayer for her.

Are you willing, as Moses was, to be an intercessor—even for someone who has been unkind to you? Today, pray for someone who has hurt you.

Dear God, make me a willing intercessor for those who criticize me. Please help . . .

June 30

DELIVERANCE

FROM

DEATH

Pull me out of the mud;
* don't let me sink any deeper!*
Rescue me from those who hate me,
* and pull me from these deep waters.*
Don't let the floods overwhelm me,
* or the deep waters swallow me,*
* or the pit of death devour me.*

PSALM 69:14-15

Earlier, David complained to God about the wickedness of those who hated and attacked him with lies. Even his own brothers were pretending not to know him. David moaned about being the "favorite topic of town gossip." But even though everyone was against him, David didn't give up. He didn't let the flood of criticism overwhelm him. He didn't let his enemies pull him down. Instead, he cried out for God to rescue him—to pull him "out of the mud."

At some time in our lives most of us have felt as David did. When you're the object of ridicule, when you've been lied about, humiliated, and mocked, when you feel you're about to be "overwhelmed by the flood," react as David did. Don't give up. Take your shame to God in prayer.

Dear Lord, please hear my prayer and pull me out of the mud . . .

July 1

GIVING GOD GLORY

Give to the Lord the glory he deserves!
Bring your offering and come to worship him.
Worship the Lord in all his holy splendor.
Let all the earth tremble before him.
The world is firmly established and cannot be shaken.
Let the heavens be glad, and let the earth rejoice!
Tell all the nations that the Lord is king.
Let the sea and everything in it shout his praise!
Let the fields and their crops burst forth with joy!
Let the trees of the forest rustle with praise before the Lord!
For he is coming to judge the earth.

1 CHRONICLES 16:29-33

Whether they are basketball players or accomplished chess players, we love to talk about champions. Often these victors have persevered through years of hard work and self-discipline before achieving their accomplishments, and now they soak up the praise that fans naturally shower on them. How much more does God deserve our enthusiastic praise? God is the loving Creator of the entire earth. In this prayer, which was sung as the Ark of God was brought into Jerusalem, David called on all of creation to join him in rejoicing over the Creator.

Plan to take a walk outside this week so you can appreciate God's creation. Give glory to God for what he has created and see how creation celebrates the Lord with you.

Dear Lord, I praise you and give you the honor you deserve from your creation . . .

July 2

Hannah's Prayer for a Child

Hannah was in deep anguish, crying bitterly as she prayed to the Lord. And she made this vow: "O Lord Almighty, if you will look down upon my sorrow and answer my prayer and give me a son, then I will give him back to you. He will be yours for his entire lifetime, and as a sign that he has been dedicated to the Lord, his hair will never be cut."

1 SAMUEL 1:10-11

Hannah, who was childless, lived in a time when women were dishonored if they were unable to bear children. Hannah's rival—her husband's other wife—flaunted her own children before her. When the whole family went up to Jerusalem for the feast, Hannah found herself unable to join in the celebration. Instead, she went into the Tabernacle and expressed her deep sorrow and longings to God. She knew whom to turn to when she was down. She knew the Almighty was the only one who could help her. She didn't arrogantly demand that God give her a son. Instead, she expressed her willingness to give back to God.

What is the cry of your heart? Have you brought it before God? Are you willing to give the answer to your prayer to him?

O Lord Almighty, look down upon me and answer my prayer . . .

July 3

**REMINDING
OURSELVES
OF GOD'S
GREATNESS**

*Nowhere among the pagan gods is there a god like you,
O Lord.
There are no other miracles like yours.
All the nations—and you made each one—
will come and bow before you, Lord;
they will praise your great and holy name.
For you are great and perform great miracles.
You alone are God.*

PSALM 86:8-10

Sometimes our prayers can become so punctuated with the word *help*, so focused on the dangers and trials, that we overlook the one we are imploring. David avoided this error. He recognized that his God was greater than all others, and the Lord had demonstrated his miraculous power in countless ways. David foresaw a day when all the nations, not just the Israelites, would acknowledge the sovereignty of God Almighty. He alone is God.

Let us lift our eyes from the problems at hand to our triumphant King. Place the difficulties that are bothering you today before your infinite, wonder-working God.

O Lord, you are great and perform great miracles. You alone are God . . .

July 4

WELCOMING THE KING OF GLORY

The earth is the Lord's, and everything in it.
The world and all its people belong to him.
For he laid the earth's foundation on the seas
and built it on the ocean depths....
Open up, ancient gates!
Open up, ancient doors,
and let the King of glory enter.
Who is the King of glory?
The Lord Almighty—
he is the King of glory.

PSALM 24:1-2, 9-10

When the president of a nation travels, it is a major event. He's accompanied by his entourage of advisers and secret service agents. When a president's entourage reaches a gated home, the president *never* gets out of his limousine to identify himself or open the gate. No, the guards simply know that this is the president. In David's day, a city's gates would be barred up while the king was away at battle. But when the king came back in victory, the gate would be flung open to welcome the returning, triumphant king. David's prayer is that the conquering King of kings would be welcomed to Jerusalem in a similar way.

Just as David welcomed the Lord, his King, so long ago, welcome God in prayer and celebrate his presence in your life.

O Lord, I welcome you into my life as King . . .

July 5

MOSES PRAISES THE LORD

"Who else among the gods is like you, O Lord?
Who is glorious in holiness like you—
so awesome in splendor,
performing such wonders?
You raised up your hand,
and the earth swallowed our enemies.
With unfailing love you will lead
this people whom you have ransomed.
You will guide them in your strength
to the place where your holiness dwells."

EXODUS 15:11-13

Freedom at last! Precious freedom. The Israelites had been slaves in Egypt for years, but now they had just witnessed a miracle: God parted the Red Sea, allowing them to pass through and escape their oppressors. They were free from their slavery, and the Promised Land lay before them! Moses led the Israelites in praising their Victor. At this celebration of freedom, Moses reminded the Israelites why they were freed. They weren't freed to do whatever they wanted. They were freed to serve God as his holy people. Moses asked that God might "guide" them to that place.

Set aside some time to celebrate your freedom in Christ. Remember that you were freed from sin to serve God as his child.

Dear Lord, don't let me stray from your path. Guide me to your holiness . . .

July 6

PLACING OUR CONFIDENCE IN GOD

My heart is confident in you, O God;
no wonder I can sing your praises!
Wake up, my soul!
Wake up, O harp and lyre!
I will waken the dawn with my song.
I will thank you, Lord, in front of all the people.
I will sing your praises among the nations.
For your unfailing love is as high as the heavens.
Your faithfulness reaches to the clouds.
Be exalted, O God, above the highest heavens.
May your glory shine over all the earth.

PSALM 57:7-11

David prayed these words when he was fleeing for his life. We would expect a man running for his life to be focused on what his enemies were doing and how he could elude their traps. But David, after describing his predicament to the Lord, focused on how powerful his Helper was. His prayer for help quickly turned to loud and heartfelt praise: "I will waken the dawn with my song. I will thank you, Lord, in front of all the people." Why was David moved to such gratitude when facing danger? Because he knew God's unfailing love was greater than his difficulty. David's prayer put his earthly trials in eternal perspective.

How could God's eternal perspective help you face the difficulties in your life? In prayer, place your confidence in your all-powerful God.

Dear God, my heart is confident in you . . .

July 7

PRAISE FOR ACCOM-PLISHMENTS

Lord, you will grant us peace,
for all we have accomplished is really from you.
O Lord our God, others have ruled us,
but we worship you alone.
Those we served before are dead and gone.
Never again will they return!
You attacked them and destroyed them,
and they are long forgotten.
We praise you, Lord!
You have made our nation great;
you have extended our borders!

ISAIAH 26:12-15

Whether it involves hitting home runs or outrunning an opponent, competitors do what's necessary to win. Some athletes take personal credit for their feats, declaring that success came only from their diligence and determination. Today's prayer offers a different attitude about who gets the credit. Isaiah prophesied that one day God's people would be victorious—but only because of what God would do for them. Instead of lauding the people for their victory, Isaiah praised God: "All we have accomplished is really from you."

What accomplishments have you experienced within the last year? Today, acknowledge that it was God who enabled you to achieve those goals. Worship him for what he has done.

Dear Lord, all we have accomplished is really from you . . .

J u l y 8

WAITING FOR GOD TO ACT

How long, O God, will you allow our enemies to mock you?
Will you let them dishonor your name forever?
Why do you hold back your strong right hand?
Unleash your powerful fist and deliver a deathblow. . . .
Arise, O God, and defend your cause.
Remember how these fools insult you all day long.
Don't overlook these things your enemies have said.
Their uproar of rebellion grows ever louder.

PSALM 74:10-11, 22-23

How often does God listen to our impatient prayers? Nothing reveals our lack of faith more than impatient "why" and "how long" prayers. Yet God arranged that even prayers like these were recorded in Scripture. Here, the psalmist cried out to the Lord to defend his holy name from those who "dishonored" and "mocked" him. He wanted God to take revenge swiftly against those people. Although the Lord doesn't always tell us when he will act, we can be confident that at the right time he will do what needs to be done.

God wants us to express our feelings and urgent requests to him. Pray against the enemies of faith with conviction. But also trust him for the future, since the final results will always remain in his able hands.

O God, why do you hold back your strong right hand?
Arise and defend your cause . . .

July 9

Trusting in God's Protection

Have mercy on me, O God, have mercy!
I look to you for protection.
I will hide beneath the shadow of your wings
until this violent storm is past.
I cry out to God Most High,
to God who will fulfill his purpose for me.
He will send help from heaven to save me,
rescuing me from those who are out to get me.
My God will send forth his unfailing love and faithfulness.

PSALM 57:1-3

David was in hiding. Saul's pursuit had driven him into a desert cave. But David knew that his hope didn't rest in how fast he could run or how creatively he could hide. Protection came from God. The darkness of a cave could not protect him as well as the shadow of God's wings. David placed his trust in God alone for his safety.

What have the violent storms of life taught you about God's faithfulness? Are you confident, as David was, that God "will fulfill his purpose" for you? Rest in the protection God offers under his wings and trust his direction for your life.

Dear Lord, help me to trust that you will fulfill your purpose for me . . .

July 10

PRAISE FOR THE GOD OF COMFORT

All praise to the God and Father of our Lord Jesus Christ. He is the source of every mercy and the God who comforts us. He comforts us in all our troubles so that we can comfort others. When others are troubled, we will be able to give them the same comfort God has given us. You can be sure that the more we suffer for Christ, the more God will shower us with his comfort through Christ.   2 CORINTHIANS 1:3-5

How often have you noticed that soon after you receive comfort for some troubling situation, you encounter someone else facing a similar situation? It is God who leads us to these people, for the comfort we provide for them seems more credible because they know we have "been there." Paul praises the Lord in his letter to the Corinthian church that God "comforts us in all our troubles so that we can comfort others" with "the same comfort God has given us."

In what ways has God comforted you in the trials you have had to go through? Pray that God may use you to comfort others.

Dear Lord, thank you for comforting me. Use me to comfort others . . .

July 11

A PRAYER FOR DISCERNMENT

I am your servant;
deal with me in unfailing love,
and teach me your principles.
Give discernment to me, your servant;
then I will understand your decrees.
Lord, it is time for you to act,
for these evil people have broken your law.
Truly, I love your commands
more than gold, even the finest gold.
Truly, each of your commandments is right.
That is why I hate every false way.

PSALM 119:124-128

The trials and struggles in our lives often force us to turn somewhere for help. Too often, however, we anxiously seek out any listening ear when we're confronted with a troublesome situation. The psalmist knew to turn to the Lord first for wisdom and discernment. He asked God, "Teach me your principles," and "Give discernment to me." He knew that living God's way would keep him from foolish actions and the path of destruction. That is why he committed himself to learning God's principles in the Scriptures and applying them to his life.

What difficult situation are you facing? God promises to give us wisdom when we ask for it (James 1:5), so pray for God's discernment in your struggle and ask him to show you how to apply his wisdom to your situation.

Dear Lord, as your servant I ask you to give me discernment . . .

July 12

**PRAISE
FROM THE
NATIONS**

Praise the Lord, all you nations.
Praise him, all you people of the earth.
For he loves us with unfailing love;
the faithfulness of the Lord endures forever.
Praise the Lord!

PSALM 117:1-2

The Lord is God over every nation, and he deserves our praise. Psalm 117, the shortest chapter in the Bible, is a simple prayer of praise encouraging people from the ends of the earth to proclaim God's greatness. The psalmist says that we should praise him because he showers his love and faithfulness upon his people.

Imagine—one day in heaven—people from every nation, every tribe, and every language group will bow before the Lord and sing his praises (Revelation 7:9-10)! Join with God's people around the globe in offering praise to the risen King.

Dear Lord, I join with all your people in praising you
for your love and faithfulness . . .

A PRAYER FOR COMFORT AND STRENGTH	*May our Lord Jesus Christ and God our Father, who loved us and in his special favor gave us everlasting comfort and good hope, comfort your hearts and give you strength in every good thing you do and say.* 2 THESSALONIANS 2:16-17

As Paul was writing to the young church at Thessalonica, he was concerned about the persecution and false teachers that inevitably would come their way. Paul never sugarcoated true Christian discipleship. He wanted more than anything for Christians to be prepared to face trials for Christ's sake. This prayer reveals a fatherly concern—expressed urgently because he was unable to be at their side. Paul prayed that God himself would comfort them and give them strength whenever they stood up for right living and against false teaching.

God's "special favor" is for all believers. We, too, can approach God with confidence, asking for God's comfort and strength. He is faithful.

Dear Lord Jesus Christ, comfort our hearts and give us the strength to do and say what is right . . .

July 14

PRAYER AS INCENSE BEFORE THE LORD

O Lord, I am calling to you. Please hurry!
Listen when I cry to you for help!
Accept my prayer as incense offered to you,
and my upraised hands as an evening offering.
Take control of what I say, O Lord,
and keep my lips sealed.
Don't let me lust for evil things;
don't let me participate in acts of wickedness.
Don't let me share in the delicacies
of those who do evil.

PSALM 141:1-4

In this psalm, David used temple imagery as he called upon God to listen to his cry for help. He asked the Lord to regard his prayer as sweet smelling incense floating from the altar into the heavens. Such incense was usually offered in the tabernacle along with a burnt offering. He also called upon God to accept his "upraised hands as an evening offering." In ancient times, people often prayed with their hands open toward heaven.

God does accept our prayers in this way. He is pleased when we come to him with our requests, and he is always willing and able to do what is best for us. Take a moment to offer up an "incense" of prayer to God and trust that he will answer.

Dear Lord, accept my prayer as incense offered to you . . .

July 15

A CALL FOR GOD TO ACT

O God, don't sit idly by,
silent and inactive!
Don't you hear the tumult of your enemies?
Don't you see what your arrogant enemies are doing?
Utterly disgrace them
until they submit to your name, O Lord.
Let them be ashamed and terrified forever.
Make them failures in everything they do,
until they learn that you alone are called the Lord,
that you alone are the Most High, supreme over all the
earth.

PSALM 83:1-2, 16-18

The nation of Israel was under attack. At least ten nations were allied against Israel. The outlook seemed hopeless. But the Israelites had been in desperate situations before this. God had crushed their enemies in the past; surely he would do it again. So the psalmist prayed. He asked God not so much for Israel's survival as for God's honor and reputation among the nations, for the plans of Israel's enemies were, in effect, plans against God.

Though God's people are no longer represented by a single nation, there are still many wicked rulers working against God's ways. Christians should pray that God will one day cause these rulers to recognize that the Lord reigns supreme over all the earth.

Almighty Lord, don't sit idly by. Make your enemies learn that you alone are the Most High . . .

July 16

THE PRAYER OF A PERSECUTED SHEPHERD

Lord, I have not abandoned my job as a shepherd for your people. I have not urged you to send disaster. It is your message I have given them, not my own. Lord, do not desert me now! You alone are my hope in the day of disaster. Bring shame and terror on all who persecute me, but give me peace. Yes, bring double destruction upon them! JEREMIAH 17:16-18

Jeremiah knew that he had been faithful to God's call to warn the people to repent—a message God's people didn't want to hear. They persecuted Jeremiah. The prophet could have defended himself, but he chose not to. He simply obeyed and waited for God to take whatever action he chose. This is the sort of behavior that Paul was talking about when he said, "Never pay back evil for evil to anyone. . . . Leave that to God. For it is written, 'I will take vengeance; I will repay those who deserve it,' says the Lord" (Romans 12:17, 19).

When you face opposition regarding something that God has called you to do, don't take matters into your own hands. Simply continue to be faithful and trust God to handle things as he sees fit.

Dear Lord, help me to honor and trust you at all times . . .

Trusting in God's Plan

Though I am surrounded by troubles,
*   you will preserve me against the anger of my enemies.*
You will clench your fist against my angry enemies!
*   Your power will save me.*
The Lord will work out his plans for my life—
*   for your faithful love, O Lord, endures forever.*
*   Don't abandon me, for you made me.*

PSALM 138:7-8

Do you believe God controls your circumstances when you feel "surrounded by troubles"? This is a difficult challenge for most people. But we must cling by faith to what we know to be true about God, even when we don't see it in action. So David says, "You *will* preserve me against the anger of my enemies." Though we are tempted to plan out our entire life as well as its possibilities, we can assert with David that "the Lord will work out his plans for my life." In a touching plea of the embattled soul, David cried, "Don't abandon me, for you made me."

Today in prayer, thank God that he has a good plan for you. In those dark moments when it seems as though he might have abandoned you, remember that God is faithful, and he will never let you go.

Dear Lord, preserve me against the anger of my enemies . . .

July 18

You know the insults I endure—
the humiliation and disgrace.
You have seen all my enemies
and know what they have said.
Their insults have broken my heart,
and I am in despair.
If only one person would show some pity;
if only one would turn and comfort me. . . .
I am suffering and in pain.
Rescue me, O God, by your saving power.
Then I will praise God's name with singing,
and I will honor him with thanksgiving.

PSALM 69:19-20, 29-30

The old African-American spiritual captures the feeling of this psalm so well: "Nobody knows the trouble I've seen, nobody knows but Jesus." This lament reflects David's sentiments. He felt that everyone had turned against him. He was being humiliated and insulted. It is clear that David was hurting inside. He wished for even one human being to show him pity and offer him comfort. But in the midst of all his pain and loneliness, he continued to pray to God. He trusted that, no matter how bad his suffering might get, God was still going to save him.

In your moment of trial, you may feel completely abandoned by those around you. But never think that God will ever abandon you. He will answer you when you call, and he knows what is best for you.

Dear God, I am suffering and in pain. Rescue me by
your saving power . . .

July 19

JEREMIAH'S
COMPLAINT
ABOUT THE
WICKED

Lord, you always give me justice when I bring a case before you. Now let me bring you this complaint: Why are the wicked so prosperous? Why are evil people so happy? You have planted them, and they have taken root and prospered. Your name is on their lips, but in their hearts they give you no credit at all. But as for me, Lord, you know my heart. You see me and test my thoughts. Drag these people away like helpless sheep to be butchered! Set them aside to be slaughtered!

JEREMIAH 12:1-3

Have you ever wondered why people who don't fear God often seem so well off in life? Have you questioned God about it? Jeremiah did. This prophet of the Lord had a hard time understanding why wicked people were prosperous and happy. After all, he had devoted his life to telling Israel that true happiness and security would come only through obedience to God. Though Jeremiah questioned God about this, it seems that ultimately he knew the final destiny of the wicked was destruction. He also knew God sees through the false religiosity of the wicked.

Ask God to show you your true heart. Can you assert, as Jeremiah did, that your thoughts are pure? If not, ask him to cleanse *you* of your evil thoughts, for these things will only cause you great harm in the end.

Dear Lord, help me not to envy the wicked, and cleanse me from my own wicked ways . . .

A PRAYER

FOR

RESTORATION

The king cried out to the man of God, "Please ask the Lord your God to restore my hand again!" So the man of God prayed to the Lord, and the king's hand became normal again.

1 KINGS 13:6

When a prophet confronted King Jeroboam over the wicked worship practices he had instituted at Bethel, Jeroboam was so brash that he dared to order his soldiers to arrest the prophet. However, the hand with which he gestured suddenly shriveled up. It was clear that Jeroboam was defying God himself. Jeroboam recognized his sin and asked the prophet to pray for him. The prophet prayed, and the Lord answered. How merciful is our God! He would have been justified in simply striking the king dead. And he certainly was not obligated to hear any prayer on behalf of this wicked man. But he heard and answered.

Though we may not have done such things as King Jeroboam had, we are still filled with sinfulness. But God is not simply out to pay us back for our wrongs but desires that we repent. He wants to restore us, but we must first be willing to recognize our wrongs.

Dear Lord, I recognize my sin and ask you to restore me . . .

PRAISE THE LORD!

Praise the Lord!
Praise God in his heavenly dwelling;
  praise him in his mighty heaven!
Praise him for his mighty works;
  praise his unequaled greatness!
Praise him with a blast of the trumpet;
  praise him with the lyre and harp!
Praise him with the tambourine and dancing;
  praise him with stringed instruments and flutes! ...
·Let everything that lives sing praises to the Lord!
Praise the Lord!

PSALM 150:1-4, 6

When we call out, "Praise the Lord!" it serves two purposes. It expresses our heartfelt adoration of our living Lord; yet it also calls upon others to do the same. We praise our God first of all for who he is—"his unequaled greatness"—and what he does—"his mighty works." We search for ways to describe the Infinite: "Praise him in his mighty heaven!" We underscore our praise to God with music: the blowing of a trumpet, the strumming of a "lyre and harp," and the playing of "stringed instruments and flutes." Nothing but a chorus of all living things would be fit to render praise to our Creator.

Meditate today on the depth and enthusiasm of the praise expressed here, and find your own words to sing his praise.

Mighty Lord, I praise you with all that is in me! ...

July 22

Give thanks to the Lord, for he is good!
His faithful love endures forever.
Cry out, "Save us, O God of our salvation!
Gather and rescue us from among the nations,
so we can thank your holy name
and rejoice and praise you."
Blessed be the Lord, the God of Israel,
from everlasting to everlasting!

And all the people shouted "Amen!" and praised the Lord.

1 CHRONICLES 16:34-36

King David had just brought the Ark of God into the city of Jerusalem. The whole community had gathered to mark this milestone in Israel's history. God had established them in their land and defeated their enemies. David gave this prayer of praise to the priests leading the worship. David prayed, "Save us, O God of our salvation! Gather and rescue us from among the nations, *so we can thank your holy name.*" Thankfulness should flow from our hearts as we consider the good things God has done for us, such as establishing us and graciously providing us with everything we need.

Recount the ways God has been good to you and your family. Thank and praise him for his goodness.

Dear Lord, I give thanks to you, for you are good! Your faithful love endures forever . . .

July 23

To the faithful you show yourself faithful;
to those with integrity you show integrity.
To the pure you show yourself pure,
but to the wicked you show yourself hostile.
You rescue those who are humble,
but you humiliate the proud.

PSALM 18:25-27

David wrote this prayer after God had delivered him from his enemy, Saul. David had refused to take Saul's life on several occasions when he had the opportunity. Instead of taking justice into his own hands, David let God enact justice in his own way and in his own time. For this, God honored him.

God is truly the Chief Justice. Though the wicked may appear to be rewarded for their crimes, one day the Lord will make everything right, bringing down the arrogant and the wicked and lifting up the righteous. On that day believers will rejoice, for their Defender will have come at last.

Take this opportunity to praise your God for his justice.

O Lord, teach me to be humble, for you humiliate the proud . . .

July 24

GREAT IS THE LORD!

Praise the Lord!
How good it is to sing praises to our God!
How delightful and how right!
The Lord is rebuilding Jerusalem
and bringing the exiles back to Israel.
He heals the brokenhearted,
binding up their wounds.
He counts the stars
and calls them all by name.
How great is our Lord! His power is absolute!
His understanding is beyond comprehension!

PSALM 147:1-5

How great is our God? How can we measure or express the extent of his majesty? His greatness is revealed through his mercy. This prayer was written right after a remnant of God's people returned from exile in Babylon. The psalmist delighted in praising God because of the miracle that was taking place before his eyes: "The Lord is rebuilding Jerusalem and bringing the exiles back to Israel." The God of mercy, who binds up the wounds of the brokenhearted, is the same mighty God who calls all the stars by name. God is wise and powerful. For all these reasons, the psalmist prayed, "How good it is to sing praises to our God!"

Consider how great the Lord of the universe is. Express your feelings to him in prayer.

O Lord, how good it is to sing praises to you! . . .

July 25

PRAISE FOR GOD'S PROTECTIVE ARMS

"There is no one like the God of Israel.
He rides across the heavens to help you,
across the skies in majestic splendor.
The eternal God is your refuge,
and his everlasting arms are under you. . . .
So Israel will live in safety,
prosperous Jacob in security. . . .
How blessed you are, O Israel!
Who else is like you, a people saved by the Lord?
He is your protecting shield
and your triumphant sword!"

DEUTERONOMY 33:26-29

At the end of his life, Moses stood before the people and reviewed their history with God, admonishing them to be faithful and pronouncing a blessing on each tribe. Then he praised God with the words above. Moses pictured God as riding "across the heavens to help [them]" and holding them in his everlasting arms. Moses declared, "How blessed you are, O Israel! Who else is like you, a people saved by the Lord?"

We need to ask ourselves the same question. How has God uniquely blessed you? Take some time to review your own history and count the ways God has upheld you and your family.

Dear Lord, I praise you for holding me in your everlasting arms . . .

God Is Near

We thank you, O God!
We give thanks because you are near.
People everywhere tell of your mighty miracles.
God says, "At the time I have planned,
I will bring justice against the wicked.
When the earth quakes and its people live in turmoil,
I am the one who keeps its foundations firm. . . ."
But as for me, I will always proclaim what God has done;
I will sing praises to the God of Israel.
For God says, "I will cut off the strength of the wicked,
but I will increase the power of the godly."

PSALM 75:1-3, 9-10

God is near. At times, he performs mighty miracles to remind us just how close he is. But there are many times when his power and justice are not readily apparent to us. This prayer addressed this situation head-on. When we find ourselves questioning whether God notices us and our plight, we should first remember to thank and praise God for his power. We should also remind ourselves of God's nearness and of the ways we see his power at work in our world. God has promised to bring justice to this earth in his own timing. As we wait for God to act, our proper posture should be praise.

In whatever situation you find yourself today, acknowledge one good thing God has done for you this past year. Genuinely thank him for it, and praise him for being near.

O Lord, thank you for being near . . .

July 27

SAMSON'S CRY FOR WATER

Now Samson was very thirsty, and he cried out to the Lord, "You have accomplished this great victory by the strength of your servant. Must I now die of thirst and fall into the hands of these pagan people?" So God caused water to gush out of a hollow in the ground at Lehi, and Samson was revived as he drank. Then he named that place "The Spring of the One Who Cried Out," and it is still in Lehi to this day. JUDGES 15:18-19

Out of fear, no one among the Israelites would stand up to their oppressors, the Philistines. Then Samson came along. God accomplished mighty deeds through Samson. He wreaked such havoc among the Philistines that they sent a whole army to capture him, but Samson killed a thousand of them with the jawbone of a donkey! After accomplishing this amazing feat, he realized that he was very thirsty. Like a grouchy child, he asked God for water: "Must I now die of thirst?" And God, who is able to supply all his people's needs, answered Samson's prayer by opening up a spring of water on the spot.

Unlike Samson, when we pray for God to meet our needs, let us do so in humility and respond with gratitude for God's response.

Dear God, please provide for me, just as you have promised . . .

July 28

APPLAUDING

GOD'S

GOODNESS

Praise the Lord!
Give thanks to the Lord, for he is good!
His faithful love endures forever.
Who can list the glorious miracles of the Lord?
Who can ever praise him half enough?

PSALM 106:1-2

There are times when we seek to offer praise and thanksgiving to God, but we find ourselves at a loss for words. The psalmist found himself in this situation: "Who can list the glorious miracles of the Lord? Who can ever praise him half enough?" In the light of God's holiness and goodness, the psalmist recounted in this psalm all the times Israel had proven unworthy of the Lord's love. But because of his goodness, God never utterly destroyed them. How could they ever praise God enough for what he had done for them?

As you ask God for mercy, remind yourself of one of the reasons God saves us—so that we can join the chorus of people continually praising his name and thanking him. Can we ever offer enough praises to God?

O God, who can ever praise you half enough? . . .

July 29

EXPRESSING FRUSTRATION TO GOD

But Abram replied, "O Sovereign Lord, what good are all your blessings when I don't even have a son? Since I don't have a son, Eliezer of Damascus, a servant in my household, will inherit all my wealth. You have given me no children, so one of my servants will have to be my heir."

Then the Lord said to him, "No, your servant will not be your heir, for you will have a son of your own to inherit everything I am giving you."

GENESIS 15:2-4

Abram's intimacy with God is demonstrated vividly in this prayer. He bared his soul before God. He told God how life looked from his perspective and how he felt about it. He even had the audacity to complain that God's blessings were not enough! Most of us wouldn't feel comfortable laying out our whole case before God in this way. But God did not rebuke Abram for his boldness. Instead he clarified his promise to him—that Abram's own son would be the heir.

Are there longings in your life that have gone unfulfilled for long periods of time? Abram's example should encourage you to tell God about them. Don't be afraid to reveal your deepest desires to the Lord. Trust in him; he will answer. Sometimes he answers in ways we can't even imagine.

O sovereign Lord, I bare my soul to you about my frustrations . . .

July 30

TRUSTING IN GOD'S UNFAILING LOVE

*"Look what happens to mighty warriors
who do not trust in God.
They trust their wealth instead
and grow more and more bold in their wickedness."
But I am like an olive tree,
thriving in the house of God.
I trust in God's unfailing love
forever and ever.
I will praise you forever, O God,
for what you have done.
I will wait for your mercies
in the presence of your people.*

PSALM 52:7-9

Where do you place your trust? Without being aware of it, many of us start hoping that our own plans may succeed, that our friends may provide us support, or that our wealth may give us the security we need. Yet in the long run, all of these will fade away. Our plans are easily disrupted. Our friends may fail us. Our clothes, cars, and home will begin to deteriorate. In the end, God is the only one who can provide true security. Those who place their trust in him will not be dismayed, for they will receive an eternal inheritance that can never be destroyed. God will never abandon them.

As you approach God in prayer today, express your complete dependence on him and your trust in him. Ask him to show you his good plan for your life.

Dear Lord, I trust in your unfailing love forever and ever . . .

July 31

The Lord, Our Stronghold

I love you, Lord; you are my strength.
The Lord is my rock, my fortress, and my savior;
my God is my rock, in whom I find protection.
He is my shield, the strength of my salvation, and my
stronghold.
I will call on the Lord, who is worthy of praise,
for he saves me from my enemies.

PSALM 18:1-3

Most of us don't depend on fortresses or strongholds to protect us, much less a shield or a boulder. But for David, such places of safety were often very important factors in his survival. When Saul's army was pursuing him, David hid behind rocks; but he reminded himself that the Lord was his true Rock—a sure defense against his enemies. He also hid in fortresses; but he reminded himself that God was his true fortress. David also used his shield to withstand the blows of his enemies; but he reminded himself that God was his true, impenetrable shield.

What do you depend on for security? Is it a large retirement account? Is it a good-paying job? Is it a family member or friends? Acknowledge to God that he is your ultimate source for security and protection.

I love you, O Lord; you are my strength . . .

August 1

PROCLAIMING GOD'S GREATNESS

Give thanks to the Lord and proclaim his greatness.
Let the whole world know what he has done.
Sing to him; yes, sing his praises.
Tell everyone about his miracles.
Exult in his holy name;
O worshipers of the Lord, rejoice!
Search for the Lord and for his strength,
and keep on searching.
Think of the wonderful works he has done,
the miracles, and the judgments he handed down.

1 CHRONICLES 16:8-12

After his army soundly defeated the Philistines, David paraded the symbol of God's presence—the Ark of the Covenant—throughout the city of Jerusalem. He established its new resting-place in a temporary "tent" in Jerusalem. In honor of the Lord's victory, David's priestly choir sang out their praise to "let the whole world know what he has done." It was a momentous day for the people of Jerusalem, and David made sure everyone knew it by loudly praising God, their Victor.

If people heard only the praise we give the Lord, would that be enough to give them a sense of God's greatness? Boldly proclaim God's greatness today.

Mighty God, I give thanks to you and proclaim your greatness . . .

**TRUSTING
IN THE
MIDST OF
TROUBLES**

Listen to my prayer, O God.
Do not ignore my cry for help!
Please listen and answer me,
for I am overwhelmed by my troubles.
My enemies shout at me,
making loud and wicked threats.
They bring trouble on me,
hunting me down in their anger. . . .
Oh, how I wish I had wings like a dove;
then I would fly away and rest!
I would fly far away
to the quiet of the wilderness.

PSALM 55:1-3, 6-7

Do you ever wish you could fly like a bird away from your problems? David did. He was completely overwhelmed by his troubles. His enemies were hunting him down and shouting loud threats at him. With his world falling apart, David was terrified that death might overpower him, and he wished he had the wings of a dove so he could fly away from his troubles to a quiet place, where he could rest. Yet even in his worst difficulties, David called upon God to rescue him.

Are you overwhelmed by troubles? Give your burdens to the Lord, and determine today to trust the Lord to save you.

O Lord, I'm overwhelmed by my troubles. Listen to my cry for help . . .

August 3

BEGGING TO BE SPARED

The priests, who minister in the Lord's presence, will stand between the people and the altar, weeping. Let them pray, "Spare your people, Lord! They belong to you, so don't let them become an object of mockery. Don't let their name become a proverb of unbelieving foreigners who say, 'Where is the God of Israel? He must be helpless!'"

Then the Lord will pity his people and be indignant for the honor of his land!

JOEL 2:17-18

When we are in trouble, we easily cry out, "Save me." Sometimes those words, however, roll off our tongues too easily. Although Joel did encourage the Israelites to ask the Lord to spare them, he first told them how they should approach God (Joel 2:12-13). Their pleas for mercy should be accompanied with genuine repentance. Rather than merely tearing their clothes to express grief, they were to have broken hearts for offending God. They were to approach him with fasting, weeping, and mourning. God was eager to forgive his people in those days, and he will be merciful to us as well when we repent of our sins.

Praise God for his abundant mercy and great compassion for sinners. Ask him to help you reflect his mercy to others.

O Lord, spare me . . .

Our Time Is Brief

"Lord, remind me how brief my time on earth will be.
Remind me that my days are numbered,
and that my life is fleeing away.
My life is no longer than the width of my hand.
An entire lifetime is just a moment to you;
human existence is but a breath."
We are merely moving shadows,
and all our busy rushing ends in nothing.
We heap up wealth for someone else to spend.
And so, Lord, where do I put my hope?
My only hope is in you.

PSALM 39:4-7

We all know people who are married to their job, not their spouse. They spend hour after hour at work, and their bosses certainly reward them for it. They accumulate big bank accounts, but their obsession with work leaves them emotionally and spiritually bankrupt. This passage comments on how foolish it is to waste one's efforts on gaining material wealth that soon will pass away. In this prayer, David saw that his time on earth was brief. "We are merely moving shadows," he said, "and all our busy rushing ends in nothing." So what are we to do? In what or in whom should we put our hope? David gives us the answer: "And so, Lord . . . my only hope is in you."

Today in prayer, place your hope in God alone.

Dear Lord, help me place my hope in you . . .

August 5

PRAYING
FOR THE
HELPLESS

Arise, O Lord!
Punish the wicked, O God!
Do not forget the helpless! . . .
The helpless put their trust in you.
You are the defender of orphans. . . .
Lord, you know the hopes of the helpless.
Surely you will listen to their cries and comfort them.
You will bring justice to the orphans and the oppressed,
so people can no longer terrify them.

PSALM 10:12, 14, 17-18

David had seen a lot of injustice in his life, but he never got used to it. In this prayer, David was angry with the wicked: "Like lions they crouch silently, waiting to pounce on the helpless" (v. 9). His heart was full of compassion for the oppressed, the widows, the orphans, the poor, the weak, and the innocent. He saw the injustice of how they were treated and pleaded for God to come to their defense.

Do you still get angry at the injustice in the world? Do you plead with God to come to the defense of the oppressed and the helpless? Has your heart become cold and indifferent? Ask God to give you a compassionate heart. Pray for God to bring justice to this world.

Dear Lord, do not forget the helpless . . .

**THIRSTING
FOR GOD**

*O God, you are my God;
I earnestly search for you.
My soul thirsts for you;
my whole body longs for you
in this parched and weary land
where there is no water.*

PSALM 63:1

Anyone who has ever been in the desert for a long time knows what thirst is like. Your mouth gets as dry as cotton, your throat hurts, and soon you begin imagining a tall, cold glass of water sparkling in the sun. Oh, how good it looks! You can almost taste it! David had experienced that kind of thirst when he stayed in the wilderness of Judah, a "parched and weary land where there is no water." In this prayer, he compared that type of thirst with his desire for God. He was agonizing, searching for the Lord with all his might. His soul thirsted, and his body longed for God.

When have you longed for the Lord that way, so much that you actually *thirst* for him? During your time in prayer, express your desire for God.

Dear Lord, my soul thirsts for you . . .

August 7

PRAYER FOR AN IMPORTANT DECISION

Then they all prayed for the right man to be chosen. "O Lord," they said, "you know every heart. Show us which of these men you have chosen as an apostle to replace Judas the traitor in this ministry, for he has deserted us and gone where he belongs." Then they cast lots, and in this way Matthias was chosen and became an apostle with the other eleven.

ACTS 1:24-26

The big decisions—what job offer we should take, what person we should marry—are the ones that produce the most anxiety. We spend hours agonizing over the pros and cons of each choice. The early church had such an important decision before them. Who would replace Judas among Jesus' twelve disciples? These early Christians wanted God's choice, so they prayed. As a group, they nominated two men who appeared to be genuine followers of Christ to them. But they realized they couldn't test the hearts of both individuals—only God could do that. So they submitted the choice to God in prayer.

What decision do you need to submit to God? Ask God to guide you in making your decision. Ask him to reveal his choice for you.

Dear Lord, you know my heart. Show me what you have chosen for me . . .

THE GREATNESS OF OUR CREATOR

Praise the Lord, I tell myself;
*   O Lord my God, how great you are!*
You are robed with honor and with majesty;
*   you are dressed in a robe of light.*
You stretch out the starry curtain of the heavens;
*   you lay out the rafters of your home in the rain clouds.*
You make the clouds your chariots;
*   you ride upon the wings of the wind.*
The winds are your messengers;
*   flames of fire are your servants.*

PSALM 104:1-4

Too often as we rush from task to task we don't take time to reflect on the greatness of God. But every once in a while we are startled by the greatness of God's world—a sudden clap of thunder or the beauty of a field of multicolored wildflowers—and we are reminded again of how glorious the God who made it must be. In a similar way, the writer of this psalm took cues from the wonders in nature to magnify and exult God.

Praise God for his power and wisdom by listing the ways you have witnessed his work in what he has created.

O Lord my God, how great you are! . . .

August 9

**RECOGNIZING
THAT GOD IS
AT WORK**

*The humble will see their God at work and be glad.
Let all who seek God's help live in joy.
For the Lord hears the cries of his needy ones;
he does not despise his people who are oppressed.
Praise him, O heaven and earth,
the seas and all that move in them.*

PSALM 69:32-34

Sometimes when we are in our deepest depression, we despair of anyone hearing our cries for help. David felt this way. His enemies had surrounded him and were even gloating over him. Yet toward the end of this prayer, David reminded himself that God does hear "the cries of his needy ones." He does work out his good plan for his people. One day, the humble will rejoice in the Lord's work. He knew the Lord heard his cries and would answer him. In this he could rejoice.

Sometime you may find your joy being sapped away by some difficult situation. Remind yourself of God's ability to hear your cry for help. Look for ways God is already working in your church and in your community. "The humble will see their God at work and be glad."

Dear God, I am glad you are at work in this world . . .

A PLEA FOR GOD'S PROTECTION

Then Jacob prayed, "O God of my grandfather Abraham and my father, Isaac–O Lord, you told me to return to my land and to my relatives, and you promised to treat me kindly. I am not worthy of all the faithfulness and unfailing love you have shown to me, your servant. When I left home, I owned nothing except a walking stick, and now my household fills two camps! O Lord, please rescue me from my brother, Esau. I am afraid that he is coming to kill me, along with my wives and children. But you promised to treat me kindly and to multiply my descendants until they become as numerous as the sands along the seashore–too many to count." GENESIS 32:9-12

Jacob had reason to be afraid of his brother Esau. Jacob had tricked his brother out of his birthright and the blessing of their father Isaac. Consequently, Jacob had to leave home because Esau was going to kill him. Years later Jacob headed home. On his way home, he heard Esau was coming to greet him. What worried Jacob was that an army of four hundred men was accompanying Esau! Convinced his brother was coming to kill him, Jacob earnestly prayed for God to protect him. His prayers were answered when Esau, instead of being angry, greeted his brother with hugs and tears.

We may not fear for our life, but there are times when we fear for our livelihood or for the welfare of our families. At such times, we can turn to God and ask him to watch over us.

Dear God, please watch over my family . . .

August 11

THE PRAYER OF AN ELDERLY MAN

Now that I am old and gray,
do not abandon me, O God.
Let me proclaim your power to this new generation,
your mighty miracles to all who come after me.
Your righteousness, O God, reaches to the highest heavens.
You have done such wonderful things.
Who can compare with you, O God?
You have allowed me to suffer much hardship,
but you will restore me to life again
and lift me up from the depths of the earth.
You will restore me to even greater honor
and comfort me once again.

PSALM 71:18-21

Whether our days on earth are few or many, God never abandons us. The writer of this psalm had lived a long life. In his old age, he felt abandoned by his friends and family Yet in his despair, he turned to God, asking the Lord to never abandon him. As this man surveyed his life, he realized how God had worked through the hardships he had suffered and through the difficult circumstances of his life, and he wanted to tell the next generation how amazing God is.

Determine today to tell someone else about God's wonderful deeds and pass on to the next generation stories of God's greatness.

Dear Lord, you have done such wonderful things. Let me proclaim your power to this new generation . . .

August 12

ENTRUSTING OUR REPUTATION TO GOD

To you, O Lord, I lift up my soul.
I trust in you, my God!
Do not let me be disgraced,
or let my enemies rejoice in my defeat.
No one who trusts in you will ever be disgraced,
but disgrace comes to those who try to deceive others.

PSALM 25:1-3

One of our greatest fears in this life is disgrace. We dread a loss of honor in the eyes of other people—whether they are friends or foes. Because of this, one of our natural instincts is to cover up our mistakes and protect our reputations. David understood that his honor was ultimately in the hands of God. God is able to keep us from disgrace. He is also able to lift us up from the disgraces we bring on ourselves. But dishonor will fall on those who deceive others to enhance their own reputations.

Instead of worrying about your reputation, your success, or your failure, trust in God. Pray for courage to live with honesty and integrity, and God will look after everything else.

Dear Lord, do not let me be disgraced. Help me to live in a way that is honorable in your eyes . . .

August 13

A Plea
for Help

Then Asa cried out to the Lord his God, "O Lord, no one but you can help the powerless against the mighty! Help us, O Lord our God, for we trust in you alone. It is in your name that we have come against this vast horde. O Lord, you are our God; do not let mere men prevail against you!"

2 CHRONICLES 14:11

King Asa was one of the few kings of Judah who feared God and banned idolatry among God's people. God rewarded him with ten years of peace, although it was not as if his kingdom's tranquillity was never threatened. When Zerah, the king of Ethiopia, assembled a huge army against him, Asa saw it as an opportunity to trust God. Because he understood it to be God's battle, not his own, he asked God for help and then acted in God's name, trusting the Lord because he had proven himself trustworthy at so many other critical junctures in Asa's life.

You may face overwhelming situations in your life today. Commit those situations to God, and pray that he would use those situations to demonstrate his power and bring honor to his name.

Help me, O Lord my God, for I trust in you alone . . .

The Lord Is a Trustworthy Ally

> Bless the Lord, who is my rock.
> He gives me strength for war
> and skill for battle.
> He is my loving ally and my fortress,
> my tower of safety, my deliverer.
> He stands before me as a shield, and I take refuge in him.
> He subdues the nations under me.
> O Lord, what are mortals that you should notice us,
> mere humans that you should care for us?

PSALM 144:1-3

When a nation is considering going into battle against a formidable enemy, it sends diplomats to its allies to solicit support. No one wants to go into battle without someone to back them up. In this prayer, David proclaimed the Lord God as his ally. He called God his "rock," "fortress," "loving ally," "deliverer," and "shield." He thanked the Lord for training him in the skills needed in combat and for giving him the strength to fight. In the confusion of the battlefield, David could rely on God to help him triumph over his enemies. Yet, he still marveled at God's willingness to come to his rescue. "O Lord, what are mortals that you should notice us?"

When have you needed God as an ally? Today, thank him for the times he has rescued you.

Dear Lord, thank you for being my loving ally and my fortress . . .

August 15

GOD'S POWERFUL, UNFAILING LOVE

*O God, we meditate on your unfailing love
as we worship in your Temple.
As your name deserves, O God,
you will be praised to the ends of the earth.
Your strong right hand is filled with victory.*

PSALM 48:9-10

The attributes of power and love appear to be opposites. We often picture a powerful ruler as a dictator or tyrant—someone who uses his power to oppress. We often imagine a loving person as someone who is gentle and meek. But this psalm speaks of God as both powerful and loving. He uses his power in a loving way—by protecting his people, while punishing those who persist in evil ways. God *will* be honored and praised, for one day he *will* triumph over his enemies. Meanwhile, we have the privilege of joining our voices to that worship *now*, regardless of our circumstances.

Meditate on God's unfailing love for you, and make a commitment this week to tell someone else what he has done for you.

O God, help me to know your powerful, unfailing love . . .

PRAISING GOD FOR KEEPING HIS PROMISES

I will praise the Lord as long as I live.
I will sing praises to my God even with my dying breath.
Don't put your confidence in powerful people;
there is no help for you there....
But happy are those who have the God of Israel as their helper,
whose hope is in the Lord their God.
He is the one who made heaven and earth,
the sea, and everything in them.
He is the one who keeps every promise forever.

PSALM 146:2-3, 5-6

All of us have been let down by someone. A friend or family member may have broken an important promise. A respected church leader may have fallen into sin. Through these experiences, we learn that we can't depend completely on other people, because sometimes they don't follow through on their promises. The writer of this prayer calls upon people to put their confidence in God, not in other people, for the Lord is always faithful. The sky above and the earth below are tokens of God's unfailing love for his people. God is faithful to keep the world going for yet another day, and he will be faithful to care for his people.

Take a few minutes to render praise to God for being faithful to you.

Dear Lord, you are the one who keeps every promise forever . . .

BOWING BEFORE THE THRONE

And all the angels were standing around the throne and around the elders and the four living beings. And they fell face down before the throne and worshiped God. They said,

"Amen! Blessing and glory and wisdom and thanksgiving and honor and power and strength belong to our God forever and forever. Amen!"

REVELATION 7:11-12

This excerpt from the book of Revelation gives us a glimpse of God's heavenly throne room. In John's vision, he saw both resurrected believers and awesome heavenly creatures bowing facedown before God's throne, praising the Lord for all that he had done. Such profound reverence for God contrasts with the great familiarity with which we often relate to God. We need to remember to whom we're speaking when we pray. As we approach God in prayer, remember that he is the ruler of the universe. We dare not be too casual with the Holy One.

The angelic beings of Revelation expressed their humility and reverence for God by bowing facedown before him. In your prayer today, join these angelic beings in giving deepest respect to your Maker.

O God, blessing and glory and wisdom and thanksgiving and honor and power and strength belong to you forever and forever . . .

RESTING IN GOD'S CARE

I am praying to you because I know you will answer, O God.
Bend down and listen as I pray.
Show me your unfailing love in wonderful ways.
You save with your strength
those who seek refuge from their enemies.
Guard me as the apple of your eye.
Hide me in the shadow of your wings.

PSALM 17:6-8

Our eyes are extremely sensitive. People react swiftly and instinctively to anything that is heading right towards their eyes. In this prayer, David asked the Lord to guard him as if he were the apple, or pupil, of God's eye. He asked to be guarded in such a way because he believed God would answer him. He envisioned God, gentle and interested, bending down to listen to his prayer. He believed that God would use his great strength to protect him. With his eyes fixed expectantly on his loving Lord, David received the shelter he desperately sought.

Use David's prayer to remind yourself that God is willing and able to keep you in his care. He is the only one who can truly guard and protect you. Commit your worries to him in prayer.

Dear Lord, guard me as the apple of your eye. Hide me in the shadow of your wings . . .

August 19

You are glorious and more majestic
than the everlasting mountains....
No wonder you are greatly feared!
Who can stand before you when your anger explodes?
From heaven you sentenced your enemies;
the earth trembled and stood silent before you....
Make vows to the Lord your God, and fulfill them.
Let everyone bring tribute to the Awesome One.

PSALM 76:4, 7-8, 11

Anyone who has spent time in the mountains develops an admiration for the forces of nature. We often feel small next to massive formations of earth and rock. God has given these impressive landscapes to us as clues to his power. This prayer asks, "Who can stand before you when your anger explodes?" If the whole earth remains silent and trembling before God's awesome power, how much more should we pray with awe and holy respect? We wouldn't want to be counted among his enemies when he renders judgment!

In prayer, praise the Lord for how powerful he is. Give to God the honor and glory he deserves. Commit today to bring tribute— whether it is a portion of your material resources or of your time— to the awesome King of kings.

O God, you are glorious and more majestic than the
everlasting mountains. I bring my tribute to you . . .

BLESSING THE LORD

Bless the Lord God, the God of Israel,
  who alone does such wonderful things.
Bless his glorious name forever!
  Let the whole earth be filled with his glory.
Amen and amen!

PSALM 72:18-19

The word *bless* is more likely to enter our prayer vocabulary when we ask God to bless ourselves or others. But Solomon in this prayer called his fellow worshipers to *bless* God. He meant that they should praise and glorify God for all that he had done for them. He *blessed* the God of Israel "who alone does such wonderful things." This blessing crowns a prayer in which Solomon asked God to bless his nation and his reign. How fitting it is that Solomon, who had received so much from the Lord, should express his indebtedness to God by blessing God's name.

As you ask God to bless you and your family, make sure you have adequately blessed God for the wonderful ways in which he continually helps you.

O Lord God, I bless you for all your wonderful deeds . . .

Jesus' Thanks for Answered Prayer

So they rolled the stone aside. Then Jesus looked up to heaven and said, "Father, thank you for hearing me. You always hear me, but I said it out loud for the sake of all these people standing here, so they will believe you sent me."

JOHN 11:41-42

The story of Jesus raising Lazarus from the dead gives us a unique glimpse into the prayer life of Jesus. He knew that his Father always heard his prayers, so as Lazarus's tomb lay open, Jesus thanked God out loud to demonstrate to his followers that God had sent him. When he commanded Lazarus to come out, he wasn't surprised that Lazarus stood up and walked toward him. But those who gathered at the tomb were astonished: How could this be? Jesus' prayer answered their questions. God the Father had sent Jesus to them. Lazarus was physical proof of Jesus' divine power.

Jesus' prayer is for our benefit as well. In prayer today, reaffirm your belief in Jesus' divine power over death. Praise and give him thanks for answering your prayers.

Dear Jesus, I believe God sent you to this earth. Thank you for hearing me . . .

SINGING PRAISES TO OUR GREAT KING

Come, let us sing to the Lord!
Let us give a joyous shout to the rock of our salvation!
Let us come before him with thanksgiving.
Let us sing him psalms of praise.
For the Lord is a great God,
the great King above all gods.
He owns the depths of the earth,
and even the mightiest mountains are his.
The sea belongs to him, for he made it.
His hands formed the dry land, too.

PSALM 95:1-5

Throughout history, kings and princes often boasted of their power by drawing attention to such things as their palace and the extent of their land. This prayer draws attention to the natural monuments that point to God's power—immovable mountains, vast seas, and rich plains. The boundaries of God's kingdom are unmatched—he owns "the depths of the earth" and "the mightiest mountains," for he formed it out of nothing in the first place! Our God existed before this earthly kingdom was created to proclaim his greatness. No power on this earth can compare to our Creator.

Think about the natural monuments you have seen that proclaim God's power. Join your voice with all his faithful people in heartfelt praise.

O Lord, I raise my voice in praise to you, for you are the great King . . .

**LONGING
FOR GOD'S
WORD**

*Your decrees are wonderful.
No wonder I obey them!
As your words are taught, they give light;
even the simple can understand them.
I open my mouth, panting expectantly,
longing for your commands.
Come and show me your mercy,
as you do for all who love your name.
Guide my steps by your word,
so I will not be overcome by any evil.*

PSALM 119:129-133

There are times in life when we long for guidance. We want someone who can clearly see the road ahead to guide us—to show us where the pitfalls and dead ends are. This is the type of longing that the psalmist had for God's Word. He yearned for God's Word to guide his every step, for he knew that it would lead him to true joy. "Your decrees are wonderful. No wonder I obey them!" he exclaimed. In today's world, it is easier to imagine longing for God's freedom than for his commands. But the psalmist understood that God's commands give true joy in life.

Reaffirm your desire for God's Word to guide your life. Pray that God might help you resist a specific sin that often overcomes you.

Dear Lord, I long for your commands. Guide my steps by your Word . . .

**PUBLISHING
GOD'S
GLORIOUS
DEEDS**

*Sing to the Lord; bless his name.
    Each day proclaim the good news that he saves.
Publish his glorious deeds among the nations.
    Tell everyone about the amazing things he does.
Great is the Lord! He is most worthy of praise!
    He is to be revered above all the gods.
The gods of other nations are merely idols,
    but the Lord made the heavens!
Honor and majesty surround him;
    strength and beauty are in his sanctuary.*

PSALM 96:2-6

Before dawn every day, newspapers lie on virtually every doorstep to greet the person inside with the day's news. If only the Good News, that Jesus came to save sinners, were published and distributed just as widely as the dismal news of our daily newspapers! The psalmist committed himself to publishing the great deeds of God each day. As God's people, we need to hear again and again about God's saving grace and tell it to the world around us as well.

Determine to start every morning by thinking of something God has done for you—how he created a brand-new day for you to enjoy, how he has saved you and given you food and shelter. Then find a way that day to publish God's wonderful deeds—to tell someone else about what he has done.

Great God, I will publish your glorious deeds among the nations . . .

August 25

**PRAISE TO
THE GOD
WHO IS
EVERYWHERE**

I can never escape from your spirit!
I can never get away from your presence!
If I go up to heaven, you are there;
if I go down to the place of the dead, you are there.
If I ride the wings of the morning,
if I dwell by the farthest oceans,
even there your hand will guide me,
and your strength will support me.

PSALM 139:7-10

David knew that it is both a wonderful and a fearful thing to realize that God is everywhere. We will never escape his presence. Sometimes, in our human weakness, we actually might try. Perhaps it is because we have a guilty conscience or are reluctant to carry out a task to which he has called us. Like Jonah, we seek to run away. But no one can run from the omnipresent God. Even if we were to run to the "place of the dead," God would be there. There is no life circumstance too dark for the light of God to penetrate. No matter where the consequences of our sins might take us, we can never travel beyond the range of his love.

Praise the Lord for being with you right now. Ask him to guide you into his righteous ways.

Dear Lord, I can never get away from your presence.
Guide me into your truth . . .

PRAISE TO OUR REDEEMER

Has the Lord redeemed you? Then speak out!
Tell others he has saved you from your enemies.
For he has gathered the exiles from many lands,
from east and west, from north and south.
Some wandered in the desert,
lost and homeless.
Hungry and thirsty,
they nearly died.
"Lord, help!" they cried in their trouble,
and he rescued them from their distress.

PSALM 107:2-6

Not many of us have experienced the hunger pains of those near starvation, but we all know what it is like to be thirsty and hungry. We know what it is like to be lost and helpless. In such a state, we quickly become frustrated and confused. When we finally find someone who can help us, a profound sense of relief washes over us. In this prayer, the psalmist described the people of Israel as hungry and lost. They called on God for help, and miraculously he answered. The psalmist expressed his gratitude by praising God and calling on everyone who was saved to speak out.

Has the Lord redeemed you? Are you excited about it? Take to heart the words of this psalm. Thank the Lord! Speak out! Tell others!

Dear Lord, thank you for redeeming me. Help me to speak out about what you have done . . .

A PLEA FOR GOD TO LISTEN

Lord, hear my prayer!
  Listen to my plea!
Don't turn away from me
  in my time of distress.
Bend down your ear
  and answer me quickly when I call to you,
  for my days disappear like smoke,
  and my bones burn like red-hot coals. . . .
But you, O Lord, will rule forever.
  Your fame will endure to every generation.

PSALM 102:1-3, 12

Like a page ripped out of a diary, this prayer gives us a glimpse into the prayer life of someone in great suffering. Many believe it is the journaled thoughts of an Israelite who was exiled to the wicked city of Babylon. The heartbeat of this prayer is simple: "Please listen. I need you." The author of this prayer asked God to "bend his ear" down to earth to hear him whisper his needs. No pretenses. No attempts to sound brave. The author of this prayer was devastated, so he cried out to God, begging him to hear his requests.

Go to your Father with your needs today. Ask for his ear to listen and his hand to comfort you as you lay out your concerns before him.

Dear Lord, hear my prayer and answer me . . .

FINDING JOY IN THE MIDST OF STRESS

O Lord, you are righteous,
and your decisions are fair.
Your decrees are perfect;
they are entirely worthy of our trust. . . .
Your justice is eternal,
and your law is perfectly true.
As pressure and stress bear down on me,
I find joy in your commands.
Your decrees are always fair;
help me to understand them, that I may live.

PSALM 119:137-138, 142-144

Have you ever wondered how God's ways fit into the pressures and stresses of real life? It is only normal, given our partial understanding of God, that we would encounter such questions. This prayer provides a wonderful model for bringing those issues truthfully before the Lord. The psalmist began his prayer by reminding himself of God's fairness and trustworthiness. When we make God's power and holiness a starting point for prayer, our daily struggles come into proper perspective. There is only one place to turn when nothing seems to make sense: God and his ways.

Commit the problems and difficulties you will face today to God. Ask him to help you find joy in his ways.

Dear Lord, as pressure and stress bear down on me, I find joy in your commands . . .

THE ELDERS' PRAISE FOR GOD

The twenty-four elders fall down and worship the one who lives forever and ever. And they lay their crowns before the throne and say,

"You are worthy, O Lord our God,
*   to receive glory and honor and power.*
For you created everything,
*   and it is for your pleasure that they exist and were created."*

REVELATION 4:10-11

Some people may have the opportunity to see the riches of a king's palace, but none of us can fully imagine what God's throne room must be like. Revelation provides us with a glimpse of it—a brilliant throne made of gemstones, a shiny sea of crystal-like glass, and a rainbow-like glow filling the entire place. Yet, what is central to John's description of God's throne room is the people's praise for God. Elders, angelic beings, and exotic living beings join their voices in an unending chorus glorifying God and declaring that the entire universe was made for his pleasure.

If the universe exists for God's pleasure, our part is clear. We should give God the adoration he deserves. Join your voice with the heavenly host today in words of praise.

O Lord our God, you are worthy to receive glory and honor and power . . .

August 30

**DECLARING
GOD AS
OUR ONLY
HOPE**

Lord, don't hold back your tender mercies from me.
My only hope is in your unfailing love and faithfulness.
For troubles surround me—
too many to count!
They pile up so high
I can't see my way out.
They are more numerous than the hairs on my head.
I have lost all my courage. . . .
As for me, I am poor and needy,
but the Lord is thinking about me right now.
You are my helper and my savior.
Do not delay, O my God.

PSALM 40:11-12, 17

As the king over all Israel, David had a mountain of riches—jewels, money, gold, and numerous servants to do his bidding. Yet David came to a place in his life where he proclaimed that God alone was his "hope." We don't know the specific situation for which this prayer was written, but we can imagine it was a landmark in David's life.

What does it take for you to claim God as your "only hope"? What would make you look solely to God for a solution to your problems? If you are facing a difficult situation, bring this before God in prayer. Then declare to God that you are trusting him to rescue you.

Dear Lord, my only hope is in your unfailing love. Don't hold back your tender mercies from me . . .

August 31

Worshiping the Lord with Gladness

Shout with joy to the Lord, O earth!
Worship the Lord with gladness.
Come before him, singing with joy.
Acknowledge that the Lord is God!
He made us, and we are his.
We are his people, the sheep of his pasture.

PSALM 100:1-3

Joy. Pleasure. Delight. Too often, we associate these emotions with earthly pleasures—such as enjoying fancy hotels, owning a brand-new car or home, or savoring fine food. The author of this prayer, however, associated joy and delight with worshiping God and learning more about his ways. He called on God's people to "worship the Lord with gladness." Our heartfelt joy in all God has given us—in all he has done for us—is like beautiful, harmonious music drifting back to God's ears. God finds pleasure in those who rejoice in what he has given them and thank him for it.

Find a new way today to praise God for his goodness. Rejoice in what God has given you and share your joy with your acquaintances and coworkers.

Dear Lord, I come before you with shouts of joy . . .

PRAISE FOR THE GOD WHO GIVES SUCCESS

"For all the earth is the Lord's,
and he has set the world in order.
He will protect his godly ones,
but the wicked will perish in darkness.
No one will succeed by strength alone.
Those who fight against the Lord will be broken.
He thunders against them from heaven;
the Lord judges throughout the earth.
He gives mighty strength to his king;
he increases the might of his anointed one."

1 SAMUEL 2:8-10

Who would ever guess these were the words of a mother who had just given her baby boy to God to be a priest? Instead of despairing over her child, Hannah praised God for blessing her with a son in the first place. Her sacrifice was success in her eyes, because she was committed to following God. Success often occurs because of some type of sacrifice, and joy often follows a period of suffering. Let Hannah's prayer remind you of the faith needed when you encounter hardship and suffering in your life. God will transform your suffering into success, your weakness into strength.

Hand over your suffering, hardships, and weaknesses to God in prayer. Ask him to use those difficulties in your life to help others.

Dear Lord, I know that no one will succeed by strength alone. You give mighty strength to your people . . .

A PRAYER FOR GOD'S GUIDANCE

Be good to your servant,
that I may live and obey your word.
Open my eyes to see
the wonderful truths in your law.
I am but a foreigner here on earth;
I need the guidance of your commands.
Don't hide them from me!
I am overwhelmed continually
with a desire for your laws. . . .
Your decrees please me;
they give me wise advice.

PSALM 119:17-20, 24

September marks the end of the lazy days of summer—a time when we begin to concentrate fully on our tasks at work or school. Life's pace quickens, and more than ever, we need to consult God's Word to find out how we should live. The author of this prayer saw himself as a "foreigner here on earth"—as someone who lived according to a higher purpose than simply accomplishing the various tasks of each day. He lived to please God and follow his commands. In them, he found wise advice; as he studied Scripture he prayed that God might reveal to him more of his wonderful truths.

The next time you set aside time to study Scripture, pray first. Ask God to help you to understand God's Word and apply it to your life.

Dear Lord, open my eyes to see your wonderful truths . . .

PRAYING

FOR

VICTORY

In times of trouble, may the Lord respond to your cry.
May the God of Israel keep you safe from all harm.
May he send you help from his sanctuary
and strengthen you from Jerusalem.
May he remember all your gifts
and look favorably on your burnt offerings.
May he grant your heart's desire
and fulfill all your plans.
May we shout for joy when we hear of your victory,
flying banners to honor our God.
May the Lord answer all your prayers.

PSALM 20:1-5

Imagine the tips of sharpened weapons gleaming in the early morning sun as God's people, armed for battle, encouraged their king with their prayers. As they assembled themselves to march out against Israel's foes, they shouted this prayer under the direction of David's director of music.

Who knows what battles the people you love might be facing today? As you think of friends and family members, picture them assembling themselves for battle—getting ready for the new school year, going to work, mulling through what they must accomplish that day. Then pray for victory in what they must do. Pray that their accomplishments might bring glory to God; then pray the same for yourself.

Dear Lord, I pray that you will give victory to . . .

September 4

ASKING GOD WHICH WAY TO TURN

Because of your unfailing love, I can enter your house;
with deepest awe I will worship at your Temple.
Lead me in the right path, O Lord,
or my enemies will conquer me.
Tell me clearly what to do,
and show me which way to turn.

PSALM 5:7-8

David wrote these words amid controversy and confusion. His enemies often tried to harass him with evil rumors and outright lies, as the rest of this psalm indicates. In those difficult and unsettling times, David immediately turned to God for direction. Surrounded by lies, David desired truth. Confronted with choices, David sought to choose the one right path.

Express your desire for God to guide you—especially during those times when life has offered you a confusing array of choices. Ask God to dispel your confusion by helping you decide "which way to turn."

Dear Lord, tell me clearly what to do. Show me which way to turn . . .

September 5

**JESUS'
PRAYER FOR
HOLY
LIVING**

"They are not part of this world any more than I am. Make them pure and holy by teaching them your words of truth. As you sent me into the world, I am sending them into the world. And I give myself entirely to you so they also might be entirely yours."

JOHN 17:16-19

Jesus prayed these words the night of his arrest. As he faced his final days when he would suffer the most, Jesus' concern was not for his own well-being but for his followers, whom he would leave behind. In front of his disciples, Jesus poured his heart out, praying for their purity and holiness in a wicked world. Jesus' prayer is for us as well. He longs for us to be his pure and holy people in a culture that revels in sexual immorality, greed, and self-centeredness. These words were among the last things Jesus said to his disciples before leaving them, and they indicate how much Jesus prized the purity and holiness of his disciples' lives.

Make Jesus' words your prayer. Pray that God will make you pure and holy by teaching you his Word, so that you may bring honor to him.

Dear Lord, make me pure and holy by teaching me your words of truth . . .

**PRAISE FOR
GOD'S
LIGHT**

Lord, you have brought light to my life;
my God, you light up my darkness.
In your strength I can crush an army;
with my God I can scale any wall.
As for God, his way is perfect.
All the Lord's promises prove true.
He is a shield for all who look to him for protection.

PSALM 18:28-30

All of us have experienced times when our lives have grown dark—when hope seemed futile and we felt alone. David knew how dark life could seem at times. When he wrote this prayer, the memories of fleeing in terror from King Saul and hiding in dark, damp caves were fresh in his mind. Yet he focused on God's light in his life—the light that dispelled the darkness of confusion. With this light, David saw clearly that God's way was perfect, even if it brought him through dark and dangerous valleys. God would always watch over him and prove himself true to his promises.

When you are traveling a dark road, remind yourself of David's experience with God—of how God led him through those dark places. Use David's prayer to remind yourself of God's light in your life.

Dear Lord, thank you for lighting up my darkness . . .

**PRAYING TO
OUR
HELPER**

Come with great power, O God, and rescue me!
Defend me with your might.
O God, listen to my prayer.
Pay attention to my plea.
For strangers are attacking me;
violent men are trying to kill me.
They care nothing for God.

PSALM 54:1-3

David had served King Saul for years and led his army to victory against Israel's enemies. Yet, suddenly, Saul turned against David and tried to kill him. As David fled, he suffered a series of betrayals, from Doeg the Edomite to the citizens of Keilah to the Ziphites (see 1 Samuel 22–23). It was during this time—when everyone seemed to be against him—that David wrote this prayer. He prayed that God would come quickly to defend him. He acknowledged that God was the only one who could keep him alive—and God did keep David alive (Psalm 54:4) and eventually placed him on Israel's throne.

The same God who defended David is willing to come to our rescue as well. Commit your problems to him today.

Come with great power, O God, and rescue me . . .

September 8

A Symphony of Praises

Praise the Lord from the earth,
you creatures of the ocean depths,
fire and hail, snow and storm,
wind and weather that obey him,
mountains and all hills,
fruit trees and all cedars,
wild animals and all livestock,
reptiles and birds,
kings of the earth and all people,
rulers and judges of the earth,
young men and maidens,
old men and children.

PSALM 148:7-12

As naturalists go to the depths of the oceans and the unexplored jungles, they find more and more exotic creatures. Meditating on how God reigns over this amazing diversity should lead us to heartfelt praise. This prayer calls upon all of God's creation— lions and tigers, bulls and cows, sparrows and pigeons—to sing their praises to God. It encourages the forces of nature—fire and wind, hail and snow—to join in. No man-made instrument can equal the chorus of God's creation. Every person—both old and young, great and small—should sing praises to the Creator. He is the one who creates and sustains each of us. At every stage of life, no matter our station, he is worthy of our praise.

Take a moment to meditate on the rich diversity of God's creation and offer him praise.

Dear Lord, I join with all creation in praising you . . .

ASKING TO BE LED ALONG GOD'S PATH

Show me the path where I should walk, O Lord;
point out the right road for me to follow.
Lead me by your truth and teach me,
for you are the God who saves me.
All day long I put my hope in you.

PSALM 25:4-5

Sometimes we're faced with several options, and we don't know which way to go. In this psalm, David asked God for guidance. Perhaps he remembered when, as a shepherd boy, he had to show the right path to his sheep who were wandering away. Just as he knew which path would lead to safety for his sheep, God knew the path that would lead to everlasting life. Just as those sheep that looked to him for direction were in the least danger, so David knew he needed to look to God for direction.

Today, God still leads us by his truth—his written Word and his Spirit, which helps us to understand it. Are you not sure which path to take? Pray as David did and read what God has already said in his written Word. He will show you the right road to follow.

Dear Father, show me the path where I should walk . . .

JEHOSHAPHAT'S CRY FOR HELP

So when the Aramean charioteers saw Jehoshaphat in his royal robes, they went after him. "There is the king of Israel!" they shouted. But Jehoshaphat cried out to the Lord to save him, and God helped him by turning the attack away from him.

2 CHRONICLES 18:31

During battle, the wicked King Ahab of Israel disguised himself as a foot soldier. This cowardly act left his ally, a brightly robed King Jehoshaphat, a sitting duck for their common enemy, the Arameans. Although God had warned Jehoshaphat about allying with Ahab, Jehoshaphat did so anyway. Despite his error, Jehoshaphat knew where to turn when he was in trouble. He cried out to God. His story should soften our pride—especially when we try to cling to our own faulty decisions. His prayer—"Lord, save me"—should become our own when we find ourselves in trouble.

Aren't you glad you never encounter "I told you so" in prayer? Turn to God for help when you know you need it—even when you don't deserve it.

Dear Lord, forgive my pride and sinfulness. Come save me . . .

**PRAYING
FOR
SPIRITUAL
WISDOM**

So we have continued praying for you ever since we first heard about you. We ask God to give you a complete understanding of what he wants to do in your lives, and we ask him to make you wise with spiritual wisdom.

COLOSSIANS 1:9

A mother with a newborn daughter showers an extraordinary amount of attention on her young child, and justifiably so. She keeps the child nearby and answers her every cry. Paul treated the Colossians as if he were their parent. Although he was under house arrest in Rome, his concern for their spiritual upbringing was evident in the tender way in which he pleaded with God the Father to give the Colossians spiritual wisdom. This spiritual wisdom is a gift from God.

Like Paul, we too ought to ask for wisdom for ourselves and the ones we love. Let Paul's love for the Colossians inspire you to pray for other believers who need God's wisdom in the situations they are facing.

Dear Lord, give spiritual wisdom to . . .

WAITING ON THE LORD IN THE MORNING

Let me hear of your unfailing love to me in the morning,
for I am trusting you.
Show me where to walk,
for I have come to you in prayer.
Save me from my enemies, Lord;
I run to you to hide me.
Teach me to do your will,
for you are my God.
May your gracious Spirit lead me forward
on a firm footing.

PSALM 143:8-10

It's autumn, and there's a wonderful crispness in the air. The mornings are brisk and invigorating, and it's delightful to walk through the leaves while they're still damp from the dew. On such a morning, it's easy to feel God's nearness. It may have been a morning like this when David prayed, "Let me hear of your unfailing love to me in the morning, for I am trusting you. Show me where to walk, for I have come to you in prayer." David longed to have fellowship with God early in the morning. He wanted God's Spirit to lead him to a path where he could find a firm footing.

Determine to start each morning with the Lord. At that time, ask God to direct your every step throughout the day.

Dear Lord, let me hear of your unfailing love to me in the morning. Show me where to walk today . . .

COMMITTING OUR CAUSE TO GOD

O Lord Almighty, you are just, and you examine the deepest thoughts of hearts and minds. Let me see your vengeance against them, for I have committed my cause to you.

JEREMIAH 11:20

Everyone has a *cause* today. We constantly receive mail and phone calls from organizations asking us to give money and time to support their cause. The prophet Jeremiah also had a cause: to deliver God's message and call the people of Israel to repent and turn to God. Jeremiah's enemies, however, were plotting to kill him. They wanted to silence him and his message. Jeremiah asked the Lord to intervene and take vengeance against those enemies, reminding God that he had committed his cause to him long ago.

If our cause honors God and if we have committed it to him, we can be sure he will honor and bless our efforts. Pray today that you're supporting the right cause. Then ask for God's blessing on it.

Dear Lord, you know my deepest thoughts. I commit my cause to you . . .

**SEEKING
GOD'S
CONFIRMATION**

Then Gideon said to God, "If you are truly going to use me to rescue Israel as you promised, prove it to me in this way. I will put some wool on the threshing floor tonight. If the fleece is wet with dew in the morning but the ground is dry, then I will know that you are going to help me rescue Israel as you promised." And it happened just that way. When Gideon got up the next morning, he squeezed the fleece and wrung out a whole bowlful of water. JUDGES 6:36-38

There are times when we simply can't believe what God is asking us to do. Such was the case with Gideon. God had told Gideon that he was to rescue Israel from the Midianites, but Gideon couldn't believe it. He "asked for a sign" to confirm God's call. When God granted him the sign, Gideon asked for yet another sign, and God answered again. Finally convinced, Gideon obeyed. He led an army of Israelites against the Midianites. God gave him a miraculous victory over them, just as he had promised.

God was gracious in answering Gideon's requests for a sign, and he is often gracious to our requests as well. But if we already know what God's will is—especially as he has revealed it in his written Word—we should not delay in carrying it out. Ask God to show you what he wants you to do and then step out in faith and do it.

Dear God, show me what you want me to do . . .

September 15

PRAYING FOR SUCCESS

"O Lord, please hear my prayer! Listen to the prayers of those of us who delight in honoring you. Please grant me success now as I go to ask the king for a great favor. Put it into his heart to be kind to me."

NEHEMIAH 1:11

Nehemiah, cupbearer for King Artaxerxes, understood that success is often dependent on numerous factors, including the response of other people. So he approached God in prayer about his plan to return to Judea to rebuild Jerusalem's walls. He knew the success of his plans would depend on God influencing the heart of the king. Later, Nehemiah boldly presented his plan to the king. "The king granted these requests," Nehemiah said, "because the gracious hand of God was on me" (Nehemiah 2:8).

God knows our needs, and he wants us to succeed in those plans that honor him. Take your plans to God in prayer. Ask that you might honor his name through your plans, and then pray that God might grant you success.

Dear Lord, I delight in honoring you. Please grant me success . . .

SINGING A NEW SONG FOR GOD'S VICTORY

Sing a new song to the Lord,
for he has done wonderful deeds.
He has won a mighty victory
by his power and holiness.
The Lord has announced his victory
and has revealed his righteousness to every nation!
He has remembered his promise to love and be faithful to
Israel.
The whole earth has seen the salvation of our God.

PSALM 98:1-3

Singing—both what we sing and how we sing—speaks volumes about the way we feel. A downcast face or halfhearted voice can make joyful lyrics sound weak and flat. A smiling and cheerful singer can liven up almost any song. Talking and thinking about what God has done for us gets our heart focused on what is good, true, and beautiful. Yet when we *sing* to him, we offer God something that pleases him greatly: heartfelt sacrifices of praise and thanksgiving. This psalm calls on people everywhere to "sing a new song" of praise to the Lord for the great victory he has won for his people.

In your prayer time today, open up a hymnal or praise book. Find a song that celebrates God's power and use it to praise your Father in heaven for his victory of salvation.

Dear Lord, I praise you for the salvation you have won
for your people . . .

PRAYING FOR OPPORTUNITIES TO SHARE CHRIST

Don't forget to pray for us, too, that God will give us many opportunities to preach about his secret plan—that Christ is also for you Gentiles. That is why I am here in chains. Pray that I will proclaim this message as clearly as I should.

COLOSSIANS 4:3-4

If telling your acquaintances about Christ sometimes seems a daunting task, remind yourself that the apostle Paul found it challenging as well. That is why Paul asked the Christians at Colosse to pray that he would have opportunities to preach the gospel and that he would proclaim the message as clearly as he should. Whether he felt he was lacking in courage or skill or something else, he knew he needed God's Spirit to work through him; and he knew that God would honor the prayers of other believers.

Today, pray for your unbelieving friends and acquaintances. Pray that you may have the opportunity to share with them succinctly and clearly the message that Christ died for their sins.

Dear Lord, help me to proclaim the gospel as clearly as I should . . .

PRAYING FOR GOD'S FAVOR

Happy are those who are strong in the Lord,
*   who set their minds on a pilgrimage to Jerusalem. . . .*
O Lord God Almighty, hear my prayer.
*   Listen, O God of Israel.*
O God, look with favor upon the king, our protector!
*   Have mercy on the one you have anointed.*
A single day in your courts
*   is better than a thousand anywhere else!*
I would rather be a gatekeeper in the house of my God
*   than live the good life in the homes of the wicked.*

PSALM 84:5, 8-10

When we describe the "good life," we usually don't start talking about being "strong in the Lord," as the psalmist did in this prayer. Instead, we describe happy families, cozy homes, world travel, or a satisfying career. None of these visions is entirely wrong. But if our visions of the good life exclude God, they are wicked. In this prayer, the psalmist reminded himself that worshiping God with the Lord's people was much better than enjoying the "good life" with the wicked. The psalmist understood that God knew perfectly what the "good life" was and would certainly grant it to his obedient children. What a good God we have! He showers blessings and rewards on those who follow him.

Thank God today for the blessings you have experienced.

O God, look with favor upon us . . .

September 19

O Lord, I am your servant;
  yes, I am your servant, the son of your handmaid,
  and you have freed me from my bonds!
I will offer you a sacrifice of thanksgiving
  and call on the name of the Lord.
I will keep my promises to the Lord
  in the presence of all his people,
in the house of the Lord,
  in the heart of Jerusalem.
Praise the Lord!

PSALM 116:16-19

Today, we don't hear too much about slavery except in a few places like Sudan. But in ancient times, a debt could cause a person to be sold into slavery. The author of this prayer compared his spiritual walk with God to being liberated from the cruelty of slavery. He responded to God by offering a sacrifice of thanksgiving. He expressed his joy by vowing to call on his Deliverer at all times, and by vowing to keep his promises to God. He honored the Lord for the great gift he had received. In a similar way, God wants us to honor him for our great gift of salvation by offering our lives to him as living sacrifices.

Thank God for saving you from your sin and commit yourself to follow him every day.

Dear Lord, I will keep my promises to you in the presence of all your people . . .

Elijah's Prayer for a Child's Life

Then Elijah cried out to the Lord, "O Lord my God, why have you brought tragedy on this widow who has opened her home to me, causing her son to die?"

And he stretched himself out over the child three times and cried out to the Lord, "O Lord my God, please let this child's life return to him." The Lord heard Elijah's prayer, and the life of the child returned, and he came back to life! 1 Kings 17:20-22

Though she had nothing to feed herself and her son, the widow of Zarephath had taken Elijah in as an extra mouth to feed during a time of famine and trusted God to provide. And indeed, God saw them through. Later, the woman's son became ill and died. So Elijah turned immediately to the Lord and pleaded for the child's life. God heard Elijah's plea and raised the poor widow's son, showing that every individual is important in the eyes of God.

Take some time to pray for someone who is experiencing heartache or tragedy in his or her life. Pray that God may apply his life-giving power to that situation. We can pray for anyone—no matter how poor, no matter how important—for God cares about that person.

O Lord, why have you brought tragedy on . . .

**ASKING FOR
GOD'S
SMILE OF
FAVOR**

*"May the Lord bless you
and protect you.
May the Lord smile on you
and be gracious to you.
May the Lord show you his favor
and give you his peace."*

NUMBERS 6:24-26

The power of a smile is real—it expresses love, affection, approval, and support. In this blessing that God himself gave to Moses, the Lord taught Moses and the Levites to pray for his favor. The Levites would pronounce the blessing on the Israelites, and God would carry out what the Levites had said. In other words, God was teaching Moses and the Levites to pray that God might smile on his people. What a picture of God! He teaches us to ask him to smile on us. He wants us to ask him to protect and bless us.

Take the words of this ancient, God-given prayer, and use it to pray for someone you know.

Dear Lord, please smile on . . .

September 22

OUR LIVES ARE IN GOD'S HANDS

Come and see what our God has done,
what awesome miracles he does for his people!
He made a dry path through the Red Sea,
and his people went across on foot.
Come, let us rejoice in who he is.
For by his great power he rules forever.
He watches every movement of the nations;
let no rebel rise in defiance.
Let the whole world bless our God
and sing aloud his praises.
Our lives are in his hands,
and he keeps our feet from stumbling.

PSALM 66:5-9

Some of the prayers in the Psalms are proclamations shouted from the place of worship for all the faithful to hear. The author of this prayer invites everyone to celebrate God and his care for his people: "Come, let us rejoice in who he is." He has performed miracles for his people. By his great power, he rules forever. At the right time, the whole world will bless our God, for he holds everyone in his hands—yes, even our lives are in his loving hands. He keeps our feet from stumbling. God is worthy of our praise.

Let us join our voices with his faithful people from the past, praising him for who he is and trusting him with our lives. Thank him for keeping you from stumbling.

Dear Lord, I thank you for holding my life in your hands and for keeping my feet from stumbling . . .

**COMMITTING
OUR
TROUBLES
TO GOD**

*O Lord, God of my salvation,
  I have cried out to you day and night.
Now hear my prayer;
  listen to my cry.
For my life is full of troubles,
  and death draws near.
I have been dismissed as one who is dead,
  like a strong man with no strength left.*

PSALM 88:1-4

Troubles, trials, and difficulties can be disheartening. And for the majority of us, life is full of troubles. Heman, the author of this prayer, knew what hardship was. He had spent days and nights crying to God about his difficulties. Heman wasn't afraid to admit his predicament, to describe his hardships, and to cry out to God for help. And though God had not rescued Heman since he first began calling out to him, Heman still prayed, looking to God for help.

When we're surrounded by troubles and difficulties, we need to follow the example of Heman and continually bring our concerns to God, for God will answer in his perfect timing.

O Lord, listen to my cry . . .

A Petition	[Jabez] was the one who prayed to the God of Israel, "Oh,
for	that you would bless me and extend my lands! Please be with
Blessing	me in all that I do, and keep me from all trouble and pain!"
	And God granted him his request. 1 Chronicles 4:10

Among the myriad of names listed in the long genealogy in
1 Chronicles, one name in particular stands out—Jabez. His mother
named him "Distress" (which is what "Jabez" means) because her
labor was so difficult; but that is not what he was best known for.
Jabez gained distinction by his *prayer*. His requests were ordinary
enough—who would not wish for prosperity and the absence of
trouble! But Jabez trusted God enough to ask God for these things.
History records that God granted his request, and obviously Jabez
told everyone about God's answer to his prayer.

Imitate the faith Jabez had in God. Boldly ask the Lord to bless
you—to be with you in whatever you do and wherever you go.

*Dear God, please bless me and be with me in all that I
do . . .*

PRAISING THE LORD FOR HIS GOODNESS

Praise the Lord!
Praise the name of the Lord!
Praise him, you who serve the Lord,
*   you who serve in the house of the Lord,*
*   in the courts of the house of our God.*
Praise the Lord, for the Lord is good;
*   celebrate his wonderful name with music.*

PSALM 135:1-3

God's goodness is evident in so many aspects of our lives, and all our blessings come from him. For these reasons, some of our prayer time should be devoted to rejoicing in his goodness. The author of this prayer did just that. He called upon all God's people gathered in the Temple for worship to praise the Lord for his goodness. Entire clans of people were dedicated to magnifying God Almighty. Some helped with the festivals and sacrifices. Others were trained musicians, leading the people in song. This prayer called upon all these people—and the common people as well—to celebrate God's goodness.

Make certain that some of your prayers this coming week are devoted to praising God for his goodness to you and your family.

Dear Lord, I praise you, for you have been good to me . . .

**PRAISING
THE GOD
WHO
KNOWS US**

*O Lord, you have examined my heart
and know everything about me.
You know when I sit down or stand up.
You know my every thought when far away.
You chart the path ahead of me
and tell me where to stop and rest.
Every moment you know where I am.
You know what I am going to say
even before I say it, Lord.*

PSALM 139:1-4

One of the greatest desires of the human heart is intimacy: knowing and being known. Our relationship with God is unique in that he alone knows us completely. It is an act of worship and submission to admit that God knows *everything* about us. Regardless of where we may find ourselves, God knows our every thought and can *direct* us where to go and give us rest. Incomprehensible as it may be to our finite minds, God's knowledge is not limited to the past and the present. To use David's words, "You know what I am going to say even before I say it." That is how intimately God knows and loves you.

In prayer today, praise the one who knows you and loves you so completely.

*O Lord, I praise you that you know everything about
me . . .*

PRAISE TO THE GOD WHO CAN SAVE US

But we worship at your throne—eternal, high, and glorious! O Lord, the hope of Israel, all who turn away from you will be disgraced and shamed. They will be buried in a dry and dusty grave, for they have forsaken the Lord, the fountain of living water.

O Lord, you alone can heal me; you alone can save. My praises are for you alone!

JEREMIAH 17:12-14

Jeremiah had the daunting task of warning God's rebellious people that there would be consequences to their sinful ways. After announcing God's judgment to the people, Jeremiah turned to God, his only hope. Turning from all the wickedness around him, he meditated on God's throne—"eternal, high, and glorious!" He reiterated the truths he had been proclaiming—that those who turn from the Lord would one day be disgraced and face death for refusing God's "fountain of living water." Jeremiah, in contrast, declared his dependence on God. Having reminded himself of these eternal truths, Jeremiah praised God.

We, too, should remember who has saved and healed us. Again and again, we need to remind ourselves in prayer of how much God has done for us.

O Lord, you alone can heal me; you alone can save . . .

September 28

OFFERING
OURSELVES
TO GOD

*Then I heard the Lord asking, "Whom should I send as a
messenger to my people? Who will go for us?"*
And I said, "Lord, I'll go! Send me."
*And he said, "Yes, go. But tell my people this: 'You will hear
my words, but you will not understand. You will see what I do,
but you will not perceive its meaning.'"*   ISAIAH 6:8-9

"I'll go! Send me." Isaiah's response to God's call was eager
enthusiasm. After being cleansed of his sins with a burning coal, Isaiah
was anxious to show his gratitude to God in tangible ways. When God
asked "Whom should I send as a messenger to my people?" Isaiah
responded with zeal. Once he had been justified in the presence of the
Holy One, he held nothing back from God. God revealed a need for
someone to go as a messenger to his people. Isaiah offered the only
thing he had—himself; and God accepted his offering.

Are you eager to respond to God's call? In prayer, imitate
Isaiah's attitude by offering your life to God.

Dear Lord, I'll go! Send me . . .

REJOICING IN GOD'S PRESENCE

Arise, O God, and scatter your enemies.
Let those who hate God run for their lives.
Drive them off like smoke blown by the wind.
Melt them like wax in fire.
Let the wicked perish in the presence of God.
But let the godly rejoice.
Let them be glad in God's presence.
Let them be filled with joy.
Sing praises to God and to his name!
Sing loud praises to him who rides the clouds.
His name is the Lord—
rejoice in his presence!

PSALM 68:1-4

Too often, we approach our prayer time with reluctance. It is almost as if we are saying, "Not again. I'm too busy to find time to talk to God." As this prayer indicates, David cultivated an attitude of joy when he approached God in prayer. He understood what a privilege it was to talk to the Almighty. God's enemies wouldn't even be able to stand in the Lord's presence. Though David was astonished by God's power, he was filled with joy because he was allowed to enter God's presence. He counted himself among the godly—those who reverence God and obey his laws.

When you enter God's presence today in prayer, thank God for listening to you.

Dear God, I am filled with joy to be in your presence . . .

PONDERING GOD'S AMAZING DEEDS

Praise the Lord!
I will thank the Lord with all my heart
*   as I meet with his godly people.*
How amazing are the deeds of the Lord!
*   All who delight in him should ponder them.*
Everything he does reveals his glory and majesty.
*   His righteousness never fails.*
Who can forget the wonders he performs?
*   How gracious and merciful is our Lord!*
He gives food to those who trust him;
*   he always remembers his covenant.*

PSALM 111:1-5

Our minds naturally go back again and again to the things we don't understand; we ponder them and try to make sense of them. The psalmist encourages believers to reflect on the amazing deeds of their God. We should express our thanks to God publicly as well as privately, letting other believers be encouraged by our reports of God's goodness to us. "Who can forget the wonders he performs?" the psalmist proclaims. God feeds us; he never forgets his covenant with us; he demonstrates his love and power to us by giving us all kinds of gifts. "How amazing are the deeds of the Lord!"

Add your own testimony to this chronicle of God's faithfulness in both your private prayers and before the people in your church.

Dear Lord, how amazing are your deeds! How can I forget the wonders you have performed? . . .

October 1

A Prayer for God to Prove Himself

At the customary time for offering the evening sacrifice, Elijah the prophet walked up to the altar and prayed, "O Lord, God of Abraham, Isaac, and Jacob, prove today that you are God in Israel and that I am your servant. Prove that I have done all this at your command. O Lord, answer me! Answer me so these people will know that you, O Lord, are God and that you have brought them back to yourself."

1 Kings 18:36-37

At the time of Elijah's prayer, Israel was being overrun by the worship of Baal. So Elijah set up a showdown between the Lord and Baal to see who would set fire to their sacrifice. The priests cried out to Baal and even cut themselves, but there was no response. Then came Elijah's turn. After drenching his sacrifice with gallons of water, he asked God to light the sacrifice, so that the Israelites would repent of their ways. God answered Elijah's prayer by sending fire down from heaven, consuming the entire altar.

We may never find ourselves in a showdown quite like Elijah's, but there are still times when we want God to show himself unmistakeably to people. Ask God to prove himself to them by answering your prayers.

Dear Lord, please answer me and show these people that you are God . . .

October 2

EXALTING THE GOD OF CREATION

The heavens tell of the glory of God.
The skies display his marvelous craftsmanship.
Day after day they continue to speak;
night after night they make him known.
They speak without a sound or a word;
their voice is silent in the skies;
yet their message has gone out to all the earth,
and their words to all the world.
The sun lives in the heavens
where God placed it.
It bursts forth like a radiant bridegroom
after his wedding.

PSALM 19:1-5

For David, the moon and the sun, the stars and the planets were all reminders of what a remarkable craftsman God was. He had created those starry heights and had set them into motion. Unlike his pagan neighbors, David didn't worship the sun, moon, and stars. No, he perceived these heavenly objects as worshiping their Creator by doing what they were made to do. If only our ears could hear creation's praises to God!

Take some time to ponder the intricate details in the world around you. Join your voice with the "voices" of the heavens in praise of your Creator.

Dear God, the heavens tell of your glory . . .

October 3

**QUIET
BEFORE
GOD**

*Lord, my heart is not proud;
my eyes are not haughty.
I don't concern myself with matters too great
or awesome for me.
But I have stilled and quieted myself,
just as a small child is quiet with its mother.
Yes, like a small child is my soul within me.*

PSALM 131:1-2

We have all seen it. A small child climbs up in her mother's arms. Full of trust and love, she is content to rest there—leaving behind her tears, worries, and even her desires. She lies content in her mother's embrace. In this prayer, David described himself as being like such a child—content to rest in God's embrace. David quieted his soul before God enough to accept his circumstances, the difficulties that were beyond his control. He left those "matters too great or awesome" for him to God. He simply trusted that God—someone wiser and more powerful than he—was looking after his needs.

Quiet your soul before God in your prayer time as David did. Leave your life in his hands.

Dear God, I have stilled and quieted myself, just as a small child is quiet with its mother . . .

October 4

PRAISE
FROM
CHILDREN

O Lord, our Lord, the majesty of your name fills the earth!
Your glory is higher than the heavens.
You have taught children and nursing infants
to give you praise.
They silence your enemies
who were seeking revenge.

PSALM 8:1-2

Were we to try to measure his glory, it would be greater than all the universe combined. Yet God enables even children to praise him. What an amazing thought! Their simple prayers of praise often shame the prayers of adults. With their sincere faith in God, they are not distracted by all the "sophisticated" things that cause adults to struggle in their praise. Perhaps that is why Jesus demands that we become like little children in order to enter God's kingdom (Matthew 18:3). And these praises of children can silence God's enemies. How can anyone contradict a simple, yet miraculous prayer from a small child's lips?

This week, find some time to listen to children praying. Let their simple prayers inspire you to express in prayer a childlike trust in God.

Dear Lord, the majesty of your name fills the earth. Teach me to give you the sincere praise of a little child . . .

October 5

HAVE MERCY ON US

After Jesus left the girl's home, two blind men followed along behind him, shouting, "Son of David, have mercy on us!"

They went right into the house where he was staying, and Jesus asked them, "Do you believe I can make you see?"

"Yes, Lord," they told him, "we do."

Then he touched their eyes and said, "Because of your faith, it will happen."

MATTHEW 9:27-29

"Have mercy on us." Though these two blind men couldn't see their surroundings, they could see that Jesus could help them, so they asked for one thing—his mercy. By calling Jesus the "Son of David," they showed that they believed Jesus was the Messiah. And these men didn't just cry out as Jesus passed by, giving up when he had passed them. They followed him right into the house where he was staying. It seems they cared more about receiving mercy from Jesus than about what others might have thought about them or about social protocol. They knew he alone was the answer to their needs.

May our own prayers be full of the faith and fervency of those two blind men, who asked for and received mercy from God.

Son of David, have mercy on me . . .

PRAISE FOR THE DIVERSITY OF CREATION

O Lord, what a variety of things you have made!
In wisdom you have made them all.
The earth is full of your creatures.

PSALM 104:24

Famous artists are often admired and remembered for the scope and variety of their work. How much more should we admire God for the incredible variety of his creation! Whether we set out to study biology, geology, or astronomy, diversity is one of the first things we notice. There are oak trees and orchids, mountains and mesas, black holes and bright stars. When we consider these vast differences in the universe, we are dumbfounded. God's wonderful creation inspires us to praise him, and God finds pleasure in those who appreciate his creation and thank him for it.

Let the endless variety of God's creation be the starting point for your meditation and praise today.

O Lord, what a variety of things you have made . . .

October 7

**PRAISING
GOD'S
TRUST-
WORTHINESS**

*Let the godly sing with joy to the Lord,
    for it is fitting to praise him.
Praise the Lord with melodies on the lyre;
    make music for him on the ten-stringed harp.
Sing new songs of praise to him;
    play skillfully on the harp and sing with joy.
For the word of the Lord holds true,
    and everything he does is worthy of our trust.
He loves whatever is just and good,
    and his unfailing love fills the earth.*

PSALM 33:1-5

What does it mean to be trustworthy and true? In a society that insists that all truth is relative, many people have given up looking for truth, much less basing their lives on it. But Scripture declares that there is something that is completely true—no matter what angle you look at it, no matter what perspective you come from. God and his Word will always remain true. That facet of God's character is what this psalm celebrates. It encourages believers everywhere to shout for joy, for their lives are securely established on God's eternal truths.

Take a moment to reflect on how few things are certain in this world and how much change is a normal part of life. Then think about how God and his Word are forever trustworthy and true, and give him praise.

Dear God, your Word holds true, and everything you do is worthy of my trust . . .

October 8

**FINDING
OUR TRUE
DESIRE**

*I look for someone to come and help me,
but no one gives me a passing thought!
No one will help me;
no one cares a bit what happens to me.
Then I pray to you, O Lord.
I say, "You are my place of refuge.
You are all I really want in life.
Hear my cry,
for I am very low.
Rescue me from my persecutors,
for they are too strong for me."*

PSALM 142:4-6

Difficult circumstances have a remarkable way of revealing what is most important in our lives. When David had fled into a cave because Saul wanted to take his life, nobody seemed to care about his plight or give him a passing thought. It was at this low point that David understood most clearly that God himself was whom he truly wanted and needed. Granted, taking refuge in the Lord doesn't mean that all our problems will be solved instantaneously. But knowing that God is with us in our trying times should comfort us and give us the strength to go on.

In those situations when it seems as if the whole world is crashing down on you, can you sincerely pray, with David, "You are all I really want in life"?

Dear Lord, you are my place of refuge. Teach me to desire you above all else . . .

DECLARING THE WONDER OF HIS NAME

"I will declare the wonder of your name to my brothers and sisters.
I will praise you among all your people."

HEBREWS 2:12

After staring hour after hour at the screens of televisions, movie theaters, and computers, we may lose our sense of wonder at nature's beauty. Even more troubling is when we allow all these things to divert our attention from how God works wonders in our lives. One reason Jesus came to earth was to point out God's wonders. His prayer was that he would "declare the wonder" of God's name. With his life, death, and resurrection, Jesus did just that, inspiring his followers to declare the wonders of God's name as well.

Determine whom you are going to tell this week about the wonderful things God has done for you and your family.

Dear Lord, I will declare the wonder of your name to my brothers and sisters . . .

$\mathcal{O}$ c t o b e r   10

A Prayer

for

Forgiveness

and Mercy

For the honor of your name, O Lord,
forgive my many, many sins. . . .
Turn to me and have mercy on me,
for I am alone and in deep distress.
My problems go from bad to worse.
Oh, save me from them all!
Feel my pain and see my trouble.
Forgive all my sins.

PSALM 25:11, 16-18

Have you ever felt as though the problems in your life were like a series of dominoes? One domino falls down, and it sets off a chain reaction that knocks down the rest of the dominoes. David felt that his problems were going from bad to worse—his enemies had surrounded him, waiting for his ultimate demise. David could see no way out. But even in his despair, he knew there was one whom he could always trust to help him. He turned to God, confessed his sins, asked for forgiveness, and pleaded for mercy.

When we are separated from God because of our sins, we need to repent and ask for forgiveness. Then, with a clean heart, we can come before him and ask for help. He will hear and answer us "for the honor of his name."

Dear God, for the honor of your name, please forgive
my many, many sins and have mercy on me . . .

AN APPEAL FOR GUIDANCE

Send out your light and your truth;
*   let them guide me.*
Let them lead me to your holy mountain,
*   to the place where you live.*
There I will go to the altar of God,
*   to God—the source of all my joy.*
I will praise you with my harp,
*   O God, my God!*
Why am I discouraged?
*   Why so sad?*
I will put my hope in God!
*   I will praise him again—*
*   my Savior and my God!*

PSALM 43:3-5

Being lost in the darkness can be a very frightening situation. But imagine if you were also being pursued by people who were out to kill you! This was the psalmist's urgent dilemma, and he didn't know which way to turn. But he did know to whom he should cry out for help. He asked God to show him the way, to guide him in the truth, and to lead him to the Lord's presence.

Pray that God will guide your steps. Set your sights on your final destination—God's dwelling place—and encourage yourself with the prospect of living joyfully in the Lord's presence.

Dear God, guide me with your light and your truth . . .

October 12

No Record of Sins

Hear my cry, O Lord.
Pay attention to my prayer.
Lord, if you kept a record of our sins,
who, O Lord, could ever survive?
But you offer forgiveness,
that we might learn to fear you.
I am counting on the Lord;
yes, I am counting on him.
I have put my hope in his word.
I long for the Lord
more than sentries long for the dawn,
yes, more than sentries long for the dawn.

PSALM 130:2-6

Even those with good financial records don't want to go through the ordeal of a tax audit. They don't want someone scrutinizing their entire financial life and demanding an answer for every tax receipt. The psalmist rejoiced that God didn't keep a record of his wrongs. What a relief to know that God wouldn't ask him to account for every sin he had committed! God forgives us if we repent of our sin—no record of wrongs, no accounting needed. This should fill us with wonder and gratitude. God is waiting to hear from us, to forgive, and to restore.

Thank God today for not keeping a record of your sins.

Dear Lord, I praise you for forgiving me, for I could not survive if you kept a record of my sins . . .

October 13

PRAYING WHEN ALL HOPE SEEMS LOST

"When I had lost all hope, I turned my thoughts once more to the Lord. And my earnest prayer went out to you in your holy Temple. Those who worship false gods turn their backs on all God's mercies. But I will offer sacrifices to you with songs of praise, and I will fulfill all my vows. For my salvation comes from the Lord alone."

JONAH 2:7-9

This amazing prayer was prayed by the prophet Jonah from the belly of the great fish that had swallowed him! Deep down, Jonah must have known that it was fruitless to try to escape God's call. On a ship headed *away* from where God had told him to go and preach, Jonah got caught in a life-threatening storm. He knew that he was the reason for the impending disaster and eventually asked to be thrown overboard to spare the others. Instead of requiring his life, God ordered a huge fish to swallow him. Jonah wasted no time. From within its belly he prayed to God, recognizing that salvation could come from no one else.

Turn your thoughts to God as Jonah did in his moment of distress. Reaffirm your dependence on God for salvation.

Dear Lord, I turn my thoughts to you, for salvation comes from you alone . . .

October 14

**TRUSTING
IN GOD**

Have mercy on me, Lord, for I am in distress.
My sight is blurred because of my tears.
My body and soul are withering away.
I am dying from grief;
my years are shortened by sadness.
Misery has drained my strength;
I am wasting away from within. . . .
But I am trusting you, O Lord,
saying, "You are my God!"
My future is in your hands.

PSALM 31:9-10, 14-15

Suffering and pain are inevitable in this life. Strained relationships, financial obligations, and situations at work can sap our strength, leaving us with little to give to others. In this prayer, David told God about the misery and suffering he was facing. His grief and sadness had weakened him, leading him to say, "I am wasting away from within." Yet even in his struggles, David found strength in the Lord by placing his future in God's hands. We, too, can trust the Lord's plans for our future.

What are the situations in your life that cause you anguish and misery? As you spend time in prayer, commit those situations to him. Place your future in God's able hands.

Dear God, my future is in your hands . . .

PLACING OUR HOPE IN GOD'S WORDS

I pray with all my heart; answer me, Lord!
I will obey your principles.
I cry out to you; save me,
that I may obey your decrees.
I rise early, before the sun is up;
I cry out for help and put my hope in your words.
I stay awake through the night,
thinking about your promise.

PSALM 119:145-148

We tend to turn to God for help when our backs are against the wall and our world is falling apart. We might even try to strike a deal with God, making promises to obey him if he only will deliver us from our current predicament. In this prayer, turning to God was not a last resort. God was the *only* solution the psalmist ever tried. He even got up early in the morning to meditate on God's promises and ask for the Lord's help. If his nights were sleepless, he focused his thoughts on what is holy and true. It was that type of commitment to God and his words that helped him get through times of difficulty.

Determine how you can make God's words a central part of your everyday life. Ask God to help you focus on his life-giving words this week.

Dear Lord, I rise early to place my hope in your words.
I will obey your principles . . .

Backing Up Words with Actions

Finally, they cried out to the Lord, saying, "We have sinned against you because we have abandoned you as our God and have served the images of Baal. . . ."

But the Israelites pleaded with the Lord and said, "We have sinned. Punish us as you see fit, only rescue us today from our enemies." Then the Israelites put aside their foreign gods and served the Lord. And he was grieved by their misery.

Judges 10:10, 15-16

Sometimes it takes more than words to convince others of a change of heart. Words have to be backed up with action. The Israelites were in such a situation with God. Again and again, they had adopted the gods of the pagan nations around them. God grew angry with the Israelites, allowing their pagan neighbors to attack them. So when the Israelites cried out to God for deliverance, they realized that they had to back up their prayers of repentance with action. They had to tear down their idols and begin serving the Lord. Then God "was grieved by their misery."

Search your heart for the idols in your life—the temporal things to which you sacrifice your time and money. Tear them down and affirm your allegiance to God alone.

Dear Lord, I have sinned. Punish me as you see fit, only rescue me today . . .

October 17

**PRAISING
GOD FOR
HIS
PROTECTION**

*I look up to the mountains—
    does my help come from there?
My help comes from the Lord,
    who made the heavens and the earth!
He will not let you stumble and fall;
    the one who watches over you will not sleep.
Indeed, he who watches over Israel
    never tires and never sleeps.
The Lord himself watches over you!
    The Lord stands beside you as your protective shade.*

PSALM 121:1-5

The role of security guards is important for protecting buildings from intruders. If guards do not pay attention to their surroundings, they could allow an intruder to sneak in undetected. In the same way, the psalmist describes the Lord as one who "never tires and never sleeps." He stands beside us to make sure we don't stumble and fall. Our God is always paying attention and will be our "protective shade" day in and day out. The psalmist knew that the Lord was able to keep him safe, for the Lord "made the heavens and the earth!"

In your prayer time, remember that God—the one who never tires or sleeps—is watching over you.

Dear Lord, thank you for watching over me . . .

October 18

A PLEA TO THE GOD WHO DECLARES US INNOCENT

Answer me when I call,
O God who declares me innocent.
Take away my distress.
Have mercy on me and hear my prayer.

PSALM 4:1

Gossip and slander ruins relationships and destroys a person's confidence. Many times, we're tempted to counter gossip with destructive words of our own. But David offers us a better solution. In this psalm, he responds to false accusations by appealing to God, who could declare him innocent. Likewise, we can look to God when we are slandered, for he is the one who decides if we are innocent or not. We do not need to fear the accusations of others. At another level, we do not need to fear the accusations of the great accuser (which is what "Satan" means), for the Lord has declared his people innocent through the death of his Son, Jesus Christ.

Spend time today thanking God for declaring you innocent.

Dear Lord, I praise you for declaring me innocent . . .

TAKING COURAGE IN GOD

Your goodness is so great!
*   You have stored up great blessings for those who honor you.*
You have done so much for those who come to you for protection,
*   blessing them before the watching world.*
You hide them in the shelter of your presence,
*   safe from those who conspire against them.*
You shelter them in your presence,
*   far from accusing tongues. . . .*
So be strong and take courage,
*   all you who put your hope in the Lord!*

PSALM 31:19-20, 24

In this prayer, David described God as a shelter that protected him from the dangers of this world—his enemies, harmful lies, and conspiracies. As king of Israel, David would have had the nation's might at his command. At the same time, he would have been the target of all kinds of attacks. David wisely sought God's protection. He knew God protects and blesses those who run to him for safety. He took courage in the fact that God would shield him from any danger he would encounter.

In prayer, ask God to protect you and your family with his presence. Pray that his protection might give you the courage to do the tasks before you.

O God, shelter me in your presence, and help me to take courage in you . . .

October 20

**HUMBLING
OURSELVES
BEFORE
GOD**

Then Job replied to the Lord:

*"I know that you can do anything, and no one can stop
you. You ask, 'Who is this that questions my wisdom with
such ignorance?' It is I. And I was talking about things I did
not understand, things far too wonderful for me.*

*"You said, 'Listen and I will speak! I have some questions
for you, and you must answer them.'*

*"I had heard about you before, but now I have seen you
with my own eyes. I take back everything I said, and I sit in
dust and ashes to show my repentance."* JOB 42:1-6

When we complain to God, we may speak without thinking and
have to take back our words. Job had plenty of time to think, yet he
still had to repent for his lack of humility. The Lord listened to
Job's complaints, criticisms, and questions, and then soundly
rebuked him, asking, "You are God's critic, but do you have the
answers?" Chastened and humbled by God, Job immediately
repented of what he said and asked the Lord to forgive him. We may
not openly challenge God as Job did, but sometimes we doubt
God's care for us. In those times, God wants us to come to him and
trust that he holds the answers and that he is good, just, and loving.

Ask for faith to overcome your doubts. Trust God and leave your
complaints in his hands.

*Dear God, I know that you can do anything, and no one
can stop you . . .*

CRYING OUT TO THE LORD

I cry out to the Lord;
I plead for the Lord's mercy.
I pour out my complaints before him
and tell him all my troubles.
For I am overwhelmed,
and you alone know the way I should turn.
Wherever I go,
my enemies have set traps for me.
I look for someone to come and help me,
but no one gives me a passing thought!
No one will help me;
no one cares a bit what happens to me.

PSALM 142:1-4

Have you ever been overwhelmed by your troubles and uncertain which way you should turn? Wherever David went, his enemies set traps for him. He searched for someone to help him, but no one gave him a passing thought. No one would help him. No one cared a bit about what was happening to him. Sound familiar? Sometimes we need to vent our frustrations about a distressing situation that has no apparent solution. Our lament is, "Everyone is against me. No one appreciates me. No one cares."

When you're feeling discouraged and low, seek the Lord. Pour out your complaints before him, and tell him all your troubles. God is big enough for your problems. He can show you the way you should go.

Dear God, I am overwhelmed. Please show me which way I should turn . . .

October 22

A PRAYER FOR FORGIVENESS

Return, O Israel, to the Lord your God, for your sins have brought you down. Bring your petitions, and return to the Lord. Say to him, "Forgive all our sins and graciously receive us, so that we may offer you the sacrifice of praise. Assyria cannot save us, nor can our strength in battle. Never again will we call the idols we have made 'our gods.' No, in you alone do the orphans find mercy."

HOSEA 14:1-3

After describing God's fierce anger over Israel's idols, the prophet Hosea made it clear that God would still welcome his people if they returned to him in humility and repentance. Hosea even taught the Israelites the prayer they should use when they returned to God. They were to turn away from their idols and confess to God that he alone could save them. Only the Lord deserved their adoration and worship.

When you are tempted to trust in your own strength and resources, come to God in humility. Recommit yourself to him and pray for his forgiveness. And know that he will graciously receive all those who genuinely repent and turn to him.

Dear Lord, forgive all my sins and graciously receive me, so that I may offer you a sacrifice of praise . . .

THANKING GOD IN ALL CIRCUMSTANCES

O God, whom I praise,
don't stand silent and aloof
while the wicked slander me
and tell lies about me.
They are all around me with their hateful words,
and they fight against me for no reason.
I love them, but they try to destroy me—
even as I am praying for them! . . .
But I will give repeated thanks to the Lord,
praising him to everyone.
For he stands beside the needy,
ready to save them from those who condemn them.

PSALM 109:1-4, 30-31

In good and bad times, when we are flush with success and also when we are brought low by failure—we are to praise God. As believers, we know that our present circumstances shouldn't affect our allegiance to him. In this prayer, David confessed that he was in deep trouble. The wicked were slandering him and telling lies about him. They returned evil for good and hatred for his love. His enemies tried to destroy him even as he prayed for them. Yet in such a predicament, David said, "I will give repeated thanks to the Lord, praising him to everyone."

Whatever your circumstances today, offer your thanks and praise to God, for he is the one who sustains you.

Dear Lord, no matter what circumstances I am in, I will give repeated thanks to you . . .

A PRAISE

AND A

REQUEST

"But in your great mercy, you did not destroy them completely or abandon them forever. What a gracious and merciful God you are!

"And now, our God, the great and mighty and awesome God, who keeps his covenant of unfailing love, do not let all the hardships we have suffered be as nothing to you. Great trouble has come upon us and upon our kings and princes and priests and prophets and ancestors from the days when the kings of Assyria first triumphed over us until now." NEHEMIAH 9:31-32

Fifty-two days after they started, the people of Israel completed rebuilding the walls of Jerusalem. For the next several weeks Nehemiah and the priests led the people in confession and in the reading of the Law. He asked them to renew their commitment to God and offer their worship to him. Nehemiah recounted how God had delivered the people time after time, and how the people had, in turn, disobeyed the Lord. In today's passage, Nehemiah praised God for being faithful to his covenant despite his people's sin. Then he asked God to once again show his people mercy and help them.

God does keep his promises. Like Nehemiah, let us pray and thank him for his faithfulness as we come before him with our requests as well.

Merciful God, you have been faithful to your covenant with me and have not abandoned me . . .

October 25

O Lord, how long will you forget me? Forever?
How long will you look the other way?
How long must I struggle with anguish in my soul,
with sorrow in my heart every day?
How long will my enemy have the upper hand?
Turn and answer me, O Lord my God!
Restore the light to my eyes, or I will die. . . .
But I trust in your unfailing love.
I will rejoice because you have rescued me.
I will sing to the Lord
because he has been so good to me.

PSALM 13:1-3, 5-6

Does it ever seem to you as if God has forgotten you? Have you prayed and prayed and seemingly received no response? David, despite his intimate relationship with God, felt that way more than once. But he didn't wallow in self-pity and hopelessness. He took those feelings of abandonment directly to God. He was honest before the Lord. He expressed his impatience: "How long must I struggle?" As he bared his soul to God, a change began to take place in him. He remembered God's faithfulness to him in the past. His cries of distress turned into songs of praise.

When you enter God's presence with all your complaints, you will undergo a similar change. Rather than feeling forgotten, you will understand the extent of God's faithfulness to and love for you.

Dear Lord, how long must I struggle with anguish in my soul? But I will trust in your unfailing love . . .

October 26

MOSES' PRAYER FOR ISRAEL

"Indeed, you love the people;
all your holy ones are in your hands.
They follow in your steps
and accept your instruction."

Just before his death, Moses gathered the people of Israel together and gave a specific blessing for each one of the tribes. But the grand theme of all his prayers appears in his introduction. He prayed that God would continue to "love the people," and in turn, Israel would accept God's instructions and follow in the Lord's steps. Moses' prayer teaches us also. The Lord does love his people and holds us safely in his hands. It is our responsibility to accept his instruction and follow in his steps.

Thank God for loving you and holding you in his hands. Ask him for strength to follow in his steps.

Dear Lord, thank you for holding me safe in your hands. Help me to follow in your steps and accept your instruction . . .

**OBSERVING
GOD'S
POWER IN
ACTION**

*Some went off in ships,
   plying the trade routes of the world.
They, too, observed the Lord's power in action,
   his impressive works on the deepest seas.
He spoke, and the winds rose,
   stirring up the waves. . . .
"Lord, help!" they cried in their trouble,
   and he saved them from their distress.
He calmed the storm to a whisper
   and stilled the waves.
What a blessing was that stillness
   as he brought them safely into harbor!*

PSALM 107:23-25, 28-30

After coming safely through a dramatic, life-threatening experience,
the whole world seems fresh and new. We have a new appreciation for
the gift of health and life. This is the perspective of the psalmist in this
passage. When some exiles were aboard a ship being tossed about by
fierce winds and relentless waves, God calmed the wind in answer to
their cries for help. We can only imagine how those windblown exiles
rejoiced over that safe harbor. They praised and thanked God and
would never take God's protection for granted again.

Recount the ways God has worked powerfully in your life. Praise
him for bringing you through the trials and hardships you have
experienced.

*Dear Lord, I have seen your power in action, and I
thank you . . .*

October 28

REJOICING IN GOD'S POWER

This prayer was sung by the prophet Habakkuk: . . .

I see God, the Holy One, moving across the deserts from Edom and Mount Paran. His brilliant splendor fills the heavens, and the earth is filled with his praise! What a wonderful God he is! Rays of brilliant light flash from his hands. He rejoices in his awesome power. Pestilence marches before him; plague follows close behind. When he stops, the earth shakes. When he looks, the nations tremble. He shatters the everlasting mountains and levels the eternal hills. . . .

The Sovereign Lord is my strength! He will make me as surefooted as a deer and bring me safely over the mountains.

HABAKKUK 3:1, 3-6, 19

Habakkuk had some tough questions for God, such as: "Why are you silent when the wicked oppress good people?" God answered Habakkuk. There will be a day when he will return to establish justice. On that day, he will rescue his people and punish the wicked. Habakkuk responded with a prayer of praise and compared God's power to a great storm that lit up the night sky with its deafening thunder—a storm so fierce that it leveled mountains and hills.

One of the reasons we pray is to understand this world from God's perspective. We can bring our tough, honest questions to God, just as Habakkuk did. Yet as we meditate on Scripture and on God's good plan, we should be inspired to praise the Almighty the same way Habakkuk did.

O God, I will be joyful in you, the God of my salvation . . .

A Prayer for a Clean Heart

How can I know all the sins lurking in my heart?
Cleanse me from these hidden faults.
Keep me from deliberate sins!
Don't let them control me.
Then I will be free of guilt
and innocent of great sin.
May the words of my mouth and the thoughts of my heart
be pleasing to you,
O Lord, my rock and my redeemer.

Psalm 19:12-14

The closer we get to God, the more we become aware of our own sin and our own unworthiness. David starts out this prayer by proclaiming the greatness of the Lord: "The heavens tell of the glory of God. The skies display his marvelous craftsmanship" (v. 1). As he praises God, David senses the sin that exists in his life. He asks the Lord to cleanse him and keep him from *all* sins—even those that are hidden deep in his own heart. In spite of his weaknesses and failures, David wants his entire life, even what he says and thinks, to be pleasing to God.

Start your prayer time today by meditating on God's perfection and holiness. Then acknowledge where you fall short and confess your sins to God. Ask him to cleanse your heart, pointing out the sins buried deep within you.

Holy God, point out all my sins and cleanse me. Make the words of my mouth and the thoughts of my heart pleasing to you . . .

JESUS'
PRAYER FOR
OUR
PROTECTION

"And now I am coming to you. I have told them many things while I was with them so they would be filled with my joy. I have given them your word. And the world hates them because they do not belong to the world, just as I do not. I'm not asking you to take them out of the world, but to keep them safe from the evil one."

JOHN 17:13-15

After their Last Supper together, Jesus was with his disciples in the upper room. Jesus knew that his "time had come." So he prayed for his disciples and asked God the Father to protect them and keep them safe from Satan. Jesus also prayed for those "who will ever believe in me because of their testimony" (v. 20). That includes us! Jesus, in the last few minutes before he faced his trial and death, prayed for his disciples' protection—and also for ours! That should be a great comfort to us. It should free us from anxiety, uncertainty, and fear. After all, if God is for us, who can be against us?

Pray that God may protect you from those who want your demise. Ask the Lord to keep you from all evil. He will certainly answer your prayers.

Dear Lord, I don't belong to the world. Please keep me safe from the evil one . . .

SUSTAINED BY GOD'S WORDS

Then I said, "Lord, you know I am suffering for your sake. Punish my persecutors! Don't let them kill me! Be merciful to me and give them what they deserve! Your words are what sustain me. They bring me great joy and are my heart's delight, for I bear your name, O Lord God Almighty. . . . I burst with indignation at their sins. Why then does my suffering continue? Why is my wound so incurable? Your help seems as uncertain as a seasonal brook. It is like a spring that has gone dry."

The Lord replied, "If you return to me, I will restore you so you can continue to serve me. . . . You are to influence them; do not let them influence you!"   JEREMIAH 15:15-19

Words can be used powerfully in both positive and negative ways. With them we can hurt and humiliate others, or we can encourage and strengthen people to carry on. In today's prayer, the prophet Jeremiah asked God to punish his persecutors and give them what they deserve. He then told the Lord, "Your words are what sustain me. They bring me great joy and are my heart's delight." God's encouraging words helped to sustain him during the persecution he was enduring.

In response to his prayer, God told Jeremiah to do the same—to "speak words that are worthy." His words were to influence the people of Israel. Think of some ways that you can use words for good and not evil. Ask the Lord for opportunities to be his spokesperson.

O Lord, help me to speak words that are worthy . . .

November 1

THANKING GOD FOR A FRIEND

May God our Father and the Lord Jesus Christ give you grace and peace.

I always thank God when I pray for you, Philemon, because I keep hearing of your trust in the Lord Jesus and your love for all of God's people.

PHILEMON 1:3-5

We are often drawn to prayer by tragedies and difficult circumstances in our lives. We tell God all about our problems and ask for his help— and rightly so. Paul was certainly in difficult circumstances when he wrote this letter to Philemon. He was under house arrest in Rome, awaiting a trial before Caesar. He certainly had much to pray for. But his attention in prayer was also focused on others. In his letter to Philemon, Paul didn't forget to tell Philemon that he was praying for him—that he was thanking God because of him.

Are there brothers or sisters in Christ who have encouraged you? Have you told them how much you appreciate them and that you are praying for them? Resolve to tell them how much they mean to you.

Dear Lord, thank you for . . .

MOSES' INTERCESSION FOR HIS PEOPLE

So Moses returned to the Lord and said, "Alas, these people have committed a terrible sin. They have made gods of gold for themselves. But now, please forgive their sin—and if not, then blot me out of the record you are keeping."

EXODUS 32:31-32

Moses had every reason to be upset with the people of Israel. While he was meeting with God on the mountain to receive God's law, the Israelites fashioned a gold calf and began to worship it. By doing so, they were not only breaking their promise to worship the living God alone, but they were also rejecting Moses' spiritual leadership. Moses could have easily asked God to destroy them on the spot. Instead, he pleaded for God's mercy on them. Moses showed great love for the Israelites, despite the fact that they had rebelled against his authority.

Among your friends, coworkers, and acquaintances, are you concerned about the best interests of others? Go to the Lord; ask him to have mercy on those who least deserve it.

Dear God, teach me to love others as Moses loved his people . . .

A Prayer
for
Harmony
in the
Church

May God, who gives this patience and encouragement, help you live in complete harmony with each other–each with the attitude of Christ Jesus toward the other. Then all of you can join together with one voice, giving praise and glory to God, the Father of our Lord Jesus Christ. Romans 15:5-6

Worshiping in a congregation whose members are excited about what God is doing is thrilling. Jesus told his disciples, "Your love for one another will prove to the world that you are my disciples" (John 13:35). In his letter to the Romans, Paul prayed that the believers in Rome would "live in complete harmony with each other—each with the attitude of Christ Jesus toward the other." Only when believers live that way will they "join together with one voice, giving praise and glory to God, the Father of our Lord Jesus Christ."

Think what an impact the church could have on a skeptical—but watching—world, if we could live in harmony as the Bible teaches. Pray for that type of harmony in your church community.

Dear Father, help me to live in harmony with my fellow believers . . .

GIVING THANKS THAT GOD IS NEAR

I will bless the Lord who guides me;
even at night my heart instructs me.
I know the Lord is always with me.
I will not be shaken, for he is right beside me.

PSALM 16:7-8

Sometimes we try to "ride out the storms" in our lives—doing this the best we can. We think, *If I can just hang on and be strong, I can get through this.* David knew he couldn't make it on his own. In the past, he had found help in the Lord God. And in this prayer, David again sought the Lord's protection: "Keep me safe, O God, for I have come to you for refuge" (v. 1). He rejoiced in the guidance and assistance the Lord had given him. Though his enemies were trying to shake and topple him, David stood firm because God was "right beside" him.

In prayer today, acknowledge that God is right beside you—upholding and guiding you. Thank him that he helps you and does not leave you to struggle on your own.

Dear Lord, I will not be shaken, for you are right beside me . . .

A REQUEST FOR GOD TO REMEMBER US

Happy are those who deal justly with others
and always do what is right.
Remember me, too, Lord, when you show favor to your
people;
come to me with your salvation.
Let me share in the prosperity of your chosen ones.
Let me rejoice in the joy of your people;
let me praise you with those who are your heritage.

PSALM 106:3-5

Feeling forgotten is one of the worst feelings—especially if the people who forgot you are your only hope. No doubt Samson felt that way when he was languishing in prison—blind and alone. In his last request, he called to the Lord, "Remember me again" (Judges 16:28). Similarly, after enduring multiple personal crises, Job pleaded with God, "Mark your calendar to think of me again!" (Job 14:13). Even the thief on the cross asked Jesus, "Remember me when you come into your Kingdom" (Luke 23:42). These people—along with the psalmist in this prayer— understood that their lives depended on God's loving concern.

Remember that the Lord never forgets his own, though we foolishly wander away from him. When you are feeling alone and rejected, call out to God and know that he watching over you.

O Father, remember me today. Let me rejoice with your
people . . .

**JESUS'
PRAYER FOR
THE
CHURCH**

*"I have told these men about you. They were in the world,
but then you gave them to me. Actually, they were always
yours, and you gave them to me; and they have kept your
word. Now they know that everything I have is a gift from
you, for I have passed on to them the words you gave me;
and they accepted them and know that I came from you, and
they believe you sent me."*

JOHN 17:6-8

In his last hours on earth, Jesus prayed to his Father on behalf of his disciples, asking the Father to protect them. In this portion of his prayer, Jesus explained to his Father how he had been obedient to the task given him of communicating God's words accurately and clearly to the twelve disciples. Jesus' job was done. Now it was the disciples' turn to share with others God's message. What a rich heritage we have as followers of Christ. Just think of it, the very words of God that were entrusted to the disciples have been passed on to us. What a precious treasure that is!

Are we treating God's words as the priceless gift it is? Are we telling others about God's message? Thank God today for his words.

Dear God, thank you for sending Jesus to earth to communicate your word to us . . .

SOLOMON'S PRAYER

"If your people offer a prayer concerning their troubles or sorrow, raising their hands toward this Temple, then hear from heaven where you live, and forgive. Give your people whatever they deserve, for you alone know the human heart. Then they will fear you and walk in your ways as long as they live in the land you gave to our ancestors."

2 CHRONICLES 6:29-31

After the building of the Temple was completed, Solomon gathered the people to dedicate it to God and pray for the nation. Though his kingdom was at peace and riches were flowing into his treasury, Solomon knew that God was the source of all those blessings. If the people didn't follow God, they would quickly lose his favor. So Solomon prayed that during those difficult times the Lord would have compassion on his people and listen to their pleas. God answered Solomon's prayer. Again and again, he came to his people's aid when they cried out to him.

Today God still takes pleasure in answering the prayers of his people. Don't hesitate to turn to him for help and ask him to hear your pleas and forgive.

Dear God, please hear me and forgive . . .

**PRAYING
FOR GOD'S
VERDICT**

*Declare me innocent, O Lord,
for I have acted with integrity;
I have trusted in the Lord without wavering.
Put me on trial, Lord, and cross-examine me.
Test my motives and affections.
For I am constantly aware of your unfailing love,
and I have lived according to your truth.*

PSALM 26:1-3

Not many people enjoy tests, and even fewer enjoy being put on trial. No one wants inquisitive lawyers cross-examining every statement and action. But David prayed that God would do just that with his life. He wanted God to declare him innocent so that the accusations of his enemies would be forever silenced. Because he had consistently tried to follow God's ways, David was confident that the Lord would protect him from these accusations. All of us will endure times when we are unjustly accused. If we have been careful to submit our ways to God, we can be confident that God will declare us innocent.

In prayer today, commit your ways to God. Ask the Lord to examine your life and help you change those areas that don't conform to his will.

Dear God, test my motives and affections. Help me to live according to your truth . . .

BOWING BEFORE THE KING OF ALL NATIONS

I will praise you among all the people;
I will fulfill my vows in the presence of those who
worship you.
The poor will eat and be satisfied.
All who seek the Lord will praise him.
Their hearts will rejoice with everlasting joy.
The whole earth will acknowledge the Lord and return to him.
People from every nation will bow down before him.
For the Lord is king!
He rules all the nations.

PSALM 22:25-28

Presidents and rulers often hold the reins of power for years. But inevitably they lose their power and pass from the scene. After a few generations, they may even be forgotten by most people. Yet there is one King who will never pass away. He will rule all the nations forever and ever. The whole earth will acknowledge his reign and bow before him, saying: "For the Lord is king! He rules all the nations." Earthly rulers rise and fall, but our Lord, the King of all nations, reigns forever.

Bow before the King of kings. Worship his holy name.

Sovereign Lord, you are King over all nations. I bow down before you . . .

**PRAYING IN
THE MIDST
OF A STORM**

*Instead, the sailors tried even harder to row the boat ashore.
But the stormy sea was too violent for them, and they
couldn't make it. Then they cried out to the Lord, Jonah's
God. "O Lord," they pleaded, "don't make us die for this
man's sin. And don't hold us responsible for his death,
because it isn't our fault. O Lord, you have sent this storm
upon him for your own good reasons."*

*Then the sailors picked Jonah up and threw him into the
raging sea, and the storm stopped at once! The sailors were
awestruck by the Lord's great power, and they offered him a
sacrifice and vowed to serve him.*　　　　JONAH 1:13-16

The sailors were desperate. As the wind and waves grew more fierce,
they feared for their lives. They tried everything, including praying to
their gods. Nothing worked—until Jonah admitted he was running
from God. What a way to witness to unbelievers! It was these pagan
sailors who encouraged Jonah, a prophet of God, to obey the living
God—not the other way around. Yet God not only brought Jonah back
to himself, he also demonstrated his power to those unbelieving sailors.
They submitted themselves to God's will, prayed that he would spare
their lives, and committed themselves to following him.

Like these sailors, recognize that the Lord is always working out
his good will—even through difficult circumstances.

*Dear God, you have sent this storm for your own good
reasons. Please spare me . . .*

DAVID'S SEARCH FOR GOD'S WILL

After this, David asked the Lord, "Should I move back to Judah?"

And the Lord replied, "Yes."

Then David asked, "Which town should I go to?"

And the Lord replied, "Hebron."

2 SAMUEL 2:1

When facing a major decision, we are often quick to consult friends or look for signs in the midst of our circumstances, but how many of us first go to God in prayer? In today's prayer, David wanted to know where to begin his reign as king. Rather than taking a survey and talking to others about where to go, David sought the Lord and his will. And the Lord was quick to reply. Although God can, and does, reveal his will through circumstances and the advice of others, he delights to answer our prayers and speak through his Word.

Today, thank God for leading you thus far. Then ask him to show you his will for you, and listen for his answer.

Dear Lord, show me where I should go . . .

REJOICING OVER GOD'S VICTORIES

Then Moses and the people of Israel sang this song to the Lord:

"I will sing to the Lord, for he has triumphed gloriously;
he has thrown both horse and rider into the sea.
The Lord is my strength and my song;
he has become my victory.
He is my God, and I will praise him;
he is my father's God, and I will exalt him!"

EXODUS 15:1-2

Moses had just seen the Lord part the Red Sea, protect the Israelites as they passed through on dry ground, and then drown Pharaoh's well-armed soldiers as the Red Sea's waters crashed down upon them. Moses had seen God demonstrate his power in a marvelous way, and he couldn't stand silent. He simply had to announce God's victory: "The Lord is my strength and my song," he sang. "He has become my victory."

What victories has God given you? In what ways have you seen God triumph over his enemies? Sometimes we forget that God is fighting with us. We find ourselves fighting the battle in our own strength. Let's remember who is our real victory. Praise the Lord as Moses did, and trust him to become your victory.

Dear Lord, you are my strength and my song. You have become my victory. I praise you . . .

November 13

**AN APPEAL
FOR JUSTICE**

O Lord, rescue me from evil people.
Preserve me from those who are violent,
those who plot evil in their hearts
and stir up trouble all day long. . . .
Don't let liars prosper here in our land.
Cause disaster to fall with great force on the violent.
But I know the Lord will surely help those they persecute;
he will maintain the rights of the poor.
Surely the godly are praising your name,
for they will live in your presence.

PSALM 140:1-2, 11-13

Almost daily we hear news reports of cruelty and injustice suffered by innocent people. Sadly, the stories are often of little children who are abandoned or abused by adults who seemingly have no conscience or remorse. When we hear of such inhuman and unspeakable acts, most of us become angry. We may even ask, "Oh, God, where is justice?" David was concerned about the injustice suffered by the poor, the innocent, and the defenseless. He asked the Lord to help those who are persecuted, to maintain the rights of the poor, and to destroy those who were committing these violent acts.

Take some time to pray for those suffering in the world today. Ask God to bring justice to that situation.

Dear God, maintain the rights of the poor. Rescue the innocent from evil people . . .

**TRUSTING
GOD TO
RESCUE**

My heart is confident in you, O God;
no wonder I can sing your praises!
Wake up, my soul!
Wake up, O harp and lyre!
I will waken the dawn with my song.
I will thank you, Lord, in front of all the people.
I will sing your praises among the nations.
For your unfailing love is higher than the heavens.
Your faithfulness reaches to the clouds.
Be exalted, O God, above the highest heavens.
May your glory shine over all the earth.

PSALM 108:1-5

The difference between winning and losing teams is often the level of confidence teammates have in each other. In this prayer David placed his confidence securely in God. He knew that he couldn't save himself. Only God could rescue him. David reminded himself that God's love was higher than the heavens, his glory was evident all over the earth. No wonder he exclaimed, "Wake up, my soul!" It is easy for us to forget the extent of God's power and love. We dwell on the problems we are going through, instead of the God who can give us victory.

In prayer today, recount the ways God has saved his people in the past. Use David's words to praise him for his power and love.

Dear Lord, your unfailing love is higher than the heavens. No wonder I can place my confidence in you . . .

November 15

HONOR TO THE KING OF NATIONS

Lord, there is no one like you! For you are great, and your name is full of power. Who would not fear you, O King of nations? That title belongs to you alone! Among all the wise people of the earth and in all the kingdoms of the world, there is no one like you.

JEREMIAH 10:6-7

Throughout history, cruel, egotistical dictators have risen to power in nations all over the earth. These despots live in wealth and splendor, while their subjects struggle to survive in poverty and hunger. They act and live as if they were gods over the people whom they rule with an iron fist. But the Bible tells us there is only one true King, and Jeremiah says that God alone is worthy of love, adoration, and worship. The title of King of nations, Jeremiah says, "belongs to you alone!"

Let us praise and exalt the name of the Lord God, who is not only King of all the earth, but also the one who causes other kings, presidents, rulers—and dictators—to rise and fall. Praise and adore the Lord, who is without equal.

Dear Lord, there is no one like you. You are the King of all the nations . . .

PRAISE TO THE CREATOR OF THE UNIVERSE

You, O God, are my king from ages past,
bringing salvation to the earth.
You split the sea by your strength
and smashed the sea monster's heads.
You crushed the heads of Leviathan
and let the desert animals eat him.
You caused the springs and streams to gush forth,
and you dried up rivers that never run dry.
Both day and night belong to you;
you made the starlight and the sun.
You set the boundaries of the earth,
and you make both summer and winter.

PSALM 74:12-17

When the forces of nature disrupt our world—whether it's a volcano, earthquake, or a flood—it inspires both awe and fear. No amount of human effort can stop the raging waters of a disastrous flood or the hot lava of a volcano. But God controls even these awesome forces. He is the one who created the earth, started it spinning on its axis, and determined its place in the solar system. The cycles of the seasons reflect his design. The variety of animal and plant species reflects his creative mind. Yet God's greatest work is the salvation he provides to those who call on his name.

We do indeed serve an all-powerful God. Offer your praises to him.

Dear God, you are my King from ages past, bringing salvation to the earth . . .

The Lord Stands beside Us

I have heard the many rumors about me. They call me "The Man Who Lives in Terror." And they say, "If you say anything, we will report it." Even my old friends are watching me, waiting for a fatal slip. "He will trap himself," they say, "and then we will get our revenge on him."

But the Lord stands beside me like a great warrior. Before him they will stumble. They cannot defeat me. They will be shamed and thoroughly humiliated. Their dishonor will never be forgotten. . . . Now I will sing out my thanks to the Lord! Praise the Lord! For though I was poor and needy, he delivered me from my oppressors. JEREMIAH 20:10-11, 13

For most of us, someone or something has struck fear in our heart at some point in our life. Those of us who had no one to stand up for us probably longed for someone to come to our rescue and make everything right. Jeremiah, who was surrounded by enemies, had such a hero. "The Lord stands beside me like a great warrior. Before him they will stumble. They cannot defeat me." God is ready to come to the aid of his children. No matter how big the enemy, he will "stand beside [us] like a great warrior."

What difficulty are you facing? Don't try to handle it all by yourself. Call upon the Lord, and he will come and help you.

Dear God, please come and stand beside me like a great warrior . . .

**PRAISE FOR
GOD'S GIFT
OF LIFE**

*You take care of the earth and water it,
    making it rich and fertile.
The rivers of God will not run dry;
    they provide a bountiful harvest of grain,
    for you have ordered it so.
You drench the plowed ground with rain,
    melting the clods and leveling the ridges.
You soften the earth with showers
    and bless its abundant crops.*

PSALM 65:9-10

By the end of November, trees have shed their leaves; crops have been harvested; and perennial plants lie dormant until next spring. It's the time of year for reflection. We often take for granted that the trees and plants will come back every year with new growth and beauty. We plant seeds in the ground and depend on the rains to come again to water the seeds so that they can produce a new harvest. Upon reflection, however, we know nothing would have life without the touch of the one who created it all. God is the Creator of all things, the giver of life to all human beings—and also to all animals and plants.

Let us not take any of God's gifts for granted. Thank him for the life he gives.

Dear God, thank you for taking care of the earth and making it fertile . . .

ASKING

GOD TO

RELIEVE

OUR

SUFFERING

Lord, have mercy on me.
See how I suffer at the hands of those who hate me.
Snatch me back from the jaws of death.
Save me, so I can praise you publicly at Jerusalem's gates,
so I can rejoice that you have rescued me. . . .
Arise, O Lord!
Do not let mere mortals defy you!
Let the nations be judged in your presence!
Make them tremble in fear, O Lord.
Let them know they are merely human.

PSALM 9:13-14, 19-20

Life is difficult enough without people seeking to attack us in one way or another. But as David quickly learned when he became king, the more responsibility and power we are given, the more enemies oppose us. When we are being attacked by our enemies, we instinctively fight back. But as this prayer shows, our first response to opposition should be to bring the situation to God in prayer. Instead of plotting how he could destroy his enemies, David identified how his current predicament could bring glory and honor to God.

What difficult and troublesome situations have you gone through? Submit those situations to God, and ask him to save you so that you may rejoice in him.

Dear Lord, you know how I am suffering. Please save me so I can rejoice in you . . .

JESUS' PRAYER FOR THE CARE OF HIS PEOPLE

"My prayer is not for the world, but for those you have given me, because they belong to you. And all of them, since they are mine, belong to you; and you have given them back to me, so they are my glory! Now I am departing the world; I am leaving them behind and coming to you. Holy Father, keep them and care for them—all those you have given me—so that they will be united just as we are. During my time here, I have kept them safe. I guarded them so that not one was lost, except the one headed for destruction, as the Scriptures foretold."

JOHN 17:9-12

Just before Jesus was arrested by Roman soldiers, he took time to pray for his followers. He asked his Father to protect those for whom he would die the next day. Listen to Jesus words: "Holy Father, keep them and care for them—all those you have given me—so that they will be united just as we are." Jesus' prayer revealed the tenor of his heart—that he cares for his disciples and desires that they live together in peace.

Jesus cares for us, his followers today, just as much as he cared for his twelve disciples while he was here on earth. Meditate on how much Jesus cares for you, and ask him to help you live in peace with your Christian brothers and sisters.

Dear Jesus, thank you for caring for me . . .

APPROACHING GOD WITH AN HONEST HEART

O Lord, hear my plea for justice.
Listen to my cry for help.
Pay attention to my prayer,
for it comes from an honest heart.
Declare me innocent,
for you know those who do right.
You have tested my thoughts and examined my heart in the night.
You have scrutinized me and found nothing amiss. . . .
But because I have done what is right, I will see you.
When I awake, I will be fully satisfied,
for I will see you face to face.

PSALM 17:1-3, 15

Like a child who longs to see his father after he has been away for a while, David longed to see God face-to-face. He wanted to thank and praise God who had rescued him. David knew God was holy and that all who enter his presence must come with an honest heart and an upright life. In this prayer, David promised to follow God's ways and even asked the Lord to examine his heart. David had certainly sinned before, even murdering an innocent man. But David didn't hide his sins; he confessed them to God. He asked God to cleanse him from sin so that he could enter the Lord's presence with praise.

Ask God to cleanse you from sin as you enter God's presence.

Dear Lord, my prayer comes from an honest heart. Test my thoughts and cleanse me of my sin . . .

**THANKS
FOR A
BOUNTIFUL
HARVEST**

*You crown the year with a bountiful harvest;
    even the hard pathways overflow with abundance.
The wilderness becomes a lush pasture,
    and the hillsides blossom with joy.
The meadows are clothed with flocks of sheep,
    and the valleys are carpeted with grain.
They all shout and sing for joy!*

PSALM 65:11-13

For farmers, harvest is a time to rejoice. The long hours of backbreaking work in the fields finally bear fruit. The acres burst forth with grain; the limbs of trees become weighed down with fruit. It is a time to rejoice in what God has provided, to sing of his goodness. In this prayer, David thanked God for all his blessings on Israel—the meadows were filled with sheep; the pastures were lush; and the fields were filled with grain. The land was so blessed by God that it appeared to be shouting out in joy.

In this month of thanksgiving, we ought to thank the Lord for our harvests of love, friendships, blessing, protection, and joy. Sing a song of praise to God today for his goodness to you.

Dear Lord, you have crowned the year with a bountiful harvest . . .

HOLY,
HOLY,
HOLY

Each of these living beings had six wings, and their wings were covered with eyes, inside and out. Day after day and night after night they keep on saying,

"Holy, holy, holy is the Lord God Almighty—
the one who always was, who is, and who is still to come."

REVELATION 4:8

Can you hear it? Be still and listen closely. The words ring out over the horizon of time itself—holy, holy, holy. The first person to hear that heavenly refrain was the prophet Isaiah. He heard those words from the angelic beings who gathered around God's throne. Then, hundreds of years later, John, while exiled on the island of Patmos, was allowed to hear this eternal chorus: "Holy, holy, holy is the Lord God Almighty." When the minutiae of life seem to outweigh their eternal meaning, when the ebb and flow of life's routine weighs you down, listen closely for heaven's refrain. Holy! Holy! Holy! The prayer of praise rings on.

Today take a moment to join the heavenly chorus in praising God, for he is holy.

Dear Lord, you are holy. You are the Lord God Almighty— the one who always was, who is, and who is still to come . . .

PRAISE FOR
BLESSINGS
THAT
OVERFLOW

You prepare a feast for me
 in the presence of my enemies.
You welcome me as a guest,
 anointing my head with oil.
 My cup overflows with blessings.
Surely your goodness and unfailing love will pursue me
 all the days of my life,
and I will live in the house of the Lord
 forever.

PSALM 23:5-6

Though wolves and lions might roam the countryside, a loyal shepherd would always protect his sheep. He would lead them to lush pastures and flowing streams, watch for predatory animals, and then guide his flock back to a place of safety. David thought of God as his loyal shepherd, providing for and protecting him. Yet God did even more than any shepherd would do. He didn't simply provide food; he arranged a feast for David in front of his enemies' jealous eyes and treated David as his guest. God didn't merely give him gifts; he gave him a cup overflowing with all sorts of blessings.

Think of the ways in which God has provided for you and blessed you more than you deserve.

Dear Lord, you have made my cup overflow with blessings. I want to live in your house forever . . .

THANKS TO GOD

Give thanks to him who alone does mighty miracles.
His faithful love endures forever.
Give thanks to him who made the heavens so skillfully.
His faithful love endures forever.
Give thanks to him who placed the earth on the water.
His faithful love endures forever.
Give thanks to him who made the heavenly lights—
His faithful love endures forever.

PSALM 136:4-7

Whether it's the air we breathe or the sand under our feet—the entire earth is God's gift to us. We owe him our thanks for his many gifts to us. In this corporate prayer, a worship leader calls on the people to thank God for one aspect of his creation. The people respond with the refrain: *His faithful love endures forever.*

Let this ancient worship leader guide your thanks to God today. Look at God's creation around you—the sky above, the sparkling stars that shine down, the soil beneath you. Let those aspects of God's creation remind you of how faithful God has been to you, how he has provided you with what you need—food, clothes, and shelter.

Dear Lord, your faithful love endures forever. I thank you for . . .

GIVING THANKS FOR GOD'S GOODNESS

Enter his gates with thanksgiving;
go into his courts with praise.
Give thanks to him and bless his name.
For the Lord is good.
His unfailing love continues forever,
and his faithfulness continues to each generation.

PSALM 100:4-5

Imagine yourself entering the gates at the entrance to the temple alongside a throng of people gathering to praise the Lord. As you near the courts of the temple, you are swept up in the words of this prayer uttered by all those around you: "Enter his gates with thanksgiving . . ." This prayer functioned as a call to worship for people entering the temple. It helped the people to focus their thoughts on God and his good gifts to them. It set a tone of thankfulness for the worship service that would follow.

Let the words of this prayer focus your thoughts on God's goodness to you. Come into his presence with thanksgiving and praise on your lips.

Dear Lord, I enter into your presence with thanksgiving and praise, for you are good . . .

DRINKING FROM THE FOUNTAIN OF SALVATION

With joy you will drink deeply from the fountain of salvation! In that wonderful day you will sing:

"Thank the Lord!
   Praise his name!
Tell the world what he has done.
   Oh, how mighty he is!
Sing to the Lord,
   for he has done wonderful things.
   Make known his praise around the world."

ISAIAH 12:3-5

This excerpt is a pause of joyful praise in an otherwise frightful prediction from God's prophet Isaiah concerning Israel's disobedience. It is the prayer the Israelites will offer to God after he saves them from their sins. Isaiah compared their change of heart to quenching one's parched throat at a fountain. Isn't it amazing how experiencing the dreadful results of sin brings a new appreciation of the joys of obeying God? The hearts of these newfound believers overflow with thanksgiving to God for all he has done.

In prayer, thank God for saving you. Ask him to satisfy your parched soul and renew your spirit.

Dear Lord, I thank you and praise your name. You have done wonderful things . . .

THANKSGIVING
FOR
ANSWERED
PRAYER

Open for me the gates where the righteous enter,
and I will go in and thank the Lord.
Those gates lead to the presence of the Lord,
and the godly enter there.
I thank you for answering my prayer
and saving me!

PSALM 118:19-21

This psalm pictures a victorious yet battle-weary king at the helm of a throng of grateful people entering the gates of the temple to thank God for saving them. During those times, the temple represented God's presence—the place where his followers would go to pray to the Lord. Today, we enter into God's presence in a car, at work, or in the aisles of a grocery store—wherever we take time to pray to him. We can be sure God hears our prayers and answers each one wherever and whenever they are uttered. And by doing so, he gives us even more reasons to pray.

Just like the victorious king in this psalm, we should enter God's presence by thanking him for answering our prayers. What answers to prayer are you thankful for today?

Dear Lord, I thank you for answering my prayers . . .

A Prayer for Good Motives

"I know, my God, that you examine our hearts and rejoice when you find integrity there. You know I have done all this with good motives, and I have watched your people offer their gifts willingly and joyously.

"O Lord, the God of our ancestors Abraham, Isaac, and Israel, make your people always want to obey you. See to it that their love for you never changes. . . ."

Then David said to the whole assembly, "Give praise to the Lord your God!" And the entire assembly praised the Lord, the God of their ancestors, and they bowed low and knelt before the Lord and the king.   1 Chronicles 29:17-18, 20

David's prayer comes at a pinnacle moment in his reign as king—the dedication of gifts for the building of the temple. As the people entered a new era in their relationship with the living God, David prayed that their motives would be pure. He knew that God was more concerned about the condition of people's hearts than the silver and gold they were giving away. Even with all the authority he possessed as king, David could not accurately judge the motives behind the Israelites' gifts. Only God could examine his heart and theirs. He prayed that God would find in their hearts integrity and a willingness to obey.

Follow David's example. Ask God to make you a person of integrity—a person who willingly obeys.

Dear Lord, examine my heart and help me always want to obey you . . .

ASKING FOR GOD'S HELP

I have chosen to be faithful;
I have determined to live by your laws.
I cling to your decrees.
Lord, don't let me be put to shame!
If you will help me,
I will run to follow your commands.

PSALM 119:30-32

Asking for help is something many of us don't like to do. We tend to think we don't need any help. "I can handle things myself," we say to ourselves. In today's prayer, the desire of the psalmist was to be faithful to God. But he confessed that he couldn't follow the commands of God on his own. He needed God's help.

Express to the Lord your desire to follow him with all your heart, soul, and mind. Then commit yourself to asking him for his guidance and assistance in the situations you face in life.

Dear Lord, please help me to follow your commands today . . .

December 1

REJOICING OVER ETERNAL BLESSINGS

"O my God, I have been bold enough to pray this prayer because you have revealed that you will build a house for me—an eternal dynasty! For you are God, O Lord. And you have promised these good things to me, your servant. And now, it has pleased you to bless me and my family so that our dynasty will continue forever before you. For when you grant a blessing, O Lord, it is an eternal blessing!"

1 CHRONICLES 17:25-27

One evening at the end of his reign, God spoke to David through a prophet and promised him an eternal dynasty. David's descendants would reign as kings forever and forever. David's immediate response to such wonderful news was to thank God. David shouted a resounding "yes" to God's marvelous promise. God's ultimate fulfillment of this promise came through his Son, Jesus Christ, who was rightfully a descendant of David.

Through Jesus, we now have "eternal blessings" as well. We serve an everlasting King, who desires to bless us with all his riches. In this month when we focus on the birth of our Savior, thank God for the eternal blessings you have in Jesus Christ, God's Son.

Dear Lord, thank you for your eternal blessings to me . . .

PRAISE FOR
THE
ANOINTED'S
VICTORY

The Lord protects his people
and gives victory to his anointed king.
Save your people!
Bless Israel, your special possession!
Lead them like a shepherd,
and carry them forever in your arms.

PSALM 28:8-9

In David's time, winning military victories was critical for the survival of the nation of Israel. If David didn't triumph over his enemies, they would ravage the nation. David trusted God to give him—the one whom God had anointed as king—victory. The Hebrew word for *anointed* is Messiah; so David's psalm is also a victory celebration of the Messiah who was to come—Jesus Christ, the ultimate Anointed One. Jesus is the Victor! He has defeated, on the cross, the devil and death itself. His victory is also ours, for he defeated the sin that enslaved us.

Think of the ways Christ has enabled you to conquer those sins that used to control you. In your prayer time today, celebrate Christ's victory over sin.

Dear Lord, thank you for giving victory to your
Anointed One and saving your people. . .

The Joys of Those Who Trust in Him

Taste and see that the Lord is good.
Oh, the joys of those who trust in him!
Let the Lord's people show him reverence,
for those who honor him will have all they need.
Even strong young lions sometimes go hungry,
but those who trust in the Lord will never lack any good thing.

PSALM 34:8-10

David invites us all to "taste and see that the Lord is good." David had recently seen God's goodness at work in his life when he wrote this prayer. Even though King Saul had sought David's death and Abimelech was considering whether he should execute David, God had spared David's life by allowing him to escape from them both. David's heart was bursting with joy because he had just experienced God's power at work in his life. Yet in his celebration, he didn't forget to invite others to find their joy in God as well—"to taste and see that the Lord is good."

How has God shown his goodness to you? What good things has God given you? Let David's prayer inspire you to find joy in the Lord.

Dear Lord, I have tasted and seen that you are good.
Thank you for providing for me . . .

December 4

THANKSGIVING FOR GOD'S PROMISES

Then King David went in and sat before the Lord and prayed, "Who am I, O Sovereign Lord, and what is my family, that you have brought me this far? And now, Sovereign Lord, in addition to everything else, you speak of giving me a lasting dynasty! Do you deal with everyone this way, O Sovereign Lord? What more can I say? You know what I am really like, Sovereign Lord. For the sake of your promise and according to your will, you have done all these great things and have shown them to me.

"How great you are, O Sovereign Lord! There is no one like you—there is no other God. We have never even heard of another god like you!"

2 SAMUEL 7:18-22

"Who am I that you have brought me this far?" This was David's response to God after hearing that the Lord was going to make his family into an eternal dynasty. God's plans for David were impressive—more than David could ever imagine. Not only would David's descendants reign as kings over the nation, but his family dynasty would last throughout eternity as well. The eternal King of kings, Jesus Christ himself, would one day come from David's royal line. There was nothing that David could have done to deserve such an honor. Such a wonderful promise came only from God's grace.

What blessings have you enjoyed from God's hand? List the ways he has blessed you beyond your wildest dreams.

Dear Lord, who am I that you have brought me this far? . . .

December 5

SHOUTING FOR JOY

Then I will praise you with music on the harp,
because you are faithful to your promises, O God.
I will sing for you with a lyre,
O Holy One of Israel.
I will shout for joy and sing your praises,
for you have redeemed me.
I will tell about your righteous deeds
all day long,
for everyone who tried to hurt me
has been shamed and humiliated.

PSALM 71:22-24

"I will shout for joy and sing your praises." Do these sound like the words of an elderly man? The author of this prayer describes himself as "old and gray" (Psalm 71:18). Yet after surveying his life in prayer, this elderly person was filled with joy. He sang God's praises for everything God had done for him. The Lord had redeemed him and brought him through all the troubles of his life, and he promised to tell others about God's righteous deeds as long as he lived.

Too often, we find ourselves praying hesitant prayers and singing small praises to God. Let the psalmist's enthusiasm inspire you to offer your own praises to God and resolve to tell others about the Lord's wonderful deeds.

Dear Lord, I will shout for joy and sing your praises today . . .

December 6

PAUL'S PRAYER FOR THE EPHESIANS

I pray that your hearts will be flooded with light so that you can understand the wonderful future he has promised to those he called. I want you to realize what a rich and glorious inheritance he has given to his people.

I pray that you will begin to understand the incredible greatness of his power for us who believe him. EPHESIANS 1:18-19

While the believers in Ephesus enjoyed the luxuries and wealth of a cosmopolitan city located on major trade routes, Paul was confined to a small room in Rome, under the constant watch of a Roman guard. But who would ever guess from Paul's prayer that he was deprived of anything? Paul's confident description of God's power does not betray a hint of hopelessness. Instead, Paul speaks of the rich inheritance and wonderful future he would have in heaven. Paul's future on earth was in the hands of Caesar. Yet Paul's ultimate hopes weren't set on this world; his hopes were set on heaven and eternity.

In your prayers, place your hopes on your eternal inheritance in heaven, just as Paul did. Pray that God might help you understand how powerful he is.

Dear Lord, help me to understand the wonderful future you have promised to me . . .

December 7

PRAISE FOR GOD'S MIGHT

The mighty oceans have roared, O Lord.
The mighty oceans roar like thunder;
the mighty oceans roar as they pound the shore.
But mightier than the violent raging of the seas,
mightier than the breakers on the shore—
the Lord above is mightier than these!
Your royal decrees cannot be changed.
The nature of your reign, O Lord, is holiness forever.

PSALM 93:3-5

People throughout the ages have admired God's handiwork when they come to the coast. There, angry, churning ocean waves break violently upon the cliffs and shoals of a shoreline, displaying the great power of these immense bodies of water. Yet, as great as these forces may be, the power of the Creator exceeds any forces found in nature. The energy found in roaring ocean waves, violent earthquakes, or volcanic eruptions can't compare to God's strength.

If God's power exceeds these natural forces, he certainly can handle our troubles. Don't allow the deafening roar of discouraging circumstances disrupt your confidence in God's power. As you pray today, remember that God is much mightier than those waves.

Dear Lord, I praise you for being mightier than all of creation . . .

MAY GOD'S PROMISE LAST FOREVER

"And now, O Lord, do as you have promised concerning me and my family. May it be a promise that will last forever. And may your name be established and honored forever so that all the world will say, 'The Lord Almighty is God over Israel!' And may the dynasty of your servant David be established in your presence."   1 CHRONICLES 17:23-24

In a world where little can be enjoyed "forever," David praised God for giving him an everlasting promise. His family would reign forever on Israel's throne. One can imagine David's delight when he realized that this promise would be fulfilled by the birth of the Messiah, Jesus Christ. Born in David's royal line, Jesus was the King of kings, who at the end of this age will reveal his eternal reign over all of creation.

Generations later, we too are moved to prayer when we consider God's eternal promises to us. May David's words help us thank God for his eternal promises—our salvation and our eternal inheritance in heaven. Spend some time thanking God for his promises that will last forever.

Dear Lord, do as you have promised to me. May your promises last forever . . .

PRAISE FOR THE ETERNAL KING

The Lord is king! He is robed in majesty.
Indeed, the Lord is robed in majesty and armed with
strength.
The world is firmly established;
it cannot be shaken.
Your throne, O Lord, has been established from time
immemorial.
You yourself are from the everlasting past.

PSALM 93:1-2

According to Jewish tradition, this psalm hints at the arrival of a Messiah, who will save God's people. Its opening lines describe the incomparable royalty of this King who would come. Christians know that this eternal King is Jesus. This King is from everlasting past; and his throne is from time immemorial. No wonder this King's majestic robe inspires such praise from the psalmist.

Our image of God can directly affect the nature of our prayers. As you pray throughout this day, let this psalm help you picture Jesus as your King, "robed in majesty" and "armed with strength." Let your imagination ignite your praises for the King.

Dear Lord, I praise you, who are robed in majesty and
armed with strength . . .

December 10

**PRAISING
GOD AND
HIS WAYS**

Then I will rejoice in the Lord.
I will be glad because he rescues me.
I will praise him from the bottom of my heart:
"Lord, who can compare with you?
Who else rescues the weak and helpless from the strong?
Who else protects the poor and needy from those who want
to rob them?" . . .
Let them continually say, "Great is the Lord,
who enjoys helping his servant."
Then I will tell everyone of your justice and goodness,
and I will praise you all day long.

PSALM 35:9-10, 27-28

Swoosh! Seconds before the clock runs out, the star player nails the game-winning shot. Instinctively, the crowd stands and cheers the strength and tenacity of their hero. In this psalm, we find David praising God for rescuing him from his enemies. "Who can compare to God?" he asked. "Who is so loving to rescue the weak?" A star athlete's accomplishments pale in comparison to God's mighty acts in this world, and one day everyone will bow before the Lord and acknowledge his power and righteousness. On that day, all honor and glory will be his. But as we wait for that day, we must help others recognize God's power and encourage them to worship him.

Let us join David in praising God for the way he has rescued us.

O Lord, no one compares with you in power and compassion . . .

December 11

GRATITUDE FOR GOD'S GIFTS

"Riches and honor come from you alone, for you rule over everything. Power and might are in your hand, and it is at your discretion that people are made great and given strength.

"O our God, we thank you and praise your glorious name! But who am I, and who are my people, that we could give anything to you? Everything we have has come from you, and we give you only what you have already given us!"

1 CHRONICLES 29:12-14

Although God prevented King David from building the great temple in Jerusalem, the king gathered some materials so that his son Solomon could build the temple. The people gave generously for the future building of the temple. David was touched by their generosity and expressed his praise to God in prayer.

At this time of the year, when people express their generosity by giving gifts to each other, David's words can help us remember that everything we have comes from God. Genuine giving expresses gratitude to God. We give in response to God's gifts to us.

Dear Lord, everything I have comes from you, and I give you only what you have already given me . . .

DANIEL'S CONFESSION FOR HIS PEOPLE

I prayed to the Lord my God and confessed: "O Lord, you are a great and awesome God! You always fulfill your promises of unfailing love to those who love you and keep your commands. But we have sinned and done wrong. We have rebelled against you and scorned your commands and regulations. We have refused to listen to your servants the prophets, who spoke your messages to our kings and princes and ancestors and to all the people of the land.

"Lord, you are in the right; but our faces are covered with shame, just as you see us now. . . .

"But the Lord our God is merciful and forgiving, even though we have rebelled against him." DANIEL 9:4-7, 9

By the time he had prayed this prayer, Daniel had already lived a full life. He had already survived the lion's den. Now his days were filled with startling visions of God's plans for the world. Still, as he read the predictions of the prophet Jeremiah, he was overwhelmed with how faithful and just God was and how faithless and wicked the Israelites were. And he was moved to pray for his people.

If we are reading God's Word attentively, our conscience should be affected by what we learn. At times, we should be moved to praise or repentance when we read Scripture. Like Daniel, we will discover how great and awesome God is and how merciful and forgiving he is to those who turn to him.

O Lord, you are a great and awesome God! You are merciful and forgiving . . .

December 13

And yet again,

FINDING HOPE IN DAVID'S HEIR

"Praise the Lord, all you Gentiles;
praise him, all you people of the earth."
And the prophet Isaiah said,
"The heir to David's throne will come,
and he will rule over the Gentiles.
They will place their hopes on him."

So I pray that God, who gives you hope, will keep you
happy and full of peace as you believe in him. May you
overflow with hope through the power of the Holy Spirit.

ROMANS 15:11-13

"May God keep you happy and full of peace." What a wonderful blessing for a Christmas card! Paul wrote this prayer for the Romans, after contemplating how Jesus came to this earth to save all people—both Jews and Gentiles. That is why Isaiah predicted that Gentiles would one day place their hope in Jesus—the great heir to David's throne. We fulfill Isaiah's prediction when we, Gentiles, sing the words of the carol, "The hopes and fears of all the years are met in thee tonight." We honor the birth of David's heir, our Lord and Savior Jesus Christ, when we place all of our hopes in Jesus for our salvation. As Christmas approaches, pray that your friends and acquaintances may find their hope and peace in Jesus alone.

Dear Lord, please give hope, happiness, and peace to . . .

JOB'S PRAISE TO GOD

Job stood up and tore his robe in grief. Then he shaved his head and fell to the ground before God. He said,

"I came naked from my mother's womb,
*   and I will be stripped of everything when I die.*
The Lord gave me everything I had,
*   and the Lord has taken it away.*
Praise the name of the Lord!"

In all of this, Job did not sin by blaming God.

JOB 1:20-22

Job had lost everything—all his animals, his servants, and even all his children. Yet, in the midst of such tragedy, Job realized everything he had was from God. Even his children were gifts from God, and so there was still reason to "praise the name of the Lord."

The tragedies of this life are not lessened by our hope in God. Losses still hurt. Our bond with Job's suffering is simply the bond of a shared humanity. What is amazing, however, is that God allowed his Son to come to this earth to suffer. God not only gives us everything we have, he gives us his Son to redeem us from our sins. Praise the name of the Lord!

Dear Lord, you have given me everything I have. Praise the name of the Lord . . .

**HANNAH'S
PRAISE TO
THE LORD**

Then Hannah prayed:

"My heart rejoices in the Lord!
Oh, how the Lord has blessed me!
Now I have an answer for my enemies,
as I delight in your deliverance.
No one is holy like the Lord!
There is no one besides you;
there is no Rock like our God."

1 SAMUEL 2:1-2

During this Advent season you will probably hear a reading of Mary's prayer, in which she thanks and praises God for allowing her to bear Jesus, God's Son (Luke 1:46-55). Her ancestor Hannah had the same feelings of gratitude towards God and shared the same prayer. Both of them were linked across the centuries as women who gave birth to special babies—the prophet Samuel to infertile Hannah, and Jesus to the virgin Mary. Hannah's prayer rings with amazement over God's miraculous intervention in her life.

In our prayers, we should imitate Hannah's example by looking for the ways God has blessed us. Our praise for God's work in our lives is the best testimony to others. Find ways this week to tell others how God has answered your prayers.

O Lord, you have richly blessed me! My heart rejoices in you . . .

December 16

WAITING FOR GOD

O Lord, hear me as I pray;
*   pay attention to my groaning.*
Listen to my cry for help, my King and my God,
*   for I will never pray to anyone but you.*
Listen to my voice in the morning, Lord.
*   Each morning I bring my requests to you and wait*
*   expectantly.*

PSALM 5:1-3

When our ship of life runs aground, we may feel as if God has deserted us. But God doesn't hide from us; instead, it's our selfishness that prevents us from recognizing him. If, in a moment of insight, we understand our predicament, we have God's promise that he will hear us when we call on him.

When we are experiencing difficulties in this life, it's certainly hard to wait on God. The Israelites, who were suffering under Roman rule, felt the same way. They couldn't wait for their Savior. But after centuries of waiting, their hopes were fulfilled in the baby born in Bethlehem. God did send his Son to save the world; all they had to do was wait for his timing.

Dear Lord, I bring my requests to you and wait
expectantly for your answer . . .

JESUS' PRAYER FOR THE UNITY OF BELIEVERS

"I am praying not only for these disciples but also for all who will ever believe in me because of their testimony. My prayer for all of them is that they will be one, just as you and I are one, Father—that just as you are in me and I am in you, so they will be in us, and the world will believe you sent me."

JOHN 17:20-21

In this month when we celebrate Jesus coming to this earth, we should remember Jesus' purpose in coming. Shortly before his arrest, Jesus prayed that those who believed in him would become united in their love for God and each other. This would show the world that Jesus was truly sent by God himself. Christian unity is not uniformity—every believer marching in lockstep; nor is it expediency, sweeping significant issues aside. As Jesus prayed here, real Christian unity is imitating the intimate communion the Father and the Son share. It is a dynamic unity—a complementary relationship of give-and-take, a sharing of life and purpose. This is the union that Jesus prayed for his disciples.

Jesus' prayer is answered whenever we show love to our fellow believers in matters both great and small.

Dear Father, help me to live in unity with other believers so that the world will believe in you . . .

Nothing Is Too Hard for God

"O Sovereign Lord! You have made the heavens and earth by your great power. Nothing is too hard for you! You are loving and kind to thousands, though children suffer for their parents' sins. You are the great and powerful God, the Lord Almighty. You have all wisdom and do great and mighty miracles. You are very aware of the conduct of all people, and you reward them according to their deeds."

JEREMIAH 32:17-19

In a time when most people were investing in liquid valuables—gold and cash—in anticipation of coming devastation—Jeremiah was instructed by God to buy some land. He did this to show that although God's people would be sent into exile, their return to the land was guaranteed by God. Having put his money on the line, Jeremiah reflected on God's faithfulness to his people. He voiced a thought we need to remember when we face difficult times—"Nothing is too hard for you!"

When we've thought through all the possibilities and think our situation is hopeless, we make a huge mistake if we discount God's power. Though your present circumstances may be challenging your trust in God, place your hope in God. Your hope will be rewarded in wonderful and surprising ways.

Dear Lord, nothing is too hard for you. You are great and powerful . . .

PRAISE FROM THE GENTILES

And he came so the Gentiles might also give glory to God for his mercies to them. That is what the psalmist meant when he wrote:

"I will praise you among the Gentiles;
I will sing praises to your name."

And in another place it is written,

"Rejoice, O you Gentiles,
along with his people, the Jews."

ROMANS 15:9-10

"Rejoice, O you Gentiles, along with his people, the Jews." To us, this statement might not seem so radical. But in Paul's day, many Jews regarded Gentiles as repulsive. But because Christ had come to this earth to save both Jews and Gentiles, Paul encouraged them to accept each other and even to pray together. He asked them to join their voices together in praising Jesus, their Savior. Jesus' birth should inspire joy in everyone—even in the hearts of those people who are completely different from us.

Rejoice in your Savior. Determine today to set aside time during this busy season to celebrate with other believers the birth of our Savior.

Dear Lord, I, too, want to add my voice to those who sing praises to your name . . .

The Lord Will Send a Redeemer

For our sins are piled up before God and testify against us. Yes, we know what sinners we are. We know that we have rebelled against the Lord. We have turned our backs on God. We know how unfair and oppressive we have been, carefully planning our deceitful lies. . . .

"The Redeemer will come to Jerusalem," says the Lord, "to buy back those in Israel who have turned from their sins."

ISAIAH 59:12-13, 20

When things begin to pile up—whether they are tasks at work or dishes in the sink—we start feeling guilty about not attending to our responsibilities. But Isaiah prayed about something far more serious. He described Israel's sins as piling up—sins that offended God and deserved punishment. Israel couldn't do anything to clean up this pile—but God could. Though the Israelites had rebelled against God, though they had turned their backs on the Almighty, God promised to send a Redeemer. Only he could buy them back from their slavery to sin. This Redeemer is Jesus—the one whose birth we celebrate on Christmas day.

In prayer today, praise God for sending Jesus to this earth to save us from our sins.

Dear Lord, my sins are piled up. Thank you for buying me back . . .

December 21

HONOR TO THE COMING KING OF KINGS

For at the right time Christ will be revealed from heaven by the blessed and only almighty God, the King of kings and Lord of lords. He alone can never die, and he lives in light so brilliant that no human can approach him. No one has ever seen him, nor ever will. To him be honor and power forever. Amen.

1 TIMOTHY 6:15-16

"Is it Christmas yet?" The anticipation in children's voices around Christmas reminds us of that "I-can-hardly-wait-until-it-gets-here" feeling. Waiting for Christmas should remind us that we who trust in Christ are also waiting for Jesus' return in glory. Just as the ancient Israelites were waiting for the birth of the coming Messiah, we are waiting for Christ's return. Only God knows the date. Only he will decide the right time. Yet one day, he will return in glory.

In the meantime, we should be as excited as children who are awaiting Christmas with just four days to go. We may not know the date when Jesus will return, but we know the day is coming! We have the right attitude when we ask the Lord with excitement, "Is it Christ's time yet?"

Dear Jesus, I am waiting for the right time when you will be revealed from heaven . . .

REJOICING IN OUR SAVIOR

Mary responded,

"Oh, how I praise the Lord.
How I rejoice in God my Savior!
For he took notice of his lowly servant girl,
and now generation after generation
will call me blessed.
For he, the Mighty One, is holy,
and he has done great things for me."

LUKE 1:46-49

Several months pregnant, Mary visited her aunt Elizabeth's house. Elizabeth was about to deliver a surprise baby herself. Her child, the future John the Baptist, leaped in the womb at the sound of Mary's voice. After Elizabeth told Mary what was going on inside her, Mary responded with a song of praise. Not only did Mary understand the greatness of God, she also believed that God had done great things for her. She realized she was part of God's good plan. Mary knew she didn't deserve the privilege of carrying the Messiah, and she expressed her amazement at God's choice.

Mary's role was unique. Only she could bear our Savior. Yet our role is surprisingly similar to Mary's. As believers, our lives should be dwelling places for Christ's Spirit.

Dear Lord, thank you for taking notice of me. I rejoice in you, my Savior . . .

December 23

MARY'S PRAISE FOR GOD'S MERCY

"His mercy goes on from generation to generation,
to all who fear him.
His mighty arm does tremendous things!
How he scatters the proud and haughty ones!
He has taken princes from their thrones
and exalted the lowly.
He has satisfied the hungry with good things
and sent the rich away with empty hands.
And how he has helped his servant Israel!
He has not forgotten his promise to be merciful.
For he promised our ancestors–Abraham and his children–
to be merciful to them forever."

LUKE 1:50-55

It's all too easy to take God's mercy for granted. It's only because God mercifully sends our land rain and good weather that it produces abundant food. It's only because of God's mercy that we enjoy good food, warm clothes, and comfortable homes. Too often we are like children, who think they receive mercy only when they get into trouble. Mary's prayer in this passage reveals that she knew to rejoice in God's mercy when she was enjoying his blessing as well.

Reflect on how merciful God has been to you and your family—the ways he has lifted you up when you were down. During this wonderful Christmas season, remember how far God was willing to go to display his mercy to a fallen world.

Dear Lord, your mighty arm does tremendous things.
You have exalted the lowly . . .

**ZECHARIAH'S
PRAISE FOR
A FULFILLED
PROMISE**

*"Praise the Lord, the God of Israel,
  because he has visited his people and redeemed them.
He has sent us a mighty Savior
  from the royal line of his servant David,
just as he promised
  through his holy prophets long ago.
Now we will be saved from our enemies
  and from all who hate us.
He has been merciful to our ancestors
  by remembering his sacred covenant with them,
  the covenant he gave to our ancestor Abraham.
We have been rescued from our enemies,
  so we can serve God without fear."*

LUKE 1:68-74

Think back on a time when you rejoiced over receiving something you had been promised long before. For Zechariah, it was God's promise to give him a son. Yet on the day of his son's birth, Zechariah had even more to rejoice over. His son's birth was only the beginning. His son—later named John the Baptist—would one day announce the coming of the Messiah—the Savior God had promised to Israel long ago. Another promise kept. Another reason to rejoice. We can only imagine what it was like for Zechariah to watch God's promises being fulfilled before his eyes.

This Christmas Eve, meditate on God's faithfulness to his promises.

Dear Lord, I praise you, for you have sent us a mighty Savior, just as you promised . . .

GLORY TO GOD IN THE HIGHEST HEAVEN

Suddenly, the angel was joined by a vast host of others—the armies of heaven—praising God:

"Glory to God in the highest heaven,
and peace on earth to all whom God favors."

LUKE 2:13-14

No doubt life for the average person wasn't all that noticeably different on the night Jesus was born. Inns and taverns were busy with their customers. Shepherds gathered around the fire to keep warm as they watched over their sheep. But in a secluded corner of Bethlehem, in an out-of-the-way stable, a baby slept in a manger. And as the shepherds settled down for a quiet night, the angels assembled into a vast choir and shattered the silence of that night by loud praises. Imagine the shepherds' response: shock, fear, and, then, awe. They knew that they had to find this extraordinary child whose birth the angels had announced.

As you celebrate Christ's birth on this joyous day, seek out Jesus as the shepherds did years ago. Use this heavenly song to rejoice in Jesus' birth.

Glory to you, God, in the highest heaven, and peace on earth to all whom you favor . . .

**SIMEON'S
PRAISE FOR
THE SAVIOR**

"Lord, now I can die in peace!
As you promised me,
I have seen the Savior
you have given to all people.
He is a light to reveal God to the nations,
and he is the glory of your people Israel!"

LUKE 2:29-32

Old Simeon wasn't some Jewish senior citizen sitting around with waning hopes that the Messiah would come in his lifetime. He was waiting expectantly! His attitude was informed by Scriptures. He understood what this tiny baby Mary and Joseph brought to the Temple meant to all the nations. This baby was the Savior of the world.

Today, people are still making the mistake of seeing only the manger and missing the message. They remember the remarkable baby Jesus, but they overlook God's very presence among us. Where others saw a little child, Simeon saw "a light to reveal God to the nations." He was ready to see God! Where others may view the Christmas season as a time to celebrate their gifts, we see it as a time to worship the newborn King of kings.

Dear Lord, I praise you for giving us a Savior. Jesus is
a light to the nations . . .

December 27

**JESUS'
PRAYER
THAT THE
WORLD
MAY KNOW
HIM**

*"I have given them the glory you gave me, so that they may
be one, as we are—I in them and you in me, all being
perfected into one. Then the world will know that you sent
me and will understand that you love them as much as you
love me. Father, I want these whom you've given me to be
with me, so they can see my glory. You gave me the glory
because you loved me even before the world began!"*

JOHN 17:22-24

As we remember Jesus' birth this week, we should remember why
Christ came to this earth in the first place. In this prayer, Jesus spoke
about his purpose for coming, asking that we, who believe in him,
might experience oneness with God and with each other. His prayer
puts into words what Jesus accomplished with his life—the
reestablishment of our relationship with God as well as the possibility
of unity between all people. Jesus became one of us so that we could
become one with God. The child whose birth we remember grew into
the one who invites us to become children in his heavenly kingdom.

As you contemplate what Jesus' life and death means to you, pray
that you may reflect Jesus' love in your life by showing love to others.

*Dear God, help me to show your love so that the world
may know that you sent your Son to save us . . .*

ANTICI-PATING THE WEDDING FEAST

Then I heard again what sounded like the shout of a huge crowd, or the roar of mighty ocean waves, or the crash of loud thunder: "Hallelujah! For the Lord our God, the Almighty, reigns. Let us be glad and rejoice and honor him. For the time has come for the wedding feast of the Lamb, and his bride has prepared herself. She is permitted to wear the finest white linen." (Fine linen represents the good deeds done by the people of God.) REVELATION 19:6-8

In Scriptures, the revelation of God calls forth one of two responses. Either we are to fall silent before his awesome presence—or we are to shout out our praises! The author of Revelation was granted a vision of that day in the future when God's people—the bride—would celebrate their union with Jesus—the Lamb. In John's vision, a voice from God's throne leads God's people in praise: "Hallelujah! For the Lord our God, the Almighty, reigns." This grand celebration commemorates the ultimate reason Jesus came to the earth. He came to buy his people back from their slavery to sin, so that they could become joyful members of his eternal kingdom.

This vision of our joyful union with Christ should always remain before us, as we serve Jesus on this earth.

Hallelujah! You reign, O Lord God. I rejoice and honor you . . .

**A PRAYER
FOR GOD TO
ANSWER**

*Answer my prayers, O Lord,
    for your unfailing love is wonderful.
Turn and take care of me,
    for your mercy is so plentiful.
Don't hide from your servant;
    answer me quickly, for I am in deep trouble!
Come and rescue me;
    free me from all my enemies.*

PSALM 69:16-18

Sometimes we're "up," and sometimes we're "down." The Scriptures, especially the Psalms, reflect the full range of human emotions, helping us to pray whatever our mood is. At times, we perceive the Lord's presence clearly and vividly; at other times, it is shadowy or hidden behind a cloud. Still, God's Word stands, whatever our circumstances, and we can carry on our conversation with the Lord through thick and thin. Although we may not literally see our Lord's face, we can be certain he is near. When Jesus left this earth, he said, "I am with you always, even to the end of the age" (Matthew 28:20). Jesus' promise to be with us always is just as true today as it was in the disciples' time. When we pray to him, we can be certain that Jesus will answer.

Dear Lord, in your mercy and unfailing love, answer my prayers . . .

December 30

CLOSE TO THE SHEPHERD

*Even when I walk
through the dark valley of death,
I will not be afraid,
for you are close beside me.
Your rod and your staff
protect and comfort me.*

PSALM 23:4

A culture that places a high value on success and self-fulfillment finds it difficult to speak of death. The Holy Scriptures, however, never attempt to hide this topic from us. At the same time, the Scriptures assure us that God is always with us. In this prayer, David voiced his belief that God was close to him, even in the "dark valley of death." He would not be afraid because he knew God was near. As this year of prayer comes to an end, we should reflect on the entire year, looking for ways God has been near to us in those "dark valleys." And when our earthly days finally have run their course, another life—filled with wonder and excitement—will open up to us. The Lord Jesus will welcome us to our eternal home.

In prayer today, thank the Lord for being near to you in the "dark valleys" of this past year. Ask the Lord to be close by your side in the year ahead.

Dear Lord, even when I walk through the dark valley of death, I will not be afraid, for you are close beside me . . .

December 31

PRAISE FOR GOD'S WONDERFUL PLAN

O Lord, I will honor and praise your name, for you are my God. You do such wonderful things! You planned them long ago, and now you have accomplished them. ISAIAH 25:1

Our year of prayer is finally over. Has this year seen the fulfillment of God's purpose in your life as you have been drawn to him in devotion, praise, and petition? We may not always know how God is going to answer our prayers. God is full of surprises! We may not always know the results—either spiritual or material—of our efforts to seek God in prayer. But we have assurance from God's Word that he is always at work in the lives of those who belong to him—of those who are called to accomplish his purpose.

No matter what happens to us, we can praise him and profess, "You are my God," just as Isaiah did. We should begin our annual cycle of prayers with this profession of faith. And we should end the cycle with the same affirmation—now more deeply felt and more clearly understood—for we are closer to learning what it means to be a servant of such a God.

You are my God, O Lord, and you do such wonderful things . . .

Index of Scripture References

Index of Devotional Titles

Topical Index of Bible Prayers